Haynes

Sewing
Manual

D1438234

First published February 2013

A catalogue record for this book is available
from the British Library

ISBN 978 0 85733 279 0

Haynes Publishing,
Sparkford, Yeovil, Somerset BA22 7JJ, UK
Tel: +44 (0) 1963 442030
Fax: +44 (0) 1963 440001
E-mail: sales@haynes.co.uk
Website: www.haynes.co.uk

Haynes North America, Inc.,
861 Lawrence Drive, Newbury Park,
California 91320, USA

Printed in the USA by Odcombe Press LP,
1299 Bridgestone Parkway, La Vergne, TN 37086

Author:	Laura Strutt
Project Manager:	Louise McIntyre
Copy editor:	Ian Heath
Design and layout:	Richard Parsons
Photography:	Thomas F J Ford
	www.thomasfjford.com
Stock photos:	Shutterstock

Acknowledgements

I would like to thank a few people who have helped me along the way
during my journey writing this book: my parents, Doug Cruickshank and
Anne Styles for their continued support and encouragement; my sister
Jenny Coomber, who alongside my mother, has taught me techniques,
encouraged me to learn and inspired my passion for textiles. Tom Ford
for his exceptional photography skills and passion for perfection; Rebecca
Burrows, dear friend and sewing enthusiast, who has always been on hand
with a needle and thread at the ready; and finally my husband John, for his
never-ending belief in my abilities and for inspiring me to chase my dreams.

Sewing
Manual

The complete step-by-step guide to sewing skills

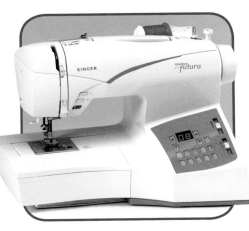

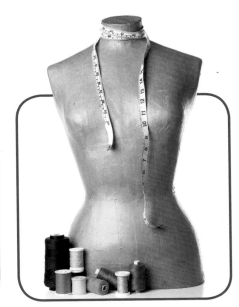

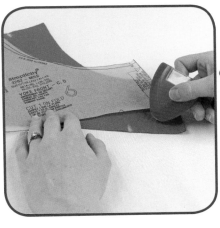

Laura Strutt

CHOOSING & USING A SEWING MACHINE • SEWING TECHNIQUES • TOOLS & EQUIPMENT • HOME FURNISHINGS • DRESSMAKING • PATCHWORKING • TROUBLESHOOTING

Contents

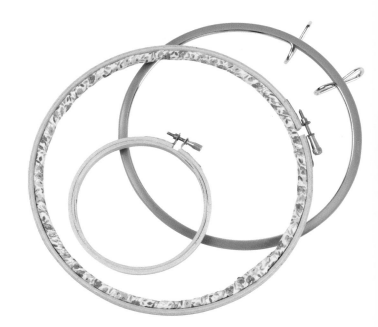

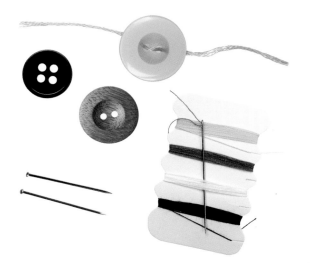

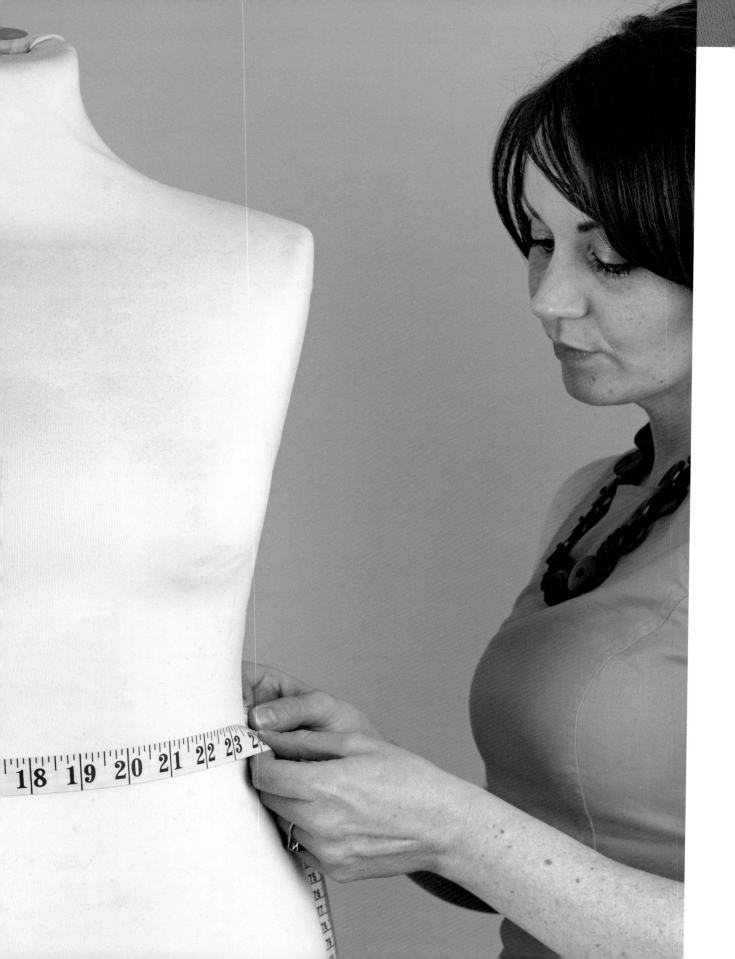

Introduction

Ever since I was a small child I've had a love for making things, and have been really fortunate to come from a family where getting busy and creative with fabrics, threads, wools, canvas, paints and even milk-bottle tops was the norm! I'm lucky to have a Mum (and Grandmothers, for that matter) who could embroider a smile on to a grumpy teddy bear, whip up fancy dress costumes that were second-to-none and create coordinated curtains for the bedroom of a teen with ever-changing tastes – all at a moment's notice. Though my interest in sewing peaked and dipped whilst growing up, being surrounded by such creativity meant it was impossible not to pick up a few stitching skills along the way.

I find it hard to believe that the little girl sitting at the old pedal-powered Singer machine, carefully stitching scraps of pink fabric together to turn a Sindy doll into a mermaid (a costume from which she later had to be cut free), would be writing a Haynes sewing manual. For me, sewing is a relaxing and enjoyable pastime, not to mention a valuable skill. There's no greater feeling than being complimented on a new dress and being able to reply, 'Thank you, I made it myself!' Not only that, but once you've mastered a few basic hand and machine stitches a whole new world of possibilities will be open to you. The 'make do and mend' ethos is back in full swing, and by taking up sewing you'll be able to join in the fun. You'll no longer have to pass up a beautiful vintage dress, simply because it has a zip that needs replacing, or throw away your favourite (and most flattering) trousers because the hem has dropped.

Stitching is no longer seen as a dated hobby, or the dreary chore that our grandmothers faced. For many returning to the craft it's a much-welcomed creative release, allowing them to take time out from busy day-to-day life to explore new techniques and discover hidden talents. Local haberdashery stores and online boutiques boast a wide array of exciting and colourful fabrics ready and waiting to inspire you. This newfound skill can be used to inject your personal style into all that surrounds you, from clothing and accessories to soft furnishings and even gifts.

I believe that sewing is a skill that's both creative and practical. Once you get started it won't be long before word gets out and your family and friends will be asking if you could make a new blind for the bathroom, darn a rip in a favourite frock, or sew a keepsake quilt for a new baby. Because there are so many different disciplines in stitching – from dressmaking and customising to appliqué and embroidery, and everything in between – you'll always find there's something new to try, different skills to learn and plenty of fabulous projects to enjoy.

Having been fortunate enough to learn the basics as a young child, I've always had the confidence to experiment with new techniques and take on increasingly challenging projects. I've had my fair share of disasters, I might add – slicing through my only tape measure whilst cutting pattern pieces, hemming a dress that had taken months to finish and rendering it too short to be decent, sewing an entire quilt block together in the wrong order to name but a few – but for me, such mishaps are all part of the experience. Then one day it occurred to me that for some people, the prospect of just slicing into some fabric (which is more often than not pretty and sometimes costly) can be a rather daunting experience, and this is the reason I decided to write this book – to show that sewing and creating wonderful projects with fabrics and threads is something that anyone can learn, with easy-to-follow instructions and a little practise.

People often tell me that they're a little frightened about using a sewing machine, that perhaps it's somehow too specialist for them, or that something dreadful might happen. But here I shall show you that your sewing machine is your friend, and you needn't be afraid of it! Of course, mistakes will be made along the way, but that's all part of the learning process. The important thing is to give it a go, to try your hand at something new – start out sewing a few simple seams and see where it takes you.

This book is designed to show you how to get to know your sewing machine and how to make it do what you want it to do, so that you can go on to create the kind of projects that interest you, be that dressmaking, quilting or whipping up a set of custom curtains. All of this is achievable by following a few simple guidelines.

So, what are you waiting for? Let's grab that sewing machine, dig out a needle and thread and give stitching a go – I know you're going to love it!

Laura Strutt

Laura Strutt
Spring 2013

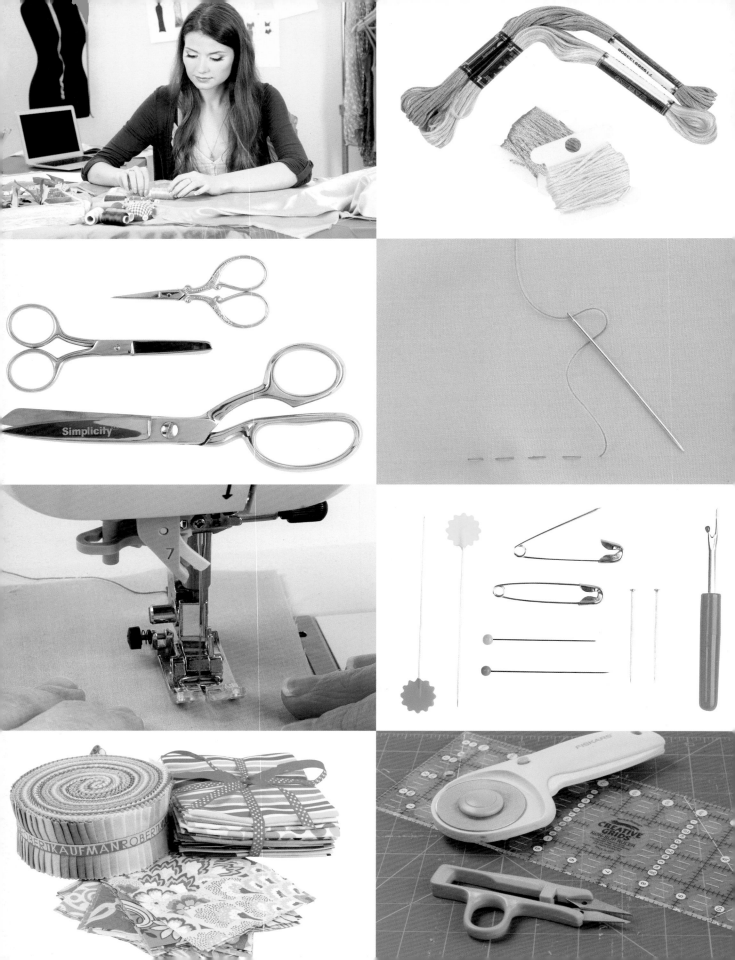

Chapter 1

Getting started

Sewing is no longer looked upon as the forgotten pastime of our grandmothers and stuffy old aunties. With the recent revival of a 'make do and mend' philosophy more and more people are turning to stitching, not only to improve their skills, but also to satisfy their creative side. What's more, with a little practice you'll soon find that not only are you able to perform functional stitching tasks – like mending dropped hems and making your own curtains – but you'll also discover that you can create and customise your own clothing and accessories. There's no better time to dig out and dust off that sewing machine and discover a whole world of skills and creativity right at your fingertips!

Sewing box basics

Before you begin to sew you'll need to gather together a basic sewing kit, which will include a few key items such as needles, threads and scissors plus, at the very least, the bits and bobs shown here.

Threads

A selection of all-purpose threads in a range of colours will allow you to quickly select the correct style and shade for your chosen project.

Scissors

Large shears with long, sharp blades (used for cutting pieces of fabric) and a small pair of sharp pointed scissors (to snip away thread ends when working close to the fabric) are both essential.

Needles

A selection of hand sewing needles is a must-have. A multipack offering a wide range of styles and sizes will ensure that you always have the correct needle to hand.

Tape measure

A long tape measure is crucial, not only for taking body measurements but to ensure correct placement of seams and sewing lines while you work.

Seam ripper

This hook-shaped tool features a sharp point and a small cutting blade inside the curve. It's used to unpick and remove unwanted stitches without damaging the fabric. It's also used for opening up buttonholes.

Thimble

Available in a range of styles, shapes and sizes, a thimble is slipped over the end of your finger to protect the tips as you stitch.

Buttons, fastenings and haberdashery items

A collection of buttons, snap fastenings and zips in a range of sizes and colours will make a handy addition to your sewing room.

Sewing supplies

You'll find before too long you also start to accumulate a variety of additional sewing supplies, depending on the type of stitching that you enjoy and do the most. It's important to stow all of your supplies in a suitable container, so that they're kept in pristine condition and are easy to lay your hands on when you need them.

Pins

Almost all projects will require pins at some stage, to hold sections of fabric together prior to stitching.

Pincushion

Whether it's a novelty shape or a traditional design, getting into the habit of returning your sharps to a pincushion will keep them safe when not in use.

Some pincushions, like this one, feature a small hanging shape that's often filled with sand. Pushing the tip of the needle in and out of this portion will help to keep it sharp.

Sewing box

Many styles of sewing box are available, from modern plastic or traditional wooden, to retro tins and hampers. What you select is entirely up to you – an old biscuit tin is great to house all your essentials. However, you may find that something with individual compartments, like the traditional wooden designs, will allow you to keep different items separate, so that threads don't become tangled up with scissors and needles.

I like to keep a few separate sewing boxes, each containing different items: a traditional cantilever box with lots of compartments is great for my general sewing essentials, a glass sweet jar to stash my ever-growing button collection, and pretty vintage boxes to store my specialist threads for embroidery or quilting.

The best tip is to start small. Sewing is really addictive and you'll gradually pick up more tools and supplies as you work, so try starting out with a medium-sized sewing box, and stow any specialist items separately in neat little tins, cases or jars.

Find out more about specialist stitching items on page 22

Sewing tools

There are several types of many sewing tools, each created to make a specific task easier. Here you will find out what items are used for different elements of sewing.

Scissors

There are a wide range of styles of scissors, each used for different applications. Use this guide to discover which tool to use for each specific project:

Fabric shears

The long blades make cutting through large sections of fabric quick and easy. These are the most popular style of scissors for stitchers, as they're used in all manner of sewing projects.

Standard scissors

Dressmakers often keep a pair of regular paper scissors in their sewing box for use when cutting tissue paper patterns or templates. This helps to prevent the blades of fabric shears becoming dull.

Keeping the blades of your scissors sharp will help to ensure crisp, neat cuts

Pinking shears

These are usually of a similar size to fabric shears, but they feature serrated blades. These leave a zigzag edging to the cut fabric, which is not only used for decorative purposes, but also for creating neat, fray-free edges.

> ## Making life easier
>
> It might seem rather silly to own several styles of scissors, or have numerous different types of needle, but they're all designed with a specific task in mind. Not only will they help you to achieve fantastic finished projects, but in many cases they'll make the process of sewing and constructing each element a lot easier.

Embroidery scissors

These small scissors with sharp pointed blades are used to snip away the ends of threads, or for cutting small pieces of fabric when precision is paramount.

Chalks, markers & pens

There will be times when you're preparing fabrics and stitching that you'll need to make marks on the surface. Sometimes you'll want these to be temporary, while at other times you'll want them to have a little more staying power. You may even require them to be permanent, depending on the task in hand.

Working with markers

Before working with air-erasable and water-soluble markers, always check the ink on a waste scrap of your chosen fabric, and follow the manufacturer's instructions to ensure that it's completely removable before getting started on your final project.

Air-erasable markers

With a fine tip like a pen, these enable you to make neat markings when accuracy is key. The coloured inks will fade after time and won't be detected on the finished project.

Water-soluble markers

Similar to air-erasable markers, these pens allow you to make precise marks on your fabrics. However, the lines can only be removed by soaking them in water, sometimes with a mild detergent. These pens are great for working embroidery motifs, as they'll remain visible until your work is completed – so you can take your time perfecting your stitches.

Fabric pencils

With specially created lead, this automatic pencil gives a clear, fine line on fabrics. All markings can be removed with the attached eraser or a damp cloth.

Tailor's chalk

Available in small blocks or, as shown here, in a powder form with a neat dispenser, this is used to transfer markings – such as notches or position markers for darts and fastenings – from sewing patterns on to fabrics. Select a coloured chalk that will be most visible on your fabric, and once you've finished working the section the marks can be easily dusted away.

Measuring tools

There is a wise saying that you should measure twice and cut once – this is a great rule to live by as a stitcher, for there is nothing worse than cutting your fabrics only to find that you have measured incorrectly. Always having a long fabric tape measure to hand will make the process of checking (and double-checking) a natural part of your sewing process.

Hand sewing needles

The type of sewing project that you're working on will determine the type of needles and pins you'll need to select. Using the wrong ones can damage your fabrics and leave visible and unwanted holes on the finished pieces. Always return all sharps to a needlebook or pincushion after using them, to keep them in top condition and to prevent nasty accidents.

General-purpose needles

Also known as 'sharps', as they have a very sharp point, these are the most common needles used for hand sewing projects. They have a medium-length shaft with a small rounded eye and, as they're used for a wide range of projects, they're available in a selection of different lengths and widths.

Embroidery needles

These look very similar to the general-purpose needle, with a medium-length shaft and a pointed tip, but they feature a slightly larger eye to accommodate the multiple strands of embroidery threads.

Tapestry needle

This needle has a large oval-shaped eye, allowing easy threading of tapestry wool or embroidery threads. The blunt tip won't pierce through fabrics but instead moves the fibres aside, making it the perfect choice for cross stitch projects, as it helps to create even stitches.

Bodkin

This wide, flat needle with a large eye is often used for drawing elastic through a channel or weaving ribbon through eyelets.

Size guide

Many general-purpose sewing needles come in packs of various lengths and widths. As a general rule, to ensure you select the correct size needle for your project you need to remember that the finer the fabric you're using, the thinner the needle you'll need to select. The larger needles are therefore best suited to heavier-weight fabrics. Test each size by pushing it through the selvedge of your chosen material; if it passes through with very little resistance and leaves only the smallest of holes on the surface then this is the correct needle for the fabric.

Specialist needles

A special needle has been designed to suit almost every different sewing application. Curved needles, with an arc-shaped shaft, are frequently used for upholstery work; beading needles, with a fine shaft and a long thin eye, are ideal for threading on beads and sequins to add accents to projects; milliners' needles are, as the name suggests, used in hat making, the greater length of the shaft makes them perfect for creating pleats and decorative details in fabrics. As these needles have been designed for specific tasks, to make stitching neater and to achieve high-quality results, it's always wise to check that you're using the right needle for the job. If you're unsure, check at your local haberdashery store when buying your fabrics and other supplies – they'll be able to help you make the right choice.

Needle care

Many people don't realise how important it is to ensure that their needle is sharp and in pristine condition when they want to sew with it. After repeated use needles will become dull, and this can affect the quality of your finished project.

Here are a few warning signs that your needle is less sharp than it needs to be:

- You have to push harder and harder to get the needle through the fabric.
- As you draw the needle through the fabric it feels as though it's snagging on the fibres.
- If you struggle to re-thread it, or the threads begin to look frayed, the eye of the needle might be squashed or distorted.

Pins

These pointy essentials are used in almost every sewing project at some stage, whether it be securing a dressmakers' pattern to fabric before cutting, aligning seams in preparation for stitching, or piecing together a patchwork quilt, it's important to have lots of pins on hand.

As with needles, there are a variety of different types of pin, each with specific properties to render a range of tasks quick and easy:

Safety pins

Not only do these versatile pins provide a quick-fix solution to mending a dropped hem or missing button, they're also used for a wide range of other tasks, including securing sections of fabric, turning through thin straps and even threading elastic through a channel.

Great for emergency repairs!

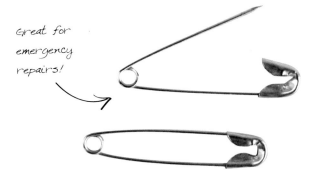

Glass head pins

With a brightly coloured ball of glass on the head, these are easy to insert and remove from fabric. They're consequently the most commonly used variety. The glass ball won't melt if it comes into contact with a hot iron when pressing fabrics. However, check that you are working with glass head pins, as the similar type with a plastic head might melt – so be sure to read the details on the packaging before use.

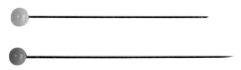

Bridal pins

These fine, almost headless pins are also known as 'satin pins'. They mark the fabric very little when used, making them an ideal choice for fine and delicate fabrics. As they don't have a coloured head they can be a little tricky to spot on the surface of some fabrics.

Quilters' pins

With their longer shaft these are used to secure the bulk of multiple layers when working with quilts. The flat heads also lie flush with the fabric, allowing a ruler to rest neatly on top while you're marking or cutting sections.

Threads

Available in all the colours of the rainbow, threads are essential for every single project. There's a vast range of threads to choose from, and you need to pick one based on the colour of the fabric you'll be using and the type of project you'll be working on.

All-purpose threads

As the name suggests, these threads are used for a wide range of projects and are suitable for both hand and machine sewing. They're available in a wide range of colours and different materials. Their thickness and the material from which they're manufactured will help you to pick exactly the right thread for your project:

Different threads

Many threads are developed in a special way to achieve the best results for specialist sewing; for example, you will find special threads for machine and hand quilting and stranded threads for embroidery alongside all-purpose threads.

Cotton

This is a medium-weight thread and is frequently used for sewing light to mid-weight cotton and linen fabrics. Most cotton threads have a smooth surface, which makes the colours really stand out on the finished stitches. A soft and durable thread that produces solid stitches without much stretch, and usually colourfast, making it easy to care for on finished projects such as garments.

Silk

A very strong yet fine thread usually selected when working with silks and wool fabrics. As it's so fine many stitchers like to use it for tacking, as it leaves very little marks on the surface of the fabric when the stitches are removed. Silk is a slightly stretchier fibre than cotton, making the stitches a little more resilient when sewing fabrics like stretch jersey, when stitches can snap as the fabric moves.

Nylon

This man-made fibre is extremely strong and is perfect for stitching medium-weight synthetic fabrics. It has a great deal of stretch, so stitches are able to move and flex with knit fabrics and return to the original shape without the risk of snapping.

Polyester

This is one of the most popular thread types, as it's both strong and has some stretch, which means that it's great for natural fabrics like cotton and linen, stretch fabrics like wool and jersey, and also man-made materials.

Other types of thread

Quilting threads

Threads for quilting are available in a wide range of colours, including variegated. Most commonly made from cotton, they're soft, strong and ideal for all kinds of quilting projects. Hand quilting thread is often coated to help it glide through the different layers when hand sewing, but avoid using these in your sewing machine – select only quilting threads specifically for machine work.

Embroidery thread

These thicker threads are stranded or plied, and are available in a wide range of solid and variegated colours. They're used to make decorative stitches in embroidery and cross-stitching. The stranded threads can be pulled apart and separated to create more delicate stitches.

Laura's top tip

Before using embroidery thread you'll need to take it from the skein and wind it round a bobbin. This will stop you getting in a tangle when you cut a length for your project. You can buy plastic bobbins or make simple ones from card. I write the shade number of the thread on the top of the bobbin so that I can accurately identify it if I need to buy any more.

Choosing thread

When you're standing in front of the rainbow-coloured shelves packed with spools of thread at your local fabric store, it's all too easy to get distracted and forget what you actually need. Here are a few simple tips to help you choose the right thread for the job:

- Buy the thread for a new project when you're buying the fabric, or take a swatch into the shop – it's a lot easier than relying on memory!
- Try to match cotton threads with cotton fabrics and silk threads with silk fabrics.
- For fabrics with stretch choose a polyester thread, as this has enough 'give' to stop the stitches from snapping.
- If the fabric is a solid colour pick a shade slightly darker.
- For gingham and check fabrics, match your thread to the most prominent colour.
- Store all your threads neat and tidy in a box. This will keep them out of direct sunlight, stop them getting dusty, and will ensure that you know where they are when you need them next!

Elastic thread

This thread is very round and has an elastic core. As it has plenty of give it's used when sewing things that will be stretched. Also used for sewing techniques such as smocking.

Clear thread

This translucent thread is used when you want stitches to be almost invisible. It can take some getting used to, as it's rather slippery, but it's great for both hand sewing and machine stitching when you're working hems, and for fabrics that are difficult to colour-match.

Fabrics

No matter what type of projects you want to work on, there are lots of inspiring fabrics out there – before too long you'll have quite a stash of different materials that you simply couldn't resist!

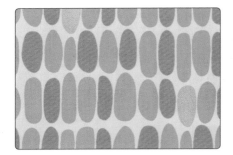

Cotton

This is perhaps the fabric that you will use most; it is ideal for clothing, quilting, appliqué and craft projects. This natural fibre is cool against the skin and carries heat away from the body, perfect for summer dresses and shirts. Cotton is available in a wide range of plain colours and prints; it's wise to launder cotton before working with it to avoid any shrinkage.

Wool

Woollen fabrics are made from natural fibres, and include tartan, cashmere and crepe. Wool is often selected when making tailored garments, like suits and coats, as not only is it fairly hardwearing, it can also be tailored with ease. Wool fabrics come in many different styles and, as they're breathable, there's a wool fabric for virtually every season.

Stretch jersey

This is characterised by its stretchy nature. Some will have 'give' in two directions (two-way stretch), while others can be pulled in four directions (four-way stretch). Stretch jersey fabrics don't fray and are great for making comfortable garments.

Fabric selection

There's a multitude of different fabrics to choose from for your sewing projects. Not only will you be selecting the colour or motif on the fabrics, you'll also need to choose the type of fabric that best suits your project. Some are extremely lightweight, while others are thicker, so ensuring that you select the correct type for the job is the foundation to a successful sewing project. These are just a selection of the most common fabrics you'll come across.

Silk

One of the strongest natural fabrics, silk has a wonderfully lustrous finish and is a versatile choice for both garments and home furnishing items. It's comfortable to wear against the skin and can be dyed in a wide range of fantastic colours.

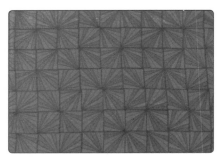

Fleece

This lightweight synthetic fibre is soft to the touch and very durable. It's great for making jackets, sweaters, hats and blankets.

Pre-cut fabrics

In fabric stores you're likely to see packs of pre-cut fabrics. These are predominantly used for patchworking and quilting. These bundles comprise of small pieces – usually strips or squares – of coordinated print cottons, and are great for piecing together into wonderful patchwork designs.

Feel and look

When buying fabric it's important to consider how the fibre feels, as well as how it looks. I unroll a small length from the bolt. This way I can see how the fabric moves, which helps me assess whether it's suitable for what I've chosen to make. For example, if you want to make a long flowing skirt but the fabric you've selected is heavy, it won't drape and flow as you'd like – it might be better for a tailored design, so you'll need to select something else for a more floaty skirt. Be sure to double-check the care instructions too. Some fabrics are dry-clean only, which might not be appropriate for your project.

Furnishing

There are many different styles of furnishing fabrics. These can be print or plain, or can feature patterns and motifs through the grain of the fabric. The most notable feature of these fabrics is that they're heavyweight. They're often extremely hardwearing and resistant to stains and snagging. Many are also fire retardant.

Oilcloth

A fabric that's been specially treated to give it a waterproof coating. Often featuring bright and bold printed cottons as a backing cloth, the treated section has a smooth, water-retardant surface. It's great for making bags, picnic mats and even raincoats.

Fabric widths

When you browse through fabrics in a store you'll notice that some are on long round bolts and others are on smaller flat cards. These will give you an indication of the width of the fabric. Dressmakers' fabrics are usually around 150cm (59in) wide to accommodate the various pieces when cutting a pattern. Craft-width fabric, which is often stored on flat cards, is typically around 115cm (45in). Be sure to check the width of the fabric before you purchase it – if it's narrow you may need to increase the amount you order to take this into account.

Preparing fabrics

Understanding fabrics and learning how to prepare
them before beginning projects will help you to
achieve really impressive finished items.

Fabric construction

As a general rule there are two main types of fabric:
woven fabrics and knitted fabrics. These terms explain the
manufacturing process used in their production, and give you
an indication of how the fabric will behave when it's made up
into a finished project. Being able to identify whether your
fabric is woven or knitted will help you to understand how
best to prepare and use it.

Finding the grain

With dressmaking in particular, it's important to look at
the way the fabric is constructed, as pattern pieces will
need to be placed in a specific manner on the fabric in
relation to its fibres. Using the grain of the fabric will
ensure that the finished garment hangs the right way.
Find out more about sewing with dressmakers'
patterns on page 90.

Woven fabrics

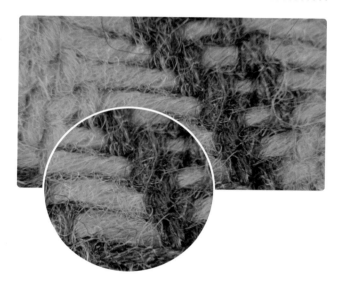

These are prepared on looms, where the different fibres are
woven together to create the fabric. These types of fabric
include cottons, denim, linen, corduroy, canvas and tweed.
The threads that make up the framework of the fabric are
called warp threads, which run vertically up and down, and
weft threads, which run horizontally across the fabric, passing
in front and then behind the warp threads to create the weave.
Each side of the weave will have a bound-off edge called
a selvedge. This prevents the threads from unravelling.

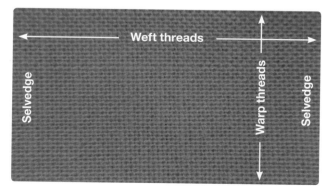

Weft threads

Selvedge

Warp threads

Selvedge

Knitted fabrics

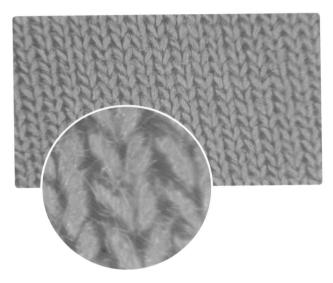

These are made on large knitting machines that work the fibres together in much the same way as in hand knitting, alternating between knit and purl rows to create a surface that's smooth on one side – the 'right' side – while the other side (the 'wrong' side) features very fine bumps. All knitted fabrics will have some stretch to them, like jersey.

Fabrics with stretch

These materials are great for a wide range of projects and are often used in dressmaking. Stretch fabrics are spilt into two different types: two-way stretch, which will stretch horizontally across the fabric; and four-way stretch, which will stretch both horizontally and vertically.

For the most part if a fabric has stretch it will be a knitted fabric. However, there are a few exceptions to this rule. You may, for instance, find a denim or a cotton that has some stretch to it. This is created by an elastic thread being mixed in with the weave. If you pull the fabric you'll quickly be able to see whether it has stretch, and whether it's two-way or four-way stretch.

Before you begin

Launder the fabric prior to use, either by hand or in the washing machine, selecting the setting that you intend to use once the project has been completed. This will test the cloth for colourfastness and shrinkage. If any of the dye in the fabric is going to run or the material is subject to initial shrinkage, it's better to find out before you begin working with it rather than after the piece is completed! Some fabrics may also have a coating on them from the production process, which will be removed by washing; this will leave the fabric much softer and easier to handle.

The washing instructions for a fabric will be indicated on its bolt, along with information about the width of the fabric and price. It's wise to get into the habit of noting this down when you buy fabric and laundering it as soon as you get home. This way the fabric will be ready when you want to use it. Once dried it should be pressed flat – neat crisply ironed fabric is much easier to cut than wrinkled fabric.

Some laundered fabrics may show signs of fraying along the cut sides. Don't worry – this is quite normal. Simply snip away the stray threads and the fabric is ready to use.

The more you sew the more you will become accustomed to the variety of fabrics and their different properties

Advanced supplies

As you discover new and exciting techniques, you'll need to stock up with some specialist sewing supplies. There is a wide range of tools designed specifically for different sewing disciplines.

Patchwork and quilting

This traditional technique comprises of the piecing together of lots of fabric shapes, joined by hand or with machine stitching. Once the fabric shapes have been pieced together they're layered with a backing fabric and a cosy wadding section between them, and then all stitched together by machine or hand to create the quilted effect.

Ruler
Large clear rulers provide both a straight edge to cut against and a selection of markings that can be used to align the ruler with the grid on the mat for a neat finish.

Self-healing mat
A solid base on which to slice and trim fabrics. It will protect your work surface, and many mats also include grid markings to assist in cutting precise shapes.

Rotary cutter
A disc-shaped blade that can be run along the length of fabric for quick, smooth and accurate cuts.

Threads
Quilters prefer to work with 100% cotton threads as they're strong yet have a smooth surface and glide easily through the layers of a quilt. They're available in a wide range of colours for both hand and machine sewing so that you can achieve the perfect finish for your project.

Snippers
These small blades are ideal for getting in close to fabrics to snip away thread ends while you're piecing together the quilt sections.

Chalks and markers
Before quilting the finished items, many quilters will mark out the placement for their stitches. This is great for stitching in straight lines and for geometric designs, as well as more fluid shapes like circles and swirls.

Charm Packs and Jelly Rolls
These handy, not to mention pretty, pre-cut fabrics are perfect for quilters. Available in colour-themed sets, they're ideal for piecing together quickly and easily to make beautiful quilts.

Needlework

The art of hand stitching takes on many different forms, including embroidery, tapestry and cross stitch. Working with a needle and stranded cottons, or thicker wools for tapestry, you can create elegant and impressive shapes and designs using different combinations of colours and stitches.

Embroidery hoops

These are secured around a section of fabric in preparation for stitching. They hold the surface of the fabric taut, which makes it easier to take the needle through the material to work the individual stitches.

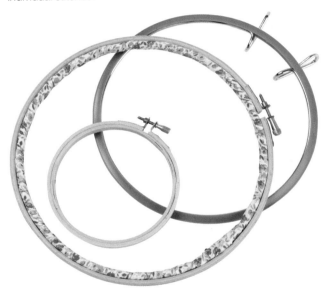

Embroidery frame

Similar to a hoop, an embroidery frame allows you to hold bigger sections of fabric at tension. They're great for large projects, tapestry and cross-stitch designs.

Embroidery scissors

Often very decorative, these little scissors have sharp, pointed blades so that you can get in close to the fabric and snip away stray thread ends.

Threads

Embroidery threads come in a range of different styles, from stranded cottons where the threads can be pulled apart and used separately to create stitches of varying thickness, to plied perle cottons that create a very solid stitch, often with more lustre.

Thread organisers

Plastic or card bobbins that are handy to keep different coloured threads neat and tidy between uses. Wrapping a skein of thread on to a bobbin will allow you to snip off your required length without getting into a tangle.

Embroidery pencil or erasable marker

Whether you're working from a template or creating a freehand design, using an embroidery pencil or erasable marker will allow you to draw out the design on the surface of the fabric to help with the placement of the stitches. These markers are temporary, so the outlines won't be visible on the surface of the finished piece.

Specialist needles

Depending on the project you're creating you'll need to select the correct needle for the job. Ensure that you pick the right sharp for embroidery, tapestry or cross stitch to make the sewing easier and neater.

Dressmaking & customising

Making clothes, whether for yourself or for others, is a great way to inject some style into your wardrobe. Not only can you select the patterns, fabrics and designs that you like best, you can also adjust them to suit your figure perfectly for a polished look.

Curve ruler

If you're altering patterns or designing your own you may need to use a curved ruler to help you create smooth, arcing shapes. A curve ruler will help you sketch out neater lines than trying to draw them freehand.

Long tape measure

Taking accurate body measurements is crucial for making finished garments that fit well. A long tape measure will enable you to measure yourself with ease, and is especially useful when taking the measurements for full-length garments.

Dressmakers' shears

Many dressmakers will invest in premium fabric shears. Working with the highest quality blades will help you to cut neatly and accurately, even when working with delicate and hard to handle fabrics. They're a great investment if you're working with expensive fabrics.

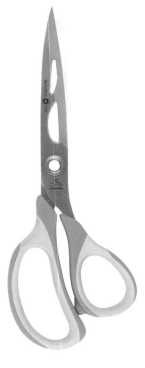

Chalks and markers

Tailors' chalks and erasable markers are great for transferring information from the pattern pieces to the fabric pieces, to aid construction. They're easily removed after the pieces have been stitched together and won't affect the finished garment.

Tool selection

Selecting the right tools for the task in hand will not only make the project easier and run more smoothly, it'll also help you achieve results that you can be really proud of.

Seam ripper

This small but incredibly handy tool is a great companion to the dressmaker. It will allow you to quickly remove temporary tacking and gather stitches – not to mention removing any mistakes!

Seam gauge

This handy tool features a little ruler and a gauge section that's used to check the seam allowances. Ensuring that all seam allowances are accurate and matching across a garment will give it a truly professional finish.

Dress form

For those who are more serious about dressmaking, investing in a dress form will help you to achieve well-fitting garments, particularly if you're making pattern alterations or creating your own designs. What's more, it'll look fantastic in your sewing room!

There is a range of different styles of dress forms, including solid bodies and adjustable ones, as shown here. Adjustable dress forms allow for different sections of the torso to be moved in and out to create the relevant measurements in the dummy to reflect your body measurements.

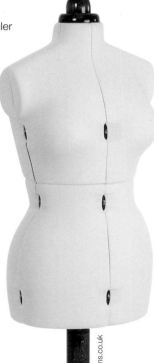

www.dressforms.co.uk

Additional materials

Some projects will call for extra supplies in order to complete them. Each will have a different property to help you achieve the required result.

Extra supplies

Depending on what you're making you might well need to use additional materials, such as adhesives or fillings, whether to add thickness to quilts, secure fabrics together in appliqué work or add stability to collars in dressmaking. These extra supplies will always be listed on a dressmaking pattern or in the instructions for the project you're making, so be sure to check that you have everything you need before you begin.

Laura's top tip

You'll notice some project instructions call for interlining and others for interfacing – it doesn't really matter too much whether it is one name or the other. The important thing is the style, so check whether you need light or heavyweight, sew-in or fusible, for your project.

Sew-in interfacing

This is available in a wide range of weights, from heavy right down to flimsy lightweight. It's sewn on to areas that require additional support or to aid a project's structure – for instance, in dressmaking it's used to support collars and cuffs.

Fusible interfacing

In much the same way as sew-in interfacing, this is used to lend support to fabric sections. One side of the interfacing is covered in small dots of adhesive, and a hot iron is used to fix it in place.

Double-sided fusible interfacing

Frequently used in appliqué, these sheets are paper-backed so that once they've been fused to a piece of fabric the paper can be removed to reveal a second section of adhesive to join it to another piece of fabric.

Toy stuffing

This is fluffy filler, used to pad out soft toys. It pulls apart easily, and as it's 100% polyester it's machine washable, making it great for children's toys. When stuffing a toy, fill it gradually, pushing the stuffing into all the corners. This way you help the filling to take the shape of the toy and ensure that it's not too soft or too firm.

Fabric glues

Strong fabric glues are available in tubes or spray cans and are ideal for securing sections of fabric together when making accessories or customisation projects.

Quilt wadding

This is what creates the lovely padded effect to a quilt. It's available in natural or man-made fibres, and also a blend of both. Many hand quilters prefer working with natural fibre wadding, as they find that a needle passes through it easier.

High and low loft

These terms are used to describe the thickness of quilt wadding, high loft being thicker than low loft. As a general rule the higher the loft, the cosier the quilt will be, while those with lower loft will have a more delicate drape.

Sewing space

We all know that old saying 'messy workplace, messy work', and this holds true for sewing. Whether you have a whole room to dedicate to your hobby, or just a small corner of your home, creating a usable and practical workplace helps to take the stress out of sewing.

A dedicated area

Creating the right environment is very important to achieving fantastic results with your projects whether you're sewing a new dress, working up a set of curtains or customising with neat hand embroidery. When you're just starting out, creating a dedicated sewing space does sound rather indulgent, and for many of us impractical. However, there are a few quick and easy tips and tricks that will ensure you have a suitable stitching zone, no matter what your space limitations are.

Good lighting

Just like reading, it's never a good idea to sew in poor light. Not only will you get eye-strain very quickly, but it's impossible to expect straight seams and pristine hand stitching when you can't see what you're doing. While natural light is great, if you plan on stitching into the small hours you'll need to ensure that you have a good overhead light. Sewing machines often feature lights to illuminate the sewing area, but you'll need to keep the lighting in the room around you to a similar level to avoid nasty headaches.

Tabletop lamps are great for both machine and hand sewing, the positionable ones being ideal for enabling you to sit comfortably while you work.

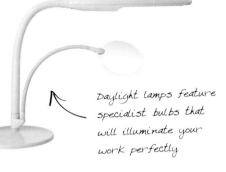

Daylight lamps feature specialist bulbs that will illuminate your work perfectly

Sewing table

Your sewing machine will work best on a sturdy, flat surface, making the dining room table a popular choice. Ensure that the table you use doesn't wobble and is strong enough to support the weight. It's also important to check that you're able to sit comfortably at the table and that there's enough space around not only for your machine, but also for the supplies that you'll need on hand.

A portable purpose-built sewing table is ideal for those with little space

Seating

Without nagging, it's all too easy to slump while you stitch, which will, over time, lead to back and shoulder aches. The need for concentration makes us sit forward too, rounding our shoulders as we hunch over our work. So just like when using a computer, you'll want to find a chair that allows you to sit straight and upright, while giving you the freedom to move your arms and control the sewing machine. The choice of chair or stool is really down to personal preference – just remember that the more comfortable you are when you're sewing, the more relaxed you'll be and the more likely you are to achieve the results you want.

Storage

Storage units needn't be dull – make them a feature in your work space. Not only will you need to keep your needles and threads neatly tucked away in a sewing box, but having a space to store your fabrics, patterns and other haberdashery supplies will not only keep them tidy, but will also mean that they won't get dirty or damaged, and that it'll be easy to find them when you need them.

Posture check

Use this handy checklist to ensure that you have good (and healthy!) posture while you sit at your sewing machine:

- When your hands are placed on the sewing area, as if to guide fabric, your elbows should create a right angle level with the needle of the machine.
- The soles of your feet should rest comfortably on the floor so that you can easily reach and press the foot pedal.
- Ensure that you have enough space between your legs and the lower part of the table. You want to be able to move your legs freely to let you control the foot pedal with comfort.
- Aim to keep your hands, wrists and arms aligned as you sew. This will help you to keep your shoulders square-on to the machine to prevent aches and pains.
- Take regular breaks. If you're concentrating on your sewing it's all too easy to hunch over your machine. If you find your shoulders are rolled and your back is hunched, take a break and have a cup of tea!

Ironing board

Whether you love it or loathe it, ironing is an essential part of sewing at a number of stages during the construction process. Having your iron and ironing board close to your sewing machine will encourage you to press your work regularly to help you to create neat and professional projects.

Chapter 2

Know your sewing machine

A sewing machine is a great investment, whether you want to create custom fashions or refresh the interior of your home. Learning how a sewing machine works will help you master its use and demystify the process of machine stitching. Whether you have a second-hand model or a brand new machine, getting to grips with its basic functions and learning how to care for it and use it properly will provide you with a great foundation for when you start work on your own sewing projects.

How it works

A sewing machine will allow you to tackle large-scale projects, work neat stitches and even achieve a professional finish. Once you master the basic controls and functions you'll be amazed at how quickly you can complete your projects.

Thread guides

Two threads make up each sewing machine stitch. The top thread comes from the spool of cotton and passes through these guides to regulate the tension of the thread before feeding it through the needle. Most modern machines feature colour-coded or numbered guides to help you thread the machine quickly and easily. The second thread comes from the bobbin (see below).

Speed controller

A slider that sets the speed the machine will work when the foot pedal is pressed, allowing control and precision when sewing.

Reverse function

Use this to set the machine working in a reverse direction, to move backwards across a stitched line. This function is used when securing the threads at the start and end of a line of stitching.

Needle and needle clamp

Sewing machine needles are removable to allow you to select from a variety of types and sizes to suit the application. The needle is held securely in place with a clamp. Most machines include a tool for tightening or loosening the clamp to access the needle.

Presser foot

Designed to hold the fabric in place as you work, this is removable, allowing you to select the one that's specifically designed for the required task.

Bobbin case

The second thread that makes up each stitch is from the bobbin. This is wound with thread and placed inside the bobbin case. A removable cover allows access to the bobbin, to monitor the thread level.

Feed dogs

These moving parts lie underneath the needle plate. With spiked teeth protruding through an opening, these help to move the fabric through the machine.

Needle plate

A metal plate that lies directly below the needle and presser foot. The small opening allows the thread from the bobbin to pass through while the needle enters to make the stitches. The metal plate is etched with a series of markings, which act as a guide for sewing straight lines and measuring seam allowances.

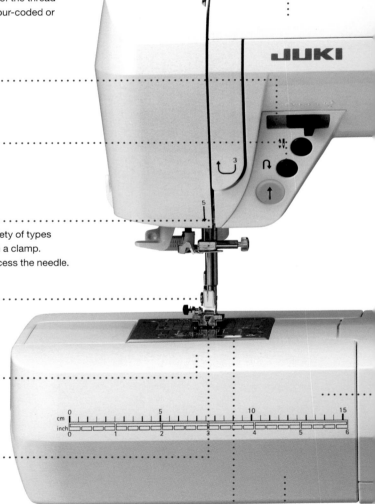

Bobbin

A small plastic or metal spool round which thread is wound. This is placed inside the bobbin case and this thread forms the lower portion of a machine stitch.

Tension control

Adjusting this dial helps to regulate the tension of the stitches by determining the speed at which the thread passes through the machine.

Machine features

There are a number of different sewing machines available, and while each offers a range of features and functions, modern computerised machines are designed for ease of use – even for a complete beginner – and will have the fundamental elements shown here in common.

Bobbin winder

Winds thread on to the bobbin from the spool of cotton, ensuring that the thread is fed evenly on to the bobbin and maintains the correct tension.

Spool holder

This pin runs through the centre of a spool of thread, allowing the thread to feed smoothly through the machine.

Screen

Computerised machines feature some form of screen, from an LCD right through to a touch screen on the high-end models. This will display the relevant information regarding the stitch style, width and length that has been selected.

Hand wheel

Turning this wheel manually operates the mechanics of the machine, moving the needle up and down and engaging the feed dogs.

Stitch selector

These controls allow you to select from the different stitches available on the machine, for example a straight stitch or a zigzag stitch. Many machines include a menu from which to make your selection. This is done by pressing the corresponding buttons or, on more basic models, turning a dial.

Stitch-length and stitch-width selector

Use these buttons (or dials) to either increase or decrease the length or width of your selected stitch.

Foot pedal

Applying pressure to the pedal operates the machine. Press it to start the machine stitching and release it to stop.

Free arm

This section of the machine can be removed to create a narrower working space, which is used when sewing smaller items or inserting sleeves.

Accessory drawer

Items such as alternative presser feet, spare bobbins and maintenance tools can be stored in the lower section of the machine for easy access.

Accessories

A number of different components and accessories will come with your machine. Each has a unique purpose and is designed to make each sewing task quick and easy.

Machine accessories

Depending on the brand and model that you have, some gadgets will be included with it, while many more can be bought as your sewing projects become more ambitious. In this section we'll look at some of the accessories available for your machine and explain what they're used for.

Machine needles

As with hand stitching, a range of different needles is used for machine sewing, and there are a number of gauges to select from too. Remember, the smaller the needle, the finer the fabric it's suited to.

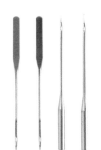

Bobbins

These can be either plastic or metal depending on your machine. Placed inside the machine, they hold the thread that will form the lower section of each stitch. If your machine requires a plastic bobbin and you insert a metal one the thread might not feed correctly though the machine, and this can affect the tension or even snap the thread. Consequently wherever possible you should use the correct style of bobbin to minimise such problems.

Standard foot

This is the most commonly used foot when working with straight or zigzag stitches, and its large flat base makes it an ideal choice for heavy fabrics.

Zip foot

Specifically designed to make inserting a zip easier, this foot fits close to either the left-hand or right-hand side of the zip, allowing you to stitch close to the teeth on the fastener.

Overcasting foot

This is used exclusively for working along the raw edge of fabrics when sewing overcasting stitches that will prevent the fabric from fraying.

Blind stitch foot

This is used when you select a blind hem stitch on your machine to work neat hems on garments. The built-in guide allows for precise placement of the stitches.

Manual buttonhole foot

Not only does this foot allow you to create buttonholes without using an automatic buttonhole feature, it can also be used when sewing decorative stitches, and even lettering.

Laura's Top Tip

Whenever I finish working on a large project I always remove the presser foot and the needle before stowing away my machine. This means that when I unpack it to begin a new project I have to insert a new needle and select the right presser foot for the job. You may think this will slow you down when all you want to do is get stuck into your next make, but if you start with a dull needle you'll notice snags as you work; and sometimes certain stitches selected with an incorrect presser foot will cause the needle to collide with the surface of the foot and snap the tip, and can even damage the machine's mechanism.

Buttonhole foot

This is used when selecting the automatic buttonhole function on your machine. The button is placed in the back of the foot, allowing the sensor to create a buttonhole to the correct size.

Quilting foot

Used when working with the feed dogs lowered, for example in free-motion embroidery and quilting where the fabric is moved freely under the needle.

Walking foot

This bulky foot is designed to 'walk' over the fabric. It's selected when sewing with fabrics that are difficult to feed through your machine, like jersey, or when it's important that the upper layer of fabric doesn't move forward, such as when quilting.

Patchwork foot

Patchwork requires a 6mm (0.25in) seam allowance, and this foot guarantees the correct allowance from the central needle position.

Smooth foot

Made from plastic, often Teflon-coated, this foot is designed to glide smoothly over tricky materials like vinyl and oilcloth.

Open toe foot

The large opening at the front of this foot gives you clear visibility for working with decorative stitches or appliqué.

Edge sewing foot

This foot has a guide section that's positioned on a line of previous stitching to assist stitch placement precision when quilting.

Rolled hem foot

The edge of this presser foot rolls the fabric under the needle ready to be straight or zigzag stitched when creating tidy hems.

Preparing to sew

Getting up and running with a sewing machine looks a little tricky at first, but before you know it you'll be filling bobbins and threading up in no time, leaving you to get on with working on your project.

When you start sewing with your machine you'll need to prepare the thread that you'll be using. Once you've selected the colour and type of thread for your project you'll need to fill a bobbin with it. The spool of thread is placed on the spool holder and threaded through the machine and through the eye of the needle. The bobbin is placed inside the machine ready to make the stitches.

Depending on the model of sewing machine, the threading process may look slightly different, but the principles will be the same. The top thread will feed through a number of different sections (many modern machines will be numbered to show you the route of the thread), and in doing so the correct tension for the stitch is achieved, which makes this element of preparation crucial. Most machines come with a bobbin-winding feature, meaning that you can fill the bobbin quickly and correctly to begin stitching.

What do the threads do?

Each sewing machine stitch is made using two threads: the spool thread, which comes from the top of the machine and threads through the needle; and the bobbin thread, which comes from the bottom of the machine. Stitches are created by the top or spool thread being pushed through the fabric and down through the hole in the needle plate. The bobbin sits in the centre of a shuttle that's rotated in time with the motion of the needle. As the needle passes down into the machine, a loop of thread is picked up by a hook on the shuttle and, as the shuttle rotates, the needle thread is looped around the thread from the bobbin. When the needle returns to the surface the stitch is created, with a spool thread lying on the top of the fabric and the bobbin thread on the underside; the section where the two are looped together joins the stitches.

Working with two threads in this way creates a strong and secure stitch. Try out using different coloured thread for the spool thread, that runs through the needle, and the bobbin thread, that creates the underside of the stitch, to help you to identify how these are made up. It's important to get the tension for both these threads correct in order to make your finished stitches neat, and threading the machine correctly is the best way to get started.

Downward stroke
The threaded needle passes through the fabric and down through a hole in the needle plate.

Upward stroke
The bobbin thread loops with the spool thread, so when the needle returns to the surface a stitch is made.

Winding the bobbin

Place the bobbin on to the bobbin winder on your sewing machine, secure the spool to the spool holder and begin to thread through the machine as directed for the bobbin winding function. Wrap the end of the thread around the bobbin in a clockwise direction until the spool thread becomes taut. Set the bobbin winder motor running – this will wind the thread until the bobbin is full. Many machines will automatically stop when the bobbin is full. Trim the end of thread and remove from the winder.

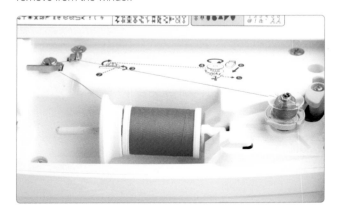

Threading the machine

1 Place the thread on to the spool holder and, if your machine has one, slide the spool holder cap into place.

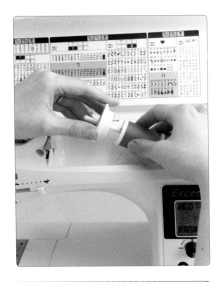

2 Pull a length of thread from the spool and, following the guide from either the machine or the manual, feed the thread through the upper section of the machine.

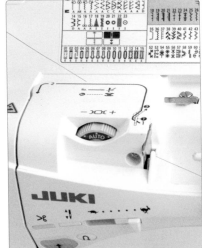

3 Easing it from the spool, work the thread through the tension section. This is a series of threading points on the left-hand side of the machine. It's important that you follow the right order to get the correct tension of the thread for sewing.

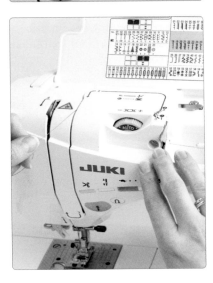

4 Draw the thread through the lever at the top left-hand side of the machine and take it back down through the threading points towards the needle.

5 Work the thread through the threading points on the needle clamp and thread the needle from front to back. Pull a small length of thread through the needle and allow it to lie towards the back of the machine.

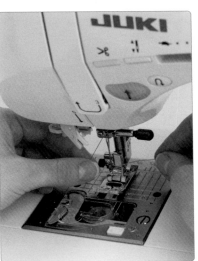

Threading

Sewing machines will all follow this basic principle of threading, where the thread travels from the spool across the top of the machine, following threading points to travel through the tension section before passing through the needle. Check with your manual to familiarise yourself with how to thread your machine. If you're finding the process a little fiddly, try using a brightly coloured thread, like red – this will stand out against the white of the sewing machine and will help you to get to grips with the process until you get the hang of it!

Inserting the bobbin

1 Remove the cover to access the bobbin case to insert the wound bobbin.

2 Check the direction that the thread feeds from the bobbin. Most drop-in bobbins will require the bobbin to rotate anticlockwise when the thread is pulled, while most front-loading bobbins will need to rotate clockwise. Check the instructions for your specific machine.

3 Place the wound bobbin into the bobbin case and pull a small length of thread from the bobbin.

4 Take the bobbin thread around the tension points marked around the bobbin case and draw the thread towards the back of the machine.

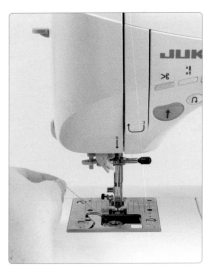

5 Finally, replace the cover securely and snip the thread end.

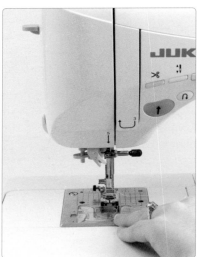

Did you know?

Some sewing machine manuals are available online, so if you've lost your manual or you're using a second-hand machine that didn't come with its guide, you may be able to get this information simply by searching online, using the make and model number of your machine. In some cases they'll be free to view, or you'll be able to purchase a downloadable version that you can store for repeated use.

Set the threads for stitching

1 Hold the end of the top thread, which has been passed through the needle, to prevent it from unthreading itself.

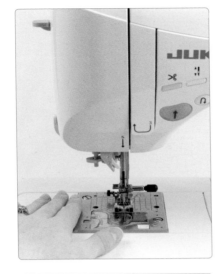

2 Rotate the hand wheel towards you to lower the needle until it passes through the needle plate and down to the bobbin. Keeping hold of the thread end, keep rotating the hand wheel until the needle returns to the surface and rises to its highest position.

3 As the needle rises a loop of bobbin thread will come up as well; pull this thread to draw it out of the bobbin case, bring both threads to the back and right-hand side of the machine, and lower the presser foot ready for stitching.

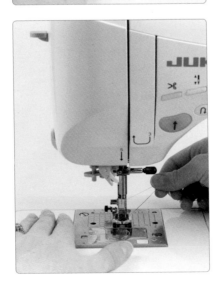

Getting the right tension

It is a common mistake to assume that just because your machine is making stitches that the tension settings are correct. Of course, if the tension settings are extremely incorrect then the threads will snap or the needle may break. However, a line of messy stitches is also a sign that the tension settings aren't quite right. This guide will show you how to read your stitches to help you assess, and correct, tension problems.

Balanced stitches

When the tension is set correctly this is described as a balanced stitch, as the upper thread, from the spool, and the lower thread, from the bobbin, are neither too tight nor too loose. This results in the join created by the two threads looping together sitting neatly in the middle of the fabric. On the right side of the fabric only the upper thread, from the spool, will be visible and from the wrong side only the bobbin thread will be visible.

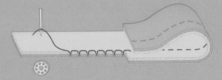

Tight tension

When the bobbin threads are being pulled to the right side of the fabric when the stitches are made this is a sign that the tension for the spool thread is too tight. Lower the tension settings and re-test the stitches.

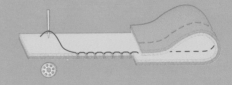

Loose tension

When the threads from the spool are pulled through the fabric and are visible on the wrong side of the line of stitches, this indicates that the spool thread is too loose. It can also mean that the bobbin thread is too tight; as it is easier to adjust the tension on the spool thread, always try tightening this and checking the results first.

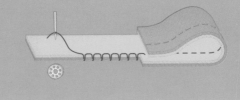

Care & maintenance

The better you take care of your machine the better it will work, and the longer it will last. Take the time to clean and care for your machine each time you use it.

Keeping your machine clean and in top condition is the key to its longevity. Regular at-home maintenance will help things run smoothly and enable you to spot any problems that you'll need to refer to your sewing machine dealer. Although you'll want to sit down at your machine and start sewing right away, there are a few simple steps you can take that will only require a few moments to carry out and will help you to stay on top of your machine care. Try to get into the habit of cleaning your machine when you finish each project. That might sound rather dull, but it means that every time you begin a new project you'll be working with a clean machine and can begin stitching right away.

The needle

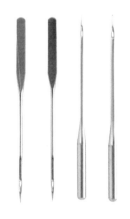

After continued usage the tip of your sewing machine needle will become blunt, and its dull tip will eventually begin to snag and damage the surface of your fabric. Remembering to change your needle before it begins to cause damage to the fabric can be tricky. A good way to remember is to check and change it every time you start a new project. As with hand sewing, there's a variety of different needles specifically designed for the fabrics that you're working with, so replacing the needle every time you begin working on something new will help you get the right needle and prevent you from working with dull sharps.

Safety first

Before carrying out any maintenance or care work on your machine, ensure that it's switched off – unplugging it from the mains will prevent you from turning it on by accident. Make sure that your hands are clean and dry before you begin, and check in your machine's user guide for any specific care instructions for your model.

Machine care kit

Most sewing machines will come with a basic care kit tucked away in the accessory drawer. This is designed to assist you in looking after your machine. Remember only to use the tools supplied in this kit and any additional or replacement tools can be obtained from your sewing machine dealer if you need them.

Small brush

A small, stiff-bristled brush that's used to dust away fibres and threads. It often features a small point at one end to help pick out stray threads or pieces of fabric.

Needle clamp key

Used to loosen and tighten the needle clamp to release the needle. The compact shape of this tool makes accessing this tricky-to-reach section quick and easy.

Small screwdriver

This handy tool is used to remove the needle plate and check the tension of the screws found around the machine.

Sewing machine oil

Some machines require a few drops of oil to keep the moving parts running smoothly. However, only sewing machine-specific oil should be used. If your machine does require oiling, a small bottle of oil will be included in the care kit. (Replacement oil can be bought from your sewing machine dealer or local haberdashery store.)

Replacing the needle

1 Use the hand wheel to turn and raise the needle into a position where you can access the clamp. Holding the needle with one hand, use the other to fit the key into the screw and turn it to loosen the needle.

2 Remove the needle by pulling straight down from the machine, and dispose of it carefully. The new needle will be inserted in the same place. Its upper part will have a flat section: with this facing away from you, push the needle into place before retightening the needle clamp.

Cleaning the thread route

1 Use the small, stiff-bristled brush to work away the dust particles. Begin at the spool holder and work your way along the machine following the thread guides.

2 Brush around the needle clamp and around the needle itself, being careful when working around the sharp tip! Most of the dust and fibres will now have fallen on to the sewing area or the needle plate. Use the small brush to sweep them clear of the machine.

Stay dust-free

While it's tempting to spritz your machine with polish to keep it looking bright and clean, the moisture and chemicals in cleaning products will damage it. I keep a clean lint-free cloth with my machine to wipe away dust from the surface. Sewing machines are often sold with a cover – either a soft vinyl one or a moulded plastic style. These are designed to add a little extra protection to your machine, by slipping these over them when they are not in use, they will create a handy barrier against dust and dirt from falling on your machine and working its way into the mechanisms.

Laura's top tip

When you can see tiny pieces of thread and fabric starting to build up around your machine you must resist the urge to blow them away. Even the small amount of moisture in your breath could cause damage to your machine. When working on a large-scale project you will soon realise how quickly the small strands of thread and bits of dust build up. I try to give my machine a quick clean with the small brush included in the care kit whenever I have to refill the bobbin during a project – especially as quite a lot of fuzz and fibres are released when the bobbin is wound.

Cleaning the bobbin case holder

1 Using the screwdriver or needle clamp key from your care kit, loosen the screws that hold the needle plate in place. Remove the needle plate, lift the bobbin from the case and place it to one side.

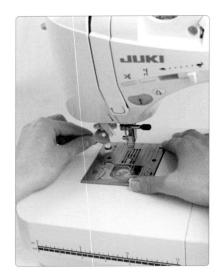

2 With the small brush, work around the bobbin case using circular movements to collect and remove any fibres or threads. Working away from you, clean the area that lies under the needle plate.

3 Work the brush carefully around the feed dogs. You may need to use the pointed tip on the end of the brush to loosen any stubborn particles.

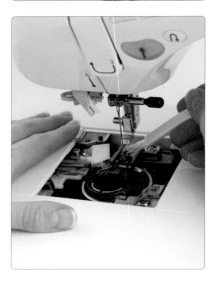

4 Once the whole section is cleaned, replace the bobbin and put the needle plate back in place. Tighten each screw in turn, gradually, to slowly get the plate into position before fully tightening them.

Laura's top tip

When taking apart any section of your machine, loosen all the screws slowly, and aim to lift the section out with the screws still in position in the corresponding holes. This will help to keep them safe until you are ready to put the removed section back into place.

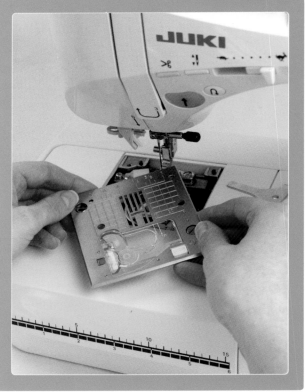

DIY servicing

Once you've gained confidence with your machine, it's wise to regularly give it a thorough check-up.

While it's always recommended that you take your machine to be serviced at your local sewing machine specialist at regular intervals, there are a number of maintenance tasks that you can carry out at home. These will allow you to spot anything that isn't working as well as it should and get it looked at by your sewing machine specialist before it turns into a major problem.

The more you use your machine the more confident you'll become in identifying each element and judging whether or not it's in good working order. If you use your machine a great deal it's wise to check it over at regular intervals – perhaps on a monthly basis.

Ensure that the machine is switched off and the power cable removed before you clean or do any maintenance work on it. The following steps are only recommended if you're fully confident with your machine.

Prepare the machine

On many sewing machines it's possible for you to remove the majority of the casing. This will allow you to take a look inside, clean the workings and check that all the components are in order.

1 Remove the thread and bobbin from the machine and set to one side. With the needle clamp key or screwdriver included in your care kit, remove the foot, needle clamp and the needle – being careful with the sharp tip of the latter. If you haven't refreshed your sewing machine needle in quite some time, it's wise to dispose of it and replace it with a new one when you begin your next project.

2 Using the needle clamp key or screwdriver, remove the needle plate and the bobbin cover. On many machines the cover panels can be easily removed using the screwdriver. However, on some models it may be more tricky, so if you find that the sections don't easily remove using the screwdriver from your kit, check with your sewing machine retailer. Place all the sections to one side.

Check for wear and tear

There are a number of key components in your machine that, with continued use, will begin to show some signs of wear and tear. It's important to keep a check on these elements, as they might start to have an effect on the quality of your projects and will need to be replaced:

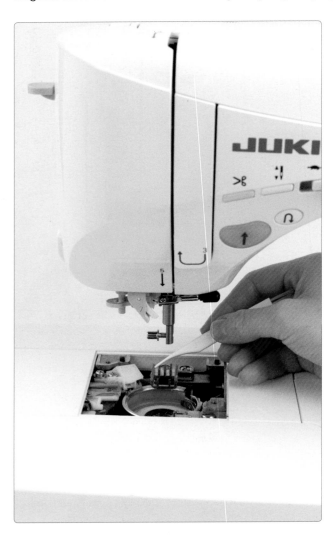

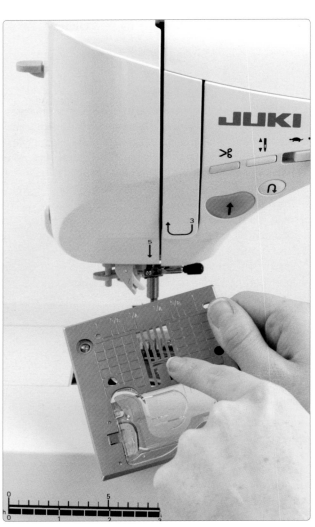

The feed dogs

Work the tip of the brush over the feed dogs. Check for missing teeth, cracks or damage to the small spikes. If any of them are damaged you'll need to get them replaced – a single crack on the feed dogs might not look like much, but it can snag and catch on your fabrics as they pass through the machine. Not only can this make sewing more tricky, but it can also cause damage to the fabric.

The needle plate

The needle plate needs to be checked for scrapes, scuffs, and marks where the needle may have hit it. Running your finger over the surface will help you to trace any damage to the metal, which might catch on your fabric and cause snags. Check around the small openings in the needle plate where the needle passes through. This should be smooth, with no rough edges for the threads to get caught on. Running the tip of the brush around this will identify if there are any areas of concern. If any of these sections have signs of wear and tear, check with your machine retailer, as it may be time to get the plate repaired or replaced.

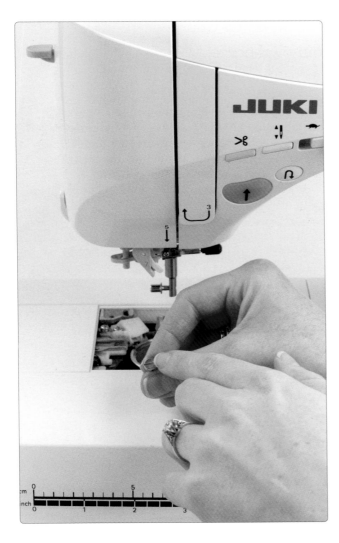

The screws

Even if you're extremely careful when removing or replacing the screws, it's possible that their heads will get damaged. Draw your fingertip over the surface. If it catches or pricks your skin it's time to get them replaced before they damage or even rip your next project. Always try to use the screwdriver or tool supplied with your machine, when removing the screws, as this has been specially designed for this task.

Clean the machine

Work very carefully around the visible areas on the machine from top to bottom with the tip of the brush (or a clean cocktail stick) to loosen any dirt and lint build-up. Carefully brush away the dirt. Try not to poke sections of the machine with your fingers – if there are stubborn particles use a pair of small tweezers to safely remove them. If your machine requires oil (this will be detailed in the manual) apply it once the machine is free from dust and dirt.

Replacing the bulb

Most machines have a small light built in to illuminate the sewing area and make stitching easier. If you need to replace the bulb make sure that the cover is completely removed to give you full access. Depending on the style of machine, the bulb can be either undone like a standard domestic light bulb, or will need to be popped out if it's an LED. Fit in the new bulb carefully so as not to knock or damage any of the moving parts inside the machine.

Reassemble the machine

Put your machine back together by working in reverse order to the sequence you followed when taking it apart. When tightening screws, begin by tightening each one on the part so that it's loosely secured, then work around the screws repeatedly tightening them a little more each time until the section is fully secured. This may seem tedious but it will help the sections align better and avoid making one part too tight and thereby risk damaging that section.

Choosing a machine

Having your own sewing machine is a great asset to your new creative pastime. It'll also help you to learn new techniques and skills at your own pace and in the comfort of your own home.

You may already have a sewing machine. Many new stitchers start out with a hand-me-down model, which is a great way to try out sewing with a machine to see which aspects of stitching you enjoy. Or maybe you have a machine and are looking to upgrade to a new model. There are so many fantastic sewing machines on the market today, available with a range of different specialist functions and features and at a variety of prices. With all the choices open to you, selecting the right machine might seem a little overwhelming, so here are some tips to help you on your way.

What are your sewing needs?

Begin by thinking about how you view your new hobby. Ask yourself a few simple questions about what you want to do and achieve, to help you direct your search for a new sewing machine.

Are you a beginner looking for a machine with the basic functions that will help you to gain confidence? Many basic machines will have enough functions to allow you to sew a whole selection of different projects, without confusing you with lots of fancy stitches and settings.

Or are you so taken with sewing that you want to try out new techniques and work on a range of projects every day? If you're very confident with your sewing, or are keen to push yourself to improve and try new things, a model with a wide range of features is a great option for you.

While the top-end machines with all the bells and whistles are very impressive, there's little point in spending the money on features that you may not use, or that might fluster you when you're trying to learn the basics. Of course, just because a basic model might be the right initial choice for you that doesn't mean that in future you can't be more ambitious with your projects and look to upgrade to a more comprehensive machine.

Will you need a computerised model?

A basic electric model is fine if you predict that you'll only use a small number of stitch styles and will only be working on a few projects. But if you think you'll be using your machine more frequently or working with a range of stitches, a computerised model might be the best option. This will make light work of the stitch selection and make creating a host of different projects quick and easy.

What's your budget?

Before shopping for a new machine it's important to have an idea of the amount of money that you're willing to spend. This will also help you to identify the level of machine that you can afford. Remember, knowing your budget doesn't necessarily mean that you're restricting your options – you can look at different brands of sewing machine to see which model has your required features and fits best into your price range.

As a guide, an electric model with basic stitching functions should cost between £150 and £200. The prices of mid-range sewing machines can vary considerably, from £200 right through to £850. As a rule the higher the price the more features it will have; between £300 and £550 is a good guide price for a mid-range machine. Top-end machines can range from £850 right through to £2,000 – and beyond for professional models. These machines will have an abundance of stitches, or specialist features that are best suited to those with lots of experience. Perhaps think of these as something to aim for in the future.

What accessories are available?

Sewing machines come with a range of accessories for different sewing projects, and additional accessories for each model can often be purchased separately to enhance it. For example, if you're keen to make your own clothes, check that the machine comes with a buttonhole function and suitable feet. If you fancy trying patchworking but don't want to spend out on a premium quilting machine right away, find a model that has compatible patchwork and quilting feet and even a quilting table.

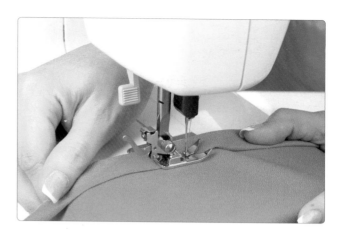

Which sewing machine brand is the best?

The majority of brands have been on the market for a great number of years, and as a result each will come with a vast heritage and experience in the mechanics of its machines. Each brand will have models with similar levels of functions. However, the features can vary from one to another. While it's impossible to say which brand is the best, it is possible to identify which is the best for you. Most stitchers will have a brand of machine that they like best – it might be due to the range of decorative stitches, the ease of use, or perhaps even how quietly the machine works when sewing at speed. The best way to find out what brand machine is best for you is to pop into a sewing machine dealership and try out various sewing machines from as many different brands as you can that fall within a similar price bracket or boast a similar range of functions. Find out what feels comfortable for you and what features you enjoy using.

Is it too cheap to be cheerful?

Sometimes you can pick up extremely cheap and unbranded sewing machines online or in stores, and I often get asked if this is a good way to get a machine on a tight budget. While it might be great to grab a machine for under £100 – or even £50 in some cases – I think that you need to check whether this really is the best option for you. OK, so you can start sewing right away, which is fantastic, but the machine will only have a very limited number of functions, and you may find that as your skills build you quickly outgrow it. If it's unbranded it may also mean that it's tricky to buy additional accessories for it, and that you won't be able to get it serviced or repaired in the future. A good thing to do is to visit your local sewing machine dealer. They're the best-informed people to help you make the right choice for your budget!

Specialist machines

Once you've been stitching for a while you may find that there's a particular type of sewing that you like the most, and want to branch out and get a dedicated machine that suits your own special interest best. Whether you're enamoured with embroidery or are partial to patchwork, there's a fabulous sewing machine out there that's designed to take your increasing skills to the next level.

Dedicated embroidery machines

If you love to add stitched embellishments and colourful designs to your makes then a dedicated embroidery machine would be a fantastic addition to your sewing room. These machines feature a huge number of built-in designs – many with a range of lettering font styles too – so you can customise and personalise to your heart's content.

Some embroidery machines allow you to create your own custom designs from scratch or download graphics from your PC on to your sewing machine ready to stitch. These can be used to add additional fancy flourishes to your projects.

Large sewing area to create your designs ↗

Home decor machine

If home stitching is your preference you'll need a machine that not only offers you a wide range of stitches, but one that's also powerful enough to handle heavyweight interior fabrics for making drapes and soft furnishings. In many cases these models will have an extra high lift presser foot. This is ideal when you're working with lots of layers of thick fabric and need to position them carefully in the sewing area for stitching. These dedicated machines will often include a range of presser feet, with many more compatible options available, so that you're able to add zips to cushions and cording to curtains. While these machines are ideal for home interior work they're also fantastic for other sewing projects, including dressmaking and general sewing.

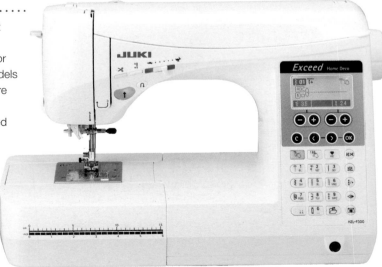

Powerful feed dogs to make sewing heavyweight fabrics easy ↗

Quilting machines

Quilting enthusiasts look for a few key features in a dedicated quilting machine, in particular a large sewing area, often with an extension table to accommodate large-scale projects. Quilting machines need to have feed dogs that can be fully lowered, enabling fabric to be moved freely under the needle when you're free-motion quilting. They also have an extra high lift presser foot, often with a knee-lift lever to enable hands-free operation. Both of these features are helpful when manoeuvring bulky layers of a quilt during sewing.

Feed dogs can be fully lowered for free-motion quilting, plus a large sewing area accommodates big projects

Overlocker

If you enjoy making lots of garments an overlocker can be the perfect companion to your sewing machine. This has a sharp blade that slices the edge off the fabric prior to stitching, and uses two, three or four threads to create a range of overlock stitch variations over the raw edge of the fabric, creating secure and extremely neat seams and edging to a very professional standard – but you need to be careful not to put your hands too close to the blade!

Select from two to four threads to create overlocking stitches

Laura's top tip

Threading an overlocker can be a pretty tricky business. You'll be working with between two and four threads on most overlockers, some of which need to travel over the top of the machine and through the needle, while the others pass through the lower section to feed through the mechanism on the underside. It's the combination of these upper and lower threads that create the overlock stitches. When you buy an overlocker it's wise to get the store to give you a run-through on how to thread it correctly; once it's been threaded you can replace the threads by simply snipping them close to the spool, knotting on a new thread and drawing it through its threading route.

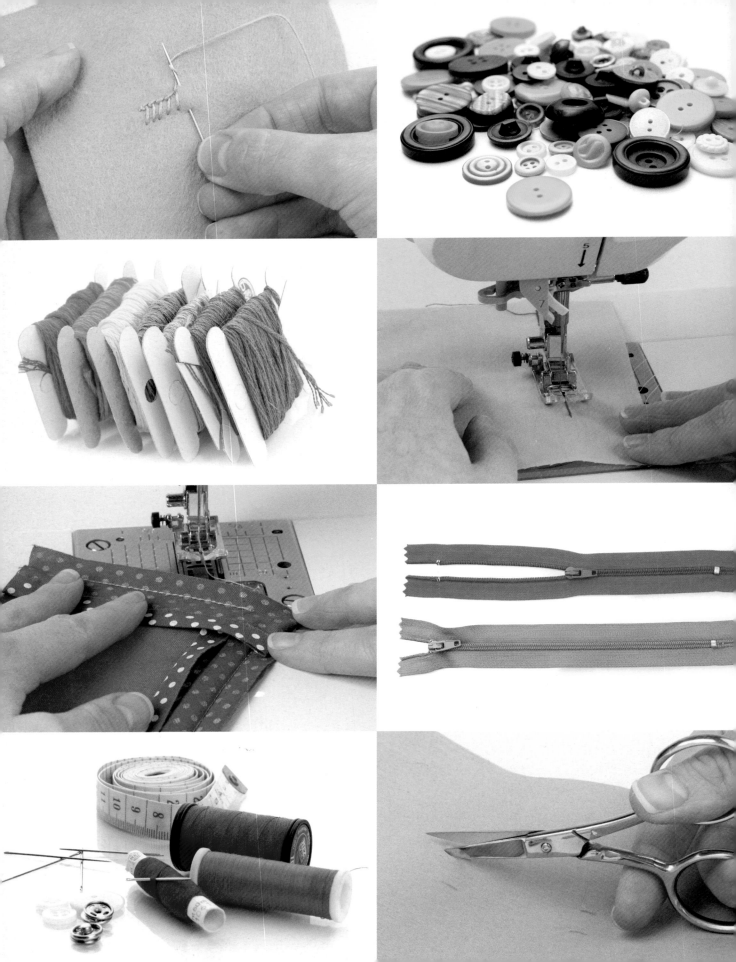

Chapter 3

Techniques

Whether you're stitching a tailor-made dress or custom-fit curtains, creating a quilt or repairing a dropped hem, there are a number of sewing techniques that you'll return to again and again. These key techniques will show you the fundamental elements of hand sewing and preparation stitching through to basic machine sewing – from straight lines and curves, to adding fastenings, gathers and pleats. Take the time to master these key techniques and you'll be amazed at the wide range of sewing projects that they'll bring within your grasp!

Hand stitches

Learning how to create a range of stitches with a needle and thread will be useful for all sorts of sewing. It's worth taking the time to practise a range of basic stitches – you'll be amazed at how often you'll use them.

Hand stitching is a fundamental element of sewing. Not only is there a wealth of projects that can be completed without the use of a sewing machine, there are also many instances when a project will require some hand sewing in preparation for machine work or for the finishing details. These stitches can be used as markers or to secure sections, and will eventually be removed, or they may be permanent stitches, as when creating buttonholes. So mastering a few basic hand stitches will help you along the road to success when you come to tackle larger, more involved makes – not to mention carrying out quick repairs, customising and embellishing projects.

Make it easy

Trying to thread a needle can be rather fiddly, but a needle threader will make light work of this task. The large metal loop is pushed through the eye, the thread is then passed through the loop. When you draw the metal loop back through the needle the thread will be sitting securely in the eye.

Threading a needle

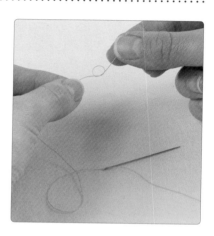

1 Carefully pass one end of thread through the eye of the needle and draw a length through so that the needle won't slip off.

2 Loop the thread into a knot at the end and pull to secure. Now you're ready to stitch.

Thread doubled

The majority of hand sewing is worked with a single thread, but if you need a more secure stitch, like sewing on buttons, for example, the thread can be doubled through the needle.

1 Thread the needle and draw sufficient thread through to align the two ends – the needle will be in the centre of the length. Tie a knot to join the two threads together.

Tailor's knot

While a basic looped knot is adequate to secure the thread end, you may want to get into the habit of tying the thread end with a tailor's knot, which is not only very small and discreet but is also extremely secure.

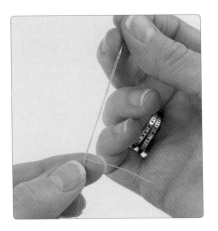

1 Thread the needle then place the end of the thread across the tip of the needle shaft and, holding the cut end still, wrap the remaining thread three times around the tip.

2 Hold the wrapped section between your thumb and forefinger and slide it down the length of the needle, past the eye and down the length of thread.

3 Once the wrapped section is 2.5cm (1in) from the end of the thread, pull up to form the secure knot. For a bulkier knot for heavier fabrics, work a second knot in the same way to sit above the first.

Fastening off

Once you've finished working your line of hand stitches you'll need to secure the thread by fastening it off with a secure knot that will sit on the wrong side of the fabric.

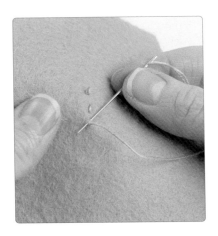

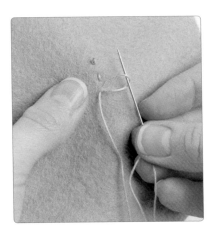

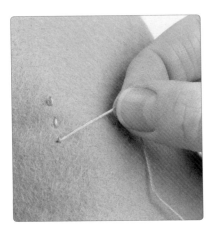

1 Complete the desired amount of stitching and push the needle through to the wrong side of the work. Turn so the wrong side is uppermost.

2 Insert the needle to the right side and back through to the wrong side to make a very small stitch. Pull the thread through, leaving a small loop on the wrong side of the work.

3 Pass the needle through the small loop in the thread and pull through. This will create a knot. Pull to tighten and repeat once or twice more to secure, then snip the thread end close to the knot.

Wrapped knot

A wrapped knot is the neatest way to secure the thread, and is created in a similar way to a tailor's knot.

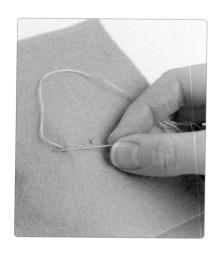

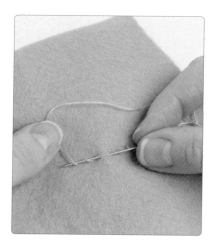

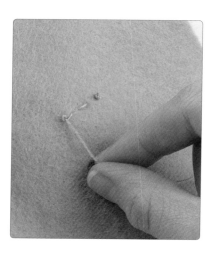

1 Pass the needle through the wrong side, down and back up to the wrong side to make a stitch, insert the needle as if to repeat, leaving a short loop of thread on the surface on the wrong side.

2 Work the needle back through the stitch, and wrap the thread twice around the tip of the needle.

3 Pull the thread through to form a knot. Gently pull so that the knot sits on the surface on the wrong side, and trim the thread end.

Running stitch

This basic stitch is used to secure fabrics together. It can also be worked as a decorative feature on your project.

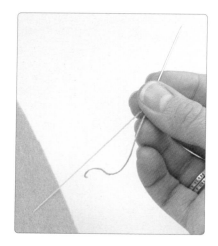

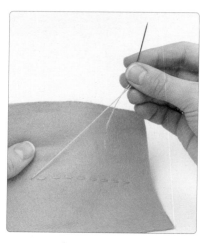

1 Bring the needle through to the right side of the fabric at the start of the stitching line and draw the thread through the fabric.

2 Insert the needle down through the fabric a small distance to the left of the point where the thread came to the surface. This will create the first stitch.

3 Continue working in this manner from right to left along the stitching line, making sure the length of the stitches and the spaces between are even.

Back stitch

This stitch is very strong and is ideal for securing key sections together in the construction of a project.

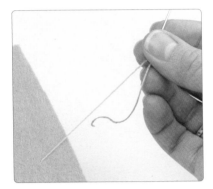

1 Bring the needle through to the right side of the fabric at the start of the stitching line. Draw the thread through the fabric.

3 Bring the needle back up through the fabric at the position that will form the left side of the second stitch. Draw the thread through.

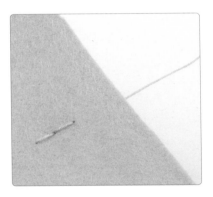

4 Insert the needle back through the fabric at the point where the first stitch ended, and draw the thread through.

2 Insert the needle down through the fabric a small distance to the left of the first part of the stitch.

5 Continue working in this manner from right to left across the fabric, ensuring each stitch ends at the exit point of the stitch before it, leaving no gaps in-between.

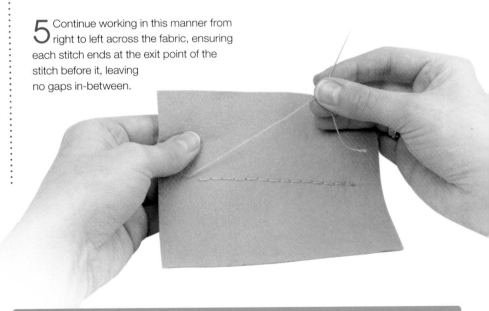

Laura's top tip

If you want your stitches to be as discreet as possible, remember to select a colour of thread that's as close as possible to the shade of the fabric. Try looking at your fabric and threads in natural daylight, as this will help you find the best match. If you're working with a print fabric, or want the stitching to be a prominent or decorative feature, pick a colour that stands out against the background, as I've done here.

Whip stitch

This stitch is used to join two sections of fabric. It's a visible seam and is often used for decorative purposes. When worked carefully the two sections of fabric will lie flat.

1 With the two pieces of fabric placed wrong sides together, draw the thread through one piece from the wrong side to the right side, sandwiching the knot in the middle of the two pieces.

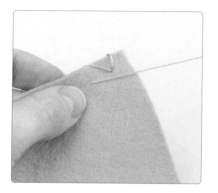

3 Bring the thread back over the raw edges, this time angling the needle so that it passes through the fabric 4mm (0.16in) to the left of the entry point, and draw the thread through to make a diagonal stitch.

4 Push the needle at an angle through both pieces of fabric and draw the thread through. This will create a stitch that slants to the left.

2 Bring the thread over the raw edges and pass the needle through both sections of fabric to create a straight stitch to secure them.

5 Continue working in this manner along the seam from right to left making diagonal stitches until the join is complete. Then fasten off.

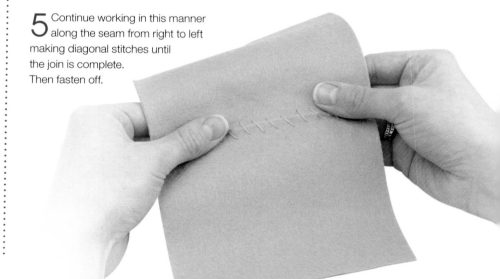

Laura's top tip

When working hand stitches I always use a single length of thread as I find this is less likely to twist and tangle as I make each stitch. A single thread will also create stitches that sit flush to the surface of the fabric for a neater finish. However, there are times when you'll need to use a length of thread held double, which produces more robust stitches so is perfect for seams in high stress areas and for sewing on buttons.

Gathering stitches

These temporary stitches are used to create and hold gathers in the fabric before the section is secured with a sewing machine.

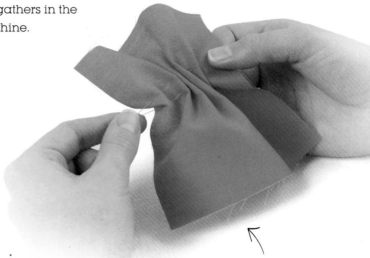

1 Secure the thread with a knot and draw the needle through the fabric from the wrong side to the right side. Working from right to left, pass the needle back through the fabric at least 1.5cm (0.6in) from the start of the stitch and draw the thread through. Continue passing the needle up and down through the fabric along the sewing line, to make 1.5cm (0.6in) stitches with gaps of a similar length between them. Leave the thread end unknotted and on the right side of the fabric and snip to leave a long length of thread. Work in the same way to create a second row of gather stitches under the first; trim the thread to leave a long end.

Gathers are often worked inside the seam allowance, and you may find that once the seam is secured the gather stitches can be left in place

2 Holding the two thread ends, gently pull to create gathers on the surface of the fabric. These ripples of fabrics can be moved and arranged along the thread to create even and neat gathers. Once the desired amount of fabric has been gathered up, knot the two loose thread ends together to secure the fabric in place.

Tacking

This is a long, temporary stitch that's used to hold sections of fabric together before working a permanent seam with a sewing machine. You'll frequently use this when making clothes and working with dressmaking patterns.

Secure the thread with a knot and draw the needle through the fabric from the wrong side to the right side. Working from right to left, pass the needle back through the fabric at least 1.5cm (0.6in) from the start of the stitch and draw the thread through. Continue passing the needle up and down through the fabric along the sewing line, to make 1.5cm (0.6in) stitches with gaps of a similar length between them. Secure with a knot and trim the thread end.

Work tacking stitching in a different colour to the thread that you'll use to sew the permanent seams. This will make it easier to identify which thread to snip when it comes to removing them

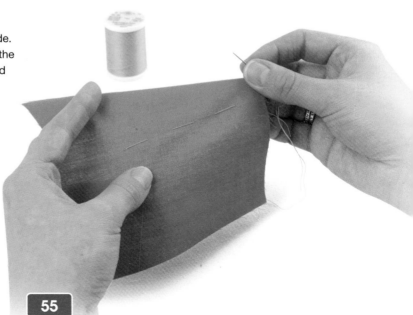

Slip stitch

This is an almost invisible stitch that's used in the finishing stages of a project. It's often used for joining small sections or for finishing seams. The needle slips between the layers to discreetly secure the sections together.

1 Secure the thread with a knot and pass the needle from wrong side to the right side through surface of the crease, draw the thread through to that the knot sits snuggly on the inside of the crease.

3 Draw the thread through this will pull the two sections of fabric together. When pulled fully, the fabric will meet and the stitching will be tucked on the inside and invisible from the right side of the project.

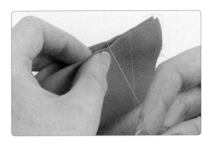

5 Continue working from right to left along the seam, pulling the thread through with each stitch to neatly join the sections. Secure well and snip away the thread end.

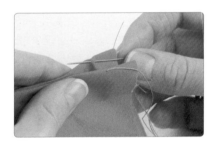

2 Insert the needle through the crease on the other side, directly opposite the first stitch.

4 Insert the needle through the crease on the first side of the fabric, directly opposite the point where the last stitch was made, bring the needle back up 5mm(0.19in) further along the crease.

Laura's top tip

I always press the seams open before turning through. When the item is turned so that the right sides are facing outermost, I fold under the fabric along the gap and re-press these, as this gives neat edges to work with.

Buttonhole stitch

The upper section of this stitch is secured with a small knot to give it extra strength. This stitch can be worked on a flat piece of fabric and the buttonhole cut in with a seam ripper, or the hole can be cut first and the stitches can be worked over the raw edges.

1 With the right side of the fabric uppermost, pass the needle from the right side of the fabric through the wrong side directly below it, leaving a loop on the surface. Bring the needle up parallel to the point where it came through and pass the needle tip to the right side, wrapping the loop around it again to create a second loop.

2 Draw the thread through and pull up to create a knot that will sit in a neat bar along the top of the stitch. Repeat to create a line of knotted bars along the length of the buttonhole.

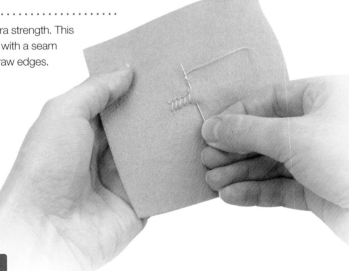

Blanket stitch

This stitch is used to neaten raw edges and is often worked as a decorative touch to finished projects.

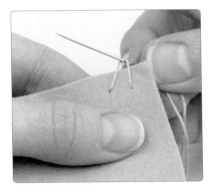

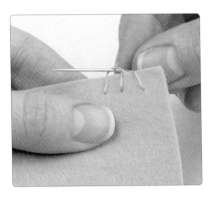

1 Secure the thread with a knot and pass the needle from the wrong side to the right side 5mm (0.19in) from the raw edge. Draw the thread through so that the knot sits snugly on the back of the project.

3 Holding the small loop of thread along the raw edge, pass the tip of the needle through the loop and gently draw the thread through. The loop will form a twist with the thread. Tighten it to draw the thread along the raw edge of the fabric.

4 Insert the needle 5mm (0.19in) to the left of the last stitch and pass it down through the fabric to create another small loop, which will form the second stitch. Pass the needle through the loop and pull up to tighten the stitch.

5 Continue working in this manner from right to left along the raw edge. To finish, pass the needle from the right side to the wrong side over the last stitch worked, and secure with a knot on the wrong side.

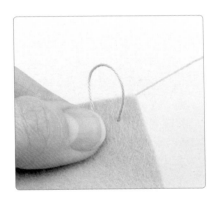

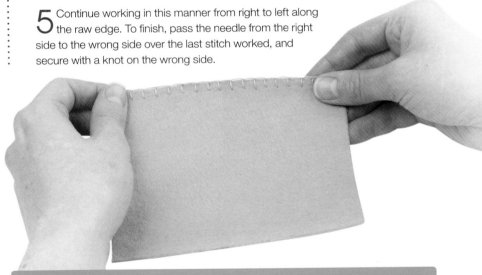

2 With the right side uppermost, pass the needle from the right side through the fabric 1cm (0.4in) along from the first stitch and draw through to leave a small loop.

Laura's top tip

Blanket stitch is a really pretty finishing touch to add to your projects. It's also useful for customising shop-bought garments and home wares. If you're using this as a decorative stitch you can use sewing cotton, stranded embroidery threads or even wool, depending on the weight of your fabric. The thicker the thread that you're using the larger each stitch can be made, so if you're edging a blanket or a throw try using wool and making each stitch 1–2cm (0.4–0.79in) apart.

Machine stitches

Sewing machines will have a wide range of stitches suitable for a variety of different tasks. It's important to get to grips with the basic settings before you move on to the more fancy stitches.

Sewing with a machine is a great way to create quick, tidy stitches, and will make light work of large-scale projects. While different sewing machines will have many different stitch styles to choose from, they'll all offer a range of basic stitches that will be a staple to many sewing projects. Here are some examples of the most commonly used machine stitches along with a few basic techniques for getting started and finishing off your stitching when machine sewing.

Fastening the threads

As with hand sewing, it's important to fasten the ends of the thread so that the stitches don't unravel. There are a couple of different ways to do this.

When the line of stitching is finished, pull the upper thread (the spool thread) to draw the bobbin thread from underneath through the fabric, and create a loop. Pull the bobbin thread through completely so that both threads are on the surface of the fabric. Knot the two threads together, pulling firmly so that the knot sits neatly on the surface of the fabric, and snip the thread ends.

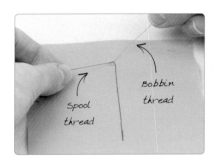

Reverse stitching

An alternative way of fastening the thread ends is reverse stitching, sometimes called back tacking. Many stitchers use it as a quick alternative to fastening off with a knot. The sewing machine's reverse function sets the feed dogs and needle mechanism to work backwards over the line of stitching, which secures the threads.

1 Begin sewing along the stitching line for 5mm (0.19in), then select the reverse function and set the machine working back over the stitches to the start of the line.

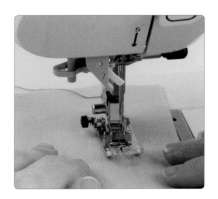

2 Deselect the reverse function to return the machine to standard stitching, and continue sewing along the stitching line.

3 Once the line of stitching has been finished, select the reverse function and work back over 5mm (0.19in) of stitches. Remove from the machine and trim the thread ends.

Laura's top tip

The zigzag stitch and the three-point zigzag stitch are great for securing the raw edges of fabrics before you piece them together. Simply work a line of stitching 4mm (0.16in) from the raw edge within the seam allowance, and then trim the fabric close to the line of stitching – being careful not to snip through any of the stitches.

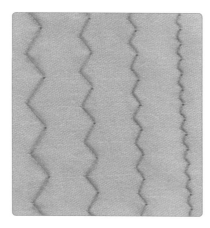

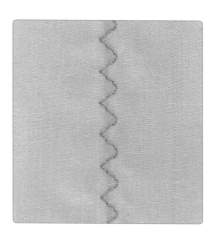

Straight stitch

This is one of the most commonly used stitches. It has many uses, from joining seams to adding decoration. The length of the stitch can be altered to suit the application.

Remember, the shorter the length, the stronger the stitch will be.

Zigzag stitch

This stitch is both functional and pretty. It's used to neaten and secure the raw edges of fabric and to add decorative elements to a project. As the needle is moving from side to side to create the stitch it's possible to adjust the width and length of the stitches as required.

Three-point zigzag stitch

Similar to zigzag, this is both a functional and decorative stitch. Each length is made up from three stitches. The width and the length of these can be adjusted to suit the project that you're working on.

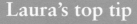

Laura's top tip

Reverse stitch can be used to secure the start and end of any line of stitching. If you work slowly and carefully you'll be able to ensure that the machine works directly into the stitches that have just been created, which leaves a neat finish on your project.

To ensure that the threads are secured aim to work back over at least four or five stitches when using the reverse stitch function, no matter what the stitch length.

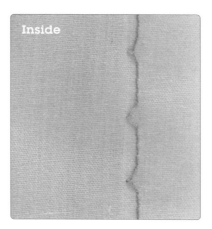

Inside

Outside

Blind hem stitch

This is used when a blind hem foot is fitted to the machine. A combination of straight and zigzag stitches are worked to secure the hem.

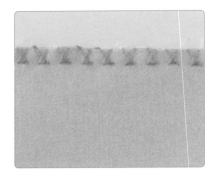

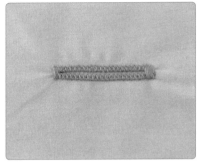

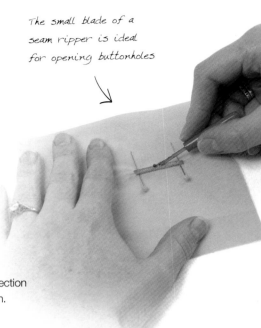

The small blade of a seam ripper is ideal for opening buttonholes

Overcasting stitch

This stitch is worked with the overcasting foot fitted to the machine. This foot has a built-in guide to work along the raw edges of fabric so that the stitches can secure them.

Buttonhole stitch

A reinforced stitch that outlines the edges of a buttonhole. Once the stitch has been worked – either manually or using an automatic buttonhole setting on your machine – you'll need to snip through the centre section of fabric to allow a button to pass through.

Laura's top tip

When working with an overcasting stitch don't be tempted to use a high-speed setting on your machine. Sew slowly and steadily, using your fingertips to carefully ease the fabric along the guide section of the foot.

Opening a buttonhole

Once you've stitched your buttonhole, the section of fabric that lies between the two bands of stitching needs to be sliced away. A seam ripper is the perfect tool for this. Insert a pin at either end of the buttonhole, in line with the short section of stitches, and push the seam ripper through the fabric from one end to the other. The curved blade will slice an opening in the fabric. As some pressure may need to be used, pins are placed at either end to stop the blade, which prevents any fabric beyond the buttonhole being ripped.

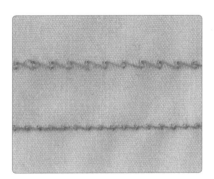

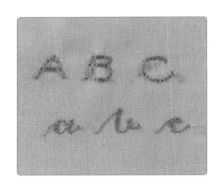

Stretch stitch

This consists of slightly offset straight stitches, which allows them to have a little more give and movement than a regular straight stitch. It's therefore very useful for stretch knits and jersey fabrics.

Decorative stitches

Some sewing machines offer a selection of decorative stitches, which can add a great finishing touch to your project.

Lettering

A number of sewing machines also offer lettering stitches, in many cases with a couple of different fonts to choose from. These are ideal for personalising your projects.

Machine sewing

Believe it or not there are countless things that you can make simply by learning to sew a straight line of stitches! Taking the time to master sewing in a straight line with your machine will also prove useful when you try your hand at more advanced techniques and projects. After all, if every seam is wonky it's going to be really tricky to get different sections to join up neatly.

Stitch width and length

The best way to work out what stitch width and length to select is to think of the strength and style of the stitch you want to use. The length of the stitch determines its durability: the shorter the stitch, the more stitches are worked across the line of sewing, making it stronger. Longer stitches have less strength and are most often used for machine tacking, creating gathers and decorative finishing work.

The width only applies to stitches that require the needle to move to the left and right of the central needle position, like a zigzag stitch for example. So when you're working a straight stitch this can be set to zero, while working overcasting stitches to secure raw edges you'll need to select a mid-width setting (usually around 5mm/0.19in), and for decorative stitches, the bigger the better – try the widest setting on your machine to create the most dramatic effects.

Tension setting

Getting the correct tension is one of the most fundamental factors in a successful sewing project. If the tension is incorrect the stitches may look messy, or the fabrics may even pucker as you sew. Some sewing machines have an automatic tension setting, which is a great time-saving feature, but there will still be some occasions when you'll need to adjust the tension yourself to get the perfect finish.

If when you use a sewing machine there are loops of thread or knots on either the right side or wrong side of the fabric, this is a sign that the tension isn't set correctly. If the thread from the bobbin is showing through to the right side of the fabric, this is a sign that the bobbin thread is too loose or that the spool thread is too tight. If the spool thread is showing on the wrong side of the work this is a sign that the needle thread is too loose or that the bobbin thread is too tight. The tension dials on the front of the machine can be adjusted to either loosen or tighten the threads to help balance out the tension. However, when you change the tension make only small adjustments, then retest the stitch, and repeat this procedure until you find the right tension.

Laura's top tip

If you're having trouble getting the tension right on your machine it might be worth checking that the machine and the bobbin are threaded correctly. If these aren't exactly right this can cause issues with the tension. Also check that the thread on the bobbin is wound correctly. If this is too tight or too loose it won't feed through the machine to make neat and even stitches. I always try to make sure that, where possible, I'm using the same thread in the bobbin as I've threaded the machine with. If these are even slightly different it can unbalance the tension.

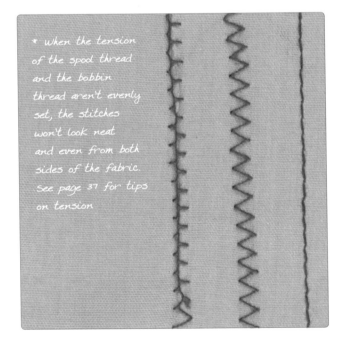

* when the tension of the spool thread and the bobbin thread aren't evenly set, the stitches won't look neat and even from both sides of the fabric. See page 37 for tips on tension

Sewing straight

As the needle moves up and down the feed dogs will engage and will move underneath the fabric to draw it through the machine. Try not to shove the fabric towards the needle, but use your hands simply to guide it. The direction that you move your hands will determine the position of the stitches.

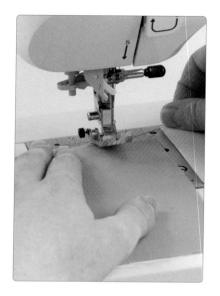

1 With a standard foot fitted, select a straight stitch and raise the presser foot. Place the fabric on to the needle plate ready for stitching. Align the raw edge with the grid on the needle plate.

2 Lower the presser foot and place your hands lightly on the surface of the fabric to either side of the foot.

3 Press the foot pedal to start stitching. Continue to work the length of stitches, keeping the raw edge of the fabric aligned with the grid on the needle plate to help keep the stitches in a straight line.

Speed control

The speed at which you sew is entirely up to you. If you're just starting out you might find that going very slowly will give you more time to get accustomed to the way sewing with a machine feels, and how you need to guide the fabric to get the stitches worked exactly where you want them. Many machines actually have a speed controller, which means you can set the maximum speed of the stitching for when the foot pedal is pressed, so that you never feel as though the machine is running away from you. When you're starting out, set this to the slowest setting until you get to grips with moving the material through the machine. You can build up speed as you work and can always change it when tackling more tricky elements of your projects. If you're stopping between sections, take your foot off the pedal. That way you won't accidentally set the machine stitching when you don't intend to! As for things going wrong, mistakes will sometimes happen, so keep your seam ripper to hand so that you can quickly unpick stitches you're unhappy with and try again.

Unpicking stitches

If you aren't happy with a line of sewing you can always unpick it. The best way to remove unwanted stitches is to slide the point of the seam ripper under a stitch and carefully push on it to slice the thread. Move along two stitches and repeat. Continue doing this along the line of stitches you want to remove, then pinch the raw ends of each thread between your thumb and finger and pull them free of the fabric. Once you've removed the threads from the surface, flip the fabric over and remove any stray bobbin threads from the wrong side.

It's important to remember that if you unpick and rework a section of stitches over and over, you'll end up with lots of needle holes in the fabric, which could spoil the look of the finished project.

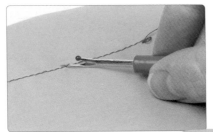

The seam ripper cuts the threads to remove stitches without damaging the fabric

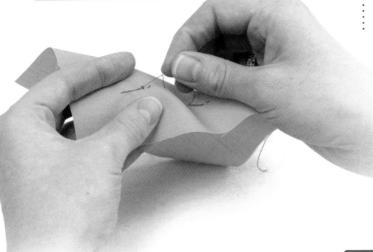

Sewing curves

Creating neat curves is required in a number of different sewing projects, and getting the line of stitching to arc evenly is important for a neat result. The grid marked on the needle plate can be used as a guide to help you achieve that perfect curve. When sewing straight lines you'll have got into the habit of aligning as much of the raw edge of the fabric as possible along the markers on the needle plate, and when sewing a curve you can still use these markers, but you'll need to ensure that the raw edge of the fabric that's directly to the right-hand side of the needle is the section that's aligned with the required marker.

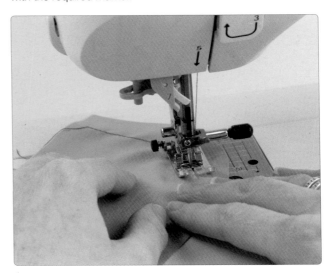

Grid markers

The lines etched on the needle plate are a handy tool that's designed to help you to position stitching exactly where you want it. Of course, some machines will have more markers on the needle plates than others, but if you find that the project you're working on requires a sewing line that isn't marked on your machine, rather than making a guess you can add a temporary marker. To do this, with the needle in its central position, raise the presser foot and use the hand wheel to lower the needle so that it's visible below the surface of the foot. Place a tape measure against the shaft of the needle, laying it flat across the sewing space on the right-hand side of your machine. Then use a piece of magic tape to mark out the position for the edge of the fabric to give you the required sewing line. Be sure to use a tape that's easy to take off, so that it doesn't damage or mark your machine when you remove it afterwards.

Sewing corners

There are many projects where you'll need to sew a precise corner. This is worked in stages. You'll need to stop the machine at the point where you want to turn to make the corner.

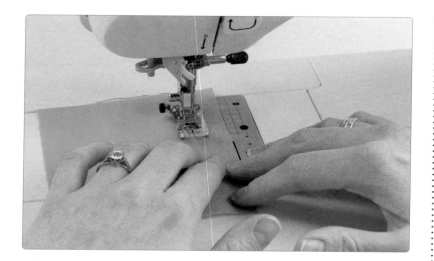

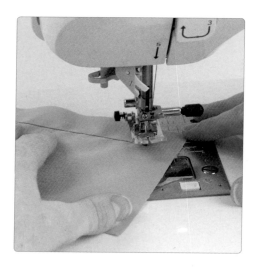

1 Begin by sewing a straight line of stitches. Use the grid on the needle plate to align with the edge of the fabric to keep the stitches straight. If you're sewing along the edge of the fabric you'll want the second line of stitching – after the corner – to be the same distance from the edge as the first. To do this, if you're sewing 1.5cm (0.6in) from the edge of the fabric you'll need to stop sewing 1.5cm (0.6in) before you reach the end, so that when you start to work up from the corner the stitching will still be 1.5cm (0.6in) from the edge.

3 Lift the presser foot, allowing you to move the fabric. Carefully pivot the fabric on the needle so that it's facing in the correct direction for the second line of stitching.

2 When you come to the point at which to make the corner, stop sewing and ensure that the needle is in the down position, pushing through the fabric. Some machines have a special button that will lower the needle back into the down position; otherwise you'll need to turn the hand wheel to carefully position the needle through the fabric.

4 Lower the presser foot and continue sewing the second line.

Seams

Every time you join two pieces of fabric together you're creating a seam. The basic principle of making a seam can be adapted to suit whatever project you're working on. There's also a range of more involved methods for making seams which each have a specific function and, when used, will really elevate the construction of your project.

Creating a basic seam

For the majority of sewing projects you'll usually work with a standard seam allowance of 1.5cm (0.6in). This means that the stitching line is 1.5cm (0.6in) in from the raw edge of the fabric. This basic seam is also known as an open seam. If the project you're working on requires a different seam allowance this will be noted in the instructions.

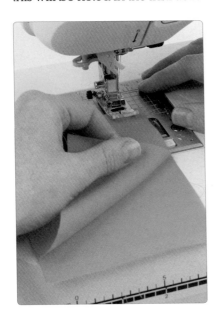

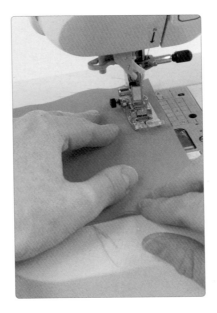

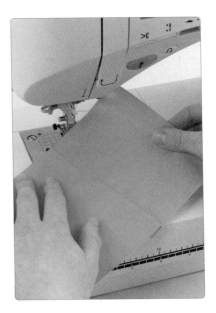

1 Place the two pieces of fabric to be joined so that the right sides of each piece are facing each other. Use pins to secure the pieces so that they don't move apart as you sew them – if you're working with slippery fabrics you can tack them together to keep them really secure.

2 Use the markers on the needle plate to align the needle so that the line of stitching will be 1.5cm (0.6in) from the raw edge. Select a straight stitch setting on your machine and sew along the length to be joined, securing the stitches at the start and end of the line with the reverse function.

3 Remove the fabric from the machine and open out. The two pieces of fabric will be neatly joined and the stitching won't be visible from the right side of the project. If you added a line of tacking stitches before machine sewing, carefully remove it now.

Finishing seams

There are a number of different ways that seams can be finished.
The simplest is to press the seams open to neaten the join.

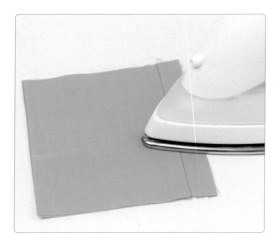

1 Once the seam is stitched, leaving the fabrics right sides together press the line of stitching with a hot iron. Position the iron over the stitches, press it down and hold for a couple of seconds before lifting it and moving it to the next section.

Laura's top tip

It might sound a little pernickety, but there's a subtle difference to the way that you press a line of stitching with an iron compared to the way that you might iron a piece of clothing. When you're ironing a garment, you smooth the plate of the iron back and forth over the fabric until the wrinkles are gone. However, when using the iron on a line of stitches you want to achieve something a little different, so you'll need to use the iron in a slightly different way. Rather than sweeping the iron over the fabric, simply position it on the line of stitches, press it down and hold it for a couple of seconds. This might sound rather odd, but the heat of the iron will set the stitches into a neat position, whereas moving the iron back and forth can distort each stitch a little. I find the best way to remember this is that if the stitching line is visible, press and hold the iron on the surface; if the fabric is visible over the stitching, move the iron freely.

2 Use your fingertips to open up the two small sections of seam allowance and lay the fabric with its right side facing up. Smooth the fabric over with your hand to make sure that the seam allowance is folded back on to itself underneath the fabric. Use the iron to gently press into the seam, pushing in towards the join. Work on one side of the fabric at a time, moving the iron along the entire length of the join before rotating the fabric to repeat on the second side.

3 Turn the fabric so that the wrong side is facing up, and, using the tip of the iron, gradually work along the centre of the seam, pressing the seam allowances neatly back on themselves. This will create a neat and tidy seam.

Taking time to press seams will give your projects a better finish

Neatening the seam allowances

On projects where the seam will be seen when looking at the wrong side of the work, such as on garments, the raw edges of the seams can be neatened to prevent them from fraying and looking messy.

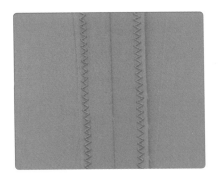

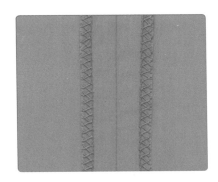

Trim with pinking shears

Trim the raw edges of the seam allowance with pinking shears. The serrated blades will give the fabric a zigzag edging that will prevent it from fraying.

Edge with zigzag stitching

A line of zigzag stitching can be worked close to the edge of the fabric's seam allowance, which is then trimmed close to the line of stitching. If you're working on a project that has lots of seams you can sew around the edges of all the pieces with a zigzag stitch before you begin to join them; this can speed up the process.

Edge with overcast stitching

If your machine has an overcast stitch function, select this and the appropriate foot and work a line of overcast stitches along the length of raw edge at the seam allowance. This will loop threads over the raw edge to secure it against fraying.

Sewing a seam on a corner

Creating a seam on a corner is done in the same manner as sewing a corner.

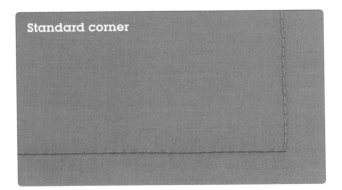

Standard corner

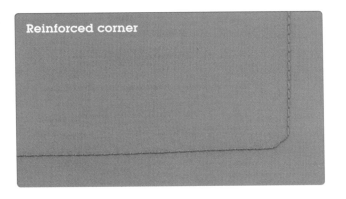

Reinforced corner

1 Standard Corner. Sew along the stitching line until you reach the point at the same distance from the edge of the fabric as the width of the seam allowance, ending with the needle in the down position. Then raise the presser foot, pivot the fabric, and continue stitching the second line.

2 Reinforced Corner. Heavyweight fabrics can be reinforced on a corner seam. Raise the foot, pivot the fabric halfway round, then lower the foot and work one or two stitches diagonal to the point of the corner. Lower the needle back into the fabric, raise the presser foot again, rotate the fabric the remainder of the way and work the second part of the corner.

Seam allowance

This is the term used to describe the amount of space between the raw edge of the fabric and the sewing line. It's very common for this to be 1.5cm (0.6in), although it can vary from project to project, and in some cases can even vary between different sections of the same project, depending on the requirements. If you're making something from scratch, and have drawn out a template or have the measurements for the finished item, you'll need to add on a seam allowance to ensure that it turns out the correct size. To do this you simply add on a border of the required seam allowance before you cut the piece. For curved shapes you simply tape two pencils together and use one to draw around the outline of the shape and the other will add the seam allowance. If the outer line this creates doesn't provide a large enough seam allowance, simply position the pencil on first 'seam' line to create another line and a larger seam allowance.

Trimming and snipping seam allowances

When turning seams through there are times when the fabric of the seam allowance will need to be trimmed or snipped to create a neater join or to reduce the bulk in that area.

Reducing bulk on a seam

If you're working with heavy fabrics the area of the seam allowance can end up rather bulky, as there will be layers of fabric on top of each other close to the seam. To reduce this you'll need to trim down one of the seam allowances so that it sits closer to the line of stitching – but be careful not to cut through any stitches!

Reducing bulk on corners

To get crisp corners when turning fabrics through, the fabric that lies in the seam allowance on the corner needs to be trimmed off to remove the excess at the point. This is also great for other angled seams, like triangles. You may need to use the end of a pencil or a knitting needle to push the fabric through neatly when turning through to the right side. On some projects where the corner seam might be sitting on the inside of the work, there'll be no corner of seam allowance to trim; here the allowance is cut from the outer edge of the seam allowance in towards the corner of stitching, to give the fabric more movement for turning through.

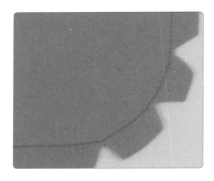

Snipping seam allowances on curves

On a curved seam, to create a neat arc on the fabric when it's turned through you'll need to make small V-shaped snips into the seam allowance. This will give the fabric the little extra movement that it needs to turn through neatly. To do this, you need to make small cuts through both layers of seam allowance, working from the raw edges towards the line of stitching. Repeat along the length of the curve. Use small sharp scissors and be careful not to snip any of the stitches.

Reinforcing a seam

On high stress areas it's sometimes necessary to reinforce a seam to give it added strength and stability.

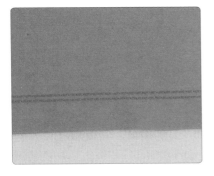

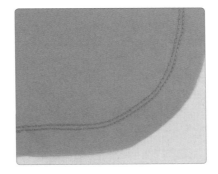

Under-stitching

There are instances when you won't want the second row of securing stitches to show on the right side of the project, for example around necklines when you don't want the seam to roll forward and allow the lining to become visible. In such cases trim the section of seam allowance on the side of the fabric that won't be seen when the item is turned through to the right side. Press the longer seam allowance over the shorter one to encase it. Work a line of straight stitching along the length, 2mm (0.08in) to the right of the original seam. The stitching will secure the seam allowances on to the fabric that will be innermost when the seam is turned through.

Double seam

The simplest method is to create a double seam. Once you've worked a seam create a second line of stitching 2mm (0.08in) to the right of the first. This will sit inside the seam allowance. This technique can be used for both straight and curved seams.

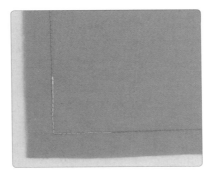

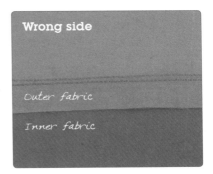

Wrong side

Outer fabric

Inner fabric

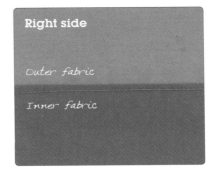

Right side

Outer fabric

Inner fabric

Top stitching

Once the seam has been turned through, a row of stitching can be worked on the right side of the seam. This will secure the fabric of the seam allowance and give the seam additional strength. The line of stitching is visible on the right side of the project, and is also used as a decorative effect. The stitching line should be positioned at the halfway point from the seam and the outer edge of the seam allowance – this will ensure all the fabric layers are secured.

Reinforcing corners

The point of a corner can be reinforced by working a second line of stitching directly on top of the first for 3cm (1.18in) either side of the corner, using the pivoting technique to turn the work to sew the second side of the corner.

The under-stitching is only visible on one side of the seam.

French seams

A French seam is used when joining delicate fabrics. It's stitched first on the right side and then again on the wrong side of the fabric, the second seam encasing the first to make it more secure and extremely neat.

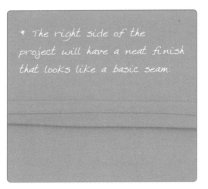

The right side of the project will have a neat finish that looks like a basic seam.

1 With the wrong sides of the fabrics facing, work a straight seam using a 5mm (0.19in) seam allowance. Trim down the seam allowance and finger press the seam so that it lies slightly open.

2 Fold the fabrics so the right sides are together – the stitched seam will be on the inside of the fold. With a 1cm (0.4in) seam allowance, work a line of stitches long the joined section.

3 Turn the fabrics to the right side and press. The first seam is fully encased by the second seam.

Laura's top tip

When working on intricate seams, like French seams, you can use your fingertips and a little pressure to gently arrange the fabric into the position it needs to be. This will hold it out of the way while you work, but it won't leave a crease on the fabric in the same way that an iron would.

Bias bound seam

Securing the raw edges on a seam will prevent the edges from unsightly fraying. This is often used to treat seams of unlined garments.

Once a seam has been stitched, place a length of bias tape along the raw edges of the seam allowance and pin in place. Sew along the length of bias tape 4mm (0.16in) in from the covered raw edges so that they're encased within the bias tape. Be careful to ensure that both the front and the back of the bias tape are being stitched. Press the bound seam open to finish.

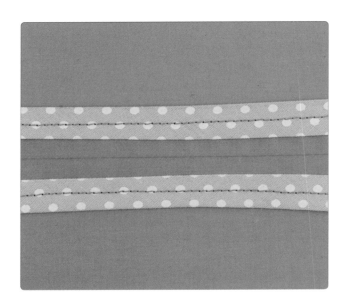

Fastenings

Whie buttons and zips are most commonly associated with dressmaking, there are a number of other projects that can really benefit from these skills, including making bags and cushions. There is a wide range of fasteners and each has special properties that are suited to a variety of different applications.

Zips

Learning to insert a zip will allow you to tackle garments like dresses, skirts and trousers. There are many different ways to insert a zip, the most commonly used being the centred zip and the concealed zip. Selecting a zip foot will allow you to work the stitches as close as possible to the fastening, giving the completed project a neat finish.

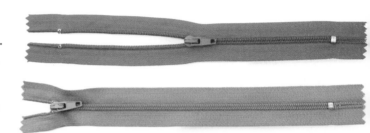

Centred zip

When stitched in position the two edges of the seam allowance meet in front of the teeth of the zip, and when it's pulled up the zip is barely visible.

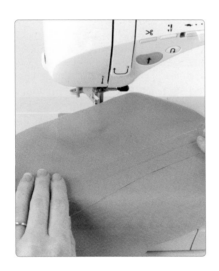

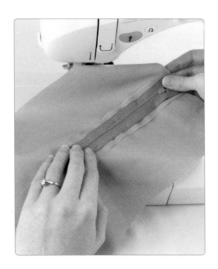

1 With the right sides of the fabric facing, join them together using a basic seam, leaving the point where the base of the zip will sit unstitched. Work a line of tacking stitches along the stitching line to temporarily hold the two sections of fabric together, and press the seam open.

2 With the wrong side of the fabric facing upwards, place the zip face down on the join, aligning the teeth with the tacked section. The base of the zip will sit at the bottom of the tacked section. Pin and tack in place along both sides of the zip.

3 With the right sides of the project uppermost, sew the zip in place, working from the top down one side. Stop the machine at the bottom of the zip and pivot on the needle to work a short line of stitches across the bottom of the zip tape. Be careful not to sew over the zip teeth. Stop and pivot to stitch the second side.

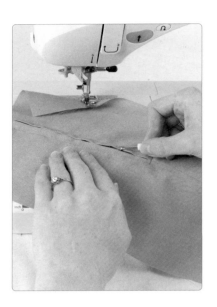

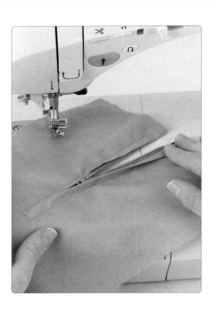

4 Turn the project and continue to sew up the second side of the zip, ending at the upper section of the zip.

5 Use a seam ripper to carefully unpick the tacking stitches from the seam allowance, and remove the unwanted threads.

6 Use the zip tab to open and close the completed fastening.

Concealed zip

This is the most discreet zip fastening there is. The teeth of the zip lie on the inside of the project and all that's visible from the right side is the small tab to pull the zip open and closed.

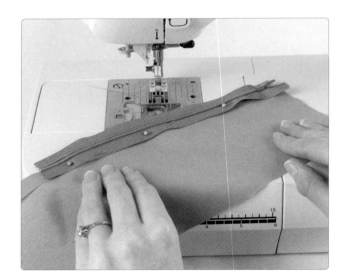

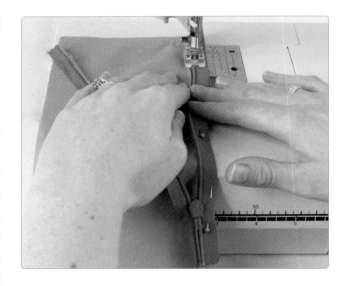

1 Press over the seam allowance on the wrong side. Place the concealed zip face down on the fabric so that the raw edges of the tape and the raw edge of the seam allowance are aligned. Pin in place carefully along the length of the zip tape.

2 Open the zip and, using a concealed zip foot, stitch as close to the teeth as possible. Ensure that the main project fabric is pushed to the left-hand side out of the sewing line. Sew as far down the zip as the foot will allow – it's impossible to sew to the bottom of a concealed zip.

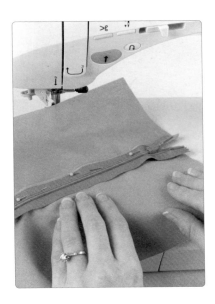

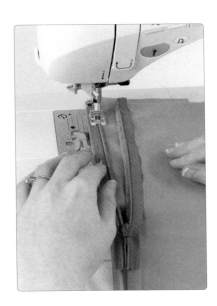

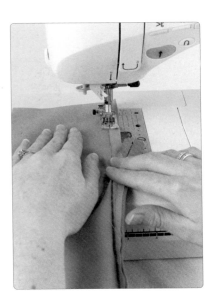

3 Pull the zip closed and align the second side of the zip tape to the seam allowance on the second side. Pin along the length of the zip to secure it in place.

4 Open the zip and, using a concealed zip foot, work along the second side, sewing as close to the teeth as possible.

5 With a straight machine stitch and returning to a standard presser foot, join the seam together below the end of the zip. It's impossible to get in really close to the end of the zip, and there's usually a small part that will remain unstitched.

Hook and eye fastenings

These very small fastenings are great for adding a finishing touch to projects. They're frequently placed in the fabric at the top of a zip to create a really professional finish to the fastening.

Pin the two separate elements of the hook and eye fastening into position and secure with tacking stitches. Secure the thread on the wrong side of the project and bring your needle through to the right side via the loops at the base of the fastening. Use buttonhole stitch to secure these loops to the fabric. Work a couple of stitches on the inside of the hook to give additional security, remove the tacks, and repeat for the second part of the fastening.

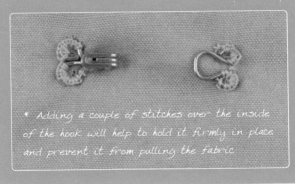

* Adding a couple of stitches over the inside of the hook will help to hold it firmly in place and prevent it from pulling the fabric

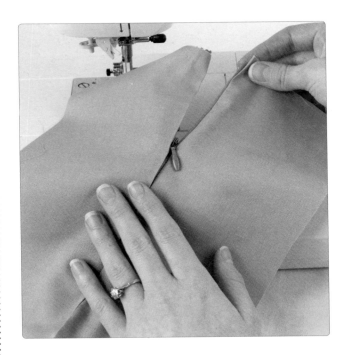

6 Working on the seam allowance on the wrong side, work 2cm (0.79in) of stitching at the bottom of the zip on each side to secure it to the seam allowance. The completed zip will be very discreet on the right side, with only the pull tab showing.

Buttons

Buttons are not only a versatile fastener but are also great for adding decorative details to your projects. There's a huge range of styles, some featuring four holes, others two; there are also buttons that have a small shank on the back, with a hole through which stitches can secure it to the fabric.

If you're just adding buttons for decorative effect you can simply sew them on, working over the holes. For a two-hole button the thread is secured on the back and the needle brought up through the fabric through one hole. The thread is then passed over the surface of the button and down through the second hole and to the wrong side of the fabric. This is repeated until the button is secure. A four-hole button is worked in much the same way, bringing the thread up through the fabric into a hole and across the button and down through the next hole to the wrong side of the fabric. To keep the stitching neat take the thread across the surface of the button, bring the needle up through one hole and pass it back down through the hole diagonally opposite, then up through the hole directly above that and down through the final unstitched hole. This will create a neat cross on the surface of the button.

Adding a thread shank to a flat button

When adding flat buttons as fastenings a thread shank needs to be created so that there's space for the fabric of the overlapping section to fit snugly underneath without pulling on the button. This is created by positioning a large tapestry needle on top of the button and stitching over it. The thickness of the tapestry needle means that the stitches are elongated and can be secured into a shank under the button.

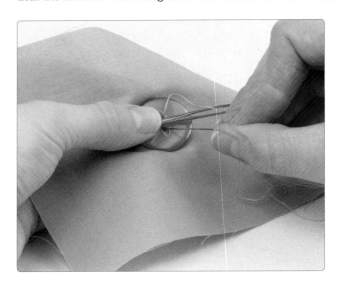

1 Secure the thread on the back of the project. Bring the thread up through the fabric and out through the hole. Lay a tapestry needle between the holes in the button and pass your sewing needle across this before passing it down through the next hole and into the fabric. Continue sewing through the button in this way, drawing the thread over the tapestry needle as you work.

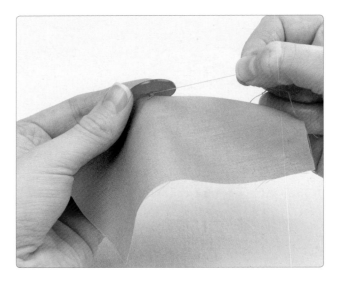

2 Remove the tapestry needle from the top of the button and push the button to the top of the resultant stitched loop. Carefully wrap the needle threads around the elongated stitches between the base of the button and the fabric to create a thread shank. Once secured, fasten off on the wrong side of the work.

Sewing on a shanked button

A shanked button has a small raised section on the back, which includes a hole through which it can be stitched to the fabric. There's no need to create an additional shank with thread, as the moulded shank raises the button above the surface of the fabric and allows the overlapping section to fit snugly underneath.

Secure the thread on the wrong side of the project, then pass the needle through to the right side of the fabric and through the hole in the shank before passing it back through to the wrong side. When affixing a shank button check that you're happy with the orientation of the button before you work the first stitch – rotate it until you're happy with its appearance on the surface before working the stitches through it.

Reinforcing a button

On thick coats and jackets, or when large heavy buttons are used, it's often wise to reinforce the button. This is a useful way to stop the button from tugging the fabric, which might eventually rip off.

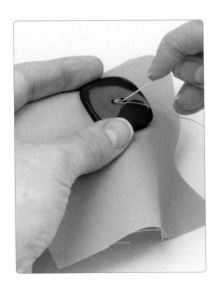

1 Secure the thread on the wrong side of the project and pass the needle through to the right side via the button on the surface. As the needle tip returns to the wrong side, slip a small button on to the needle and pull through so that it sits flush on the wrong side of the fabric.

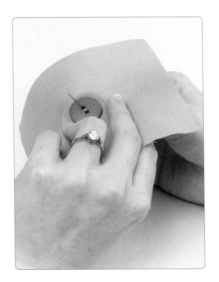

2 Pass the needle back through the other hole in the small button on the wrong side of the fabric, and through to the button on the right side. Continue stitching the buttons in place, ensuring that the needle always passes through the large button on the right side and the small button on the wrong side. Secure on the wrong side of the work to finish.

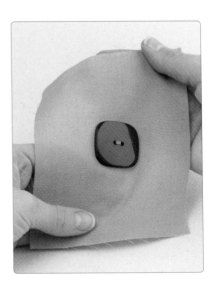

3 Only the main button is visible on the right side of the project with the smaller button secured to the back for added support.

Snap fastenings

These clever little fasteners are available in a wide range of sizes and can be either metal or plastic, with small holes around the outer edge for easy application. They can be used to join fabric sections by pressing the two corresponding parts together, and are opened by pulling them apart. They can also be added to clothing – for example, if a blouse gapes open along the buttonband a snap can be sewn between the buttons to hold the material together without being noticeable from the right side.

Place the two snap parts in the required positions and tack in place to prevent them from slipping. Secure the thread on the back of the project and bring the needle up to the right side of the fabric through the hole in the snap. Secure with small stitches through the hole, and continue around until the whole snap is firmly in place. Then remove the tacking stitches. Repeat for the second half of the snap.

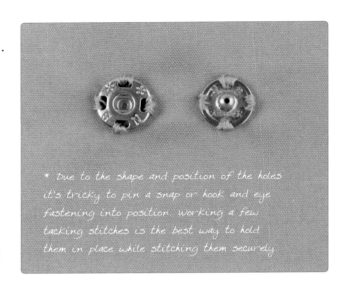

Due to the shape and position of the holes it's tricky to pin a snap or hook and eye fastening into position. Working a few tacking stitches is the best way to hold them in place while stitching them securely

Magnetic snaps

With a strong magnet to hold its parts together, these snaps are great for adding quick and secure fastenings to bags and purses. Since the magnet is quite strong, back the fabric with a small piece of interfacing to prevent it from tearing when you open and close the fastening. Also, the metal bars on the back of these fastenings that are used to secure them should be affixed to the lining of your project so that the metal isn't visible from the right side.

1 Use pins or chalks to mark the positions of each half of the snap fastener. Use a seam ripper or small sharp scissors to make small cuts in the fabric for the metal bars.

2 Position the snap on the fabric with its bars passing through the openings.

3 Slide the washer on to the back of the snap – the bars will pass through the holes on the back of the washer. Push the washer flush to the surface of the fabric and carefully press down the bars to secure the snap into position.

4 Complete the fastening by securing the second snap in the same way.

Tucks, gathers & pleats

These are all fantastic ways to add decorative details to clothing, accessories and even soft furnishings, and knowing how to accomplish them will enable you to take on more challenging and exciting projects.

Tucks

Folding the fabric and stitching it in place will create neat little tucks that lie on the surface. This decorative effect can be as subtle or as dramatic as you want – you simply have to work with larger or smaller folds of fabric to create the tucks.

1 With a ruler and chalk or erasable marker, draw out on the right side of the fabric the lines that will form the tucks. Be careful to keep the spacing of the lines even, as this will mark out the sewing line. Fold the fabric over on each line and press with an iron to create a crease.

Every pair of lines will be folded together to create a tuck. Work with 2.5 cm (1in) gaps between each line to create narrow tucks

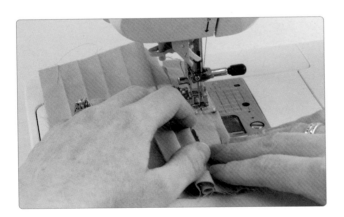

2 With the right side facing upwards, fold the fabric to align the first marked line with the second. Pin the tuck together along its length. Fold the fabric so that the tuck is to the right-hand side and the remainder of the fabric is on the left-hand side, clear of the machine needle.

3 With a straight machine stitch, sew along the length, working over the marked lines to hold the tuck in place. Work one tuck at a time, pinning then stitching until all of the tucks are created.

Different tuck styles

You can change the look of your tucks by making the sections larger or smaller. The wider you space each pair of lines the bigger the tuck will be on the surface; smaller gaps between the lines will make more discreet tucks. You can enlarge the space between tucks by increasing the space between each pair of lines drawn. Experiment with different widths and spaces to create different effects. If you want to keep the tucks the same size you'll need to ensure that each pair of lines is equally spaced, regardless of the spacing between the pairs.

Create rippled tucks

Once you've sewn a section of tucks you can stitch them in place on the surface to create ripples.

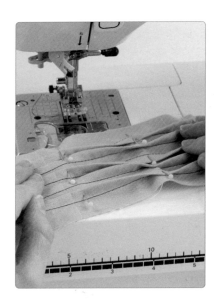

1 Working on the right side of the tucked fabric, use a ruler and chalk to draw evenly spaced lines through the tucks. Then, using your fingertips, press the tucks to lie in one direction and pin either side of the line. Move to the next line and finger-press the tucks in the other direction, to create a ripple. Repeat pressing and pinning to alternate along the length of tucked fabric.

2 With a straight stitch, work along the marked lines to carefully sew the tucks into position. Smooth the fabric as you sew to ensure that all the tucks are facing in the correct direction for each line of stitching.

3 Continue along the length of the fabric, sewing the tucks down in alternating directions to create a rippled effect.

Gathers

This produces a rippled effect on the surface of the fabric. They're created by drawing up a length of fabric along a machine- or hand-stitched line, and are often used in making skirts and dresses.

1 Prepare the fabric by working two lines of gathering stitches within the seam allowance along the top and pulling the threads to create ruffles.

3 With the right sides facing, place the length of gathered fabric on the flat fabric that it will be joined to. Pin it in place carefully to ensure that the gathered section is aligned along the raw edge of the fabric. If the fabrics you're using are slippery, tack the two sections together to hold them in place for sewing. Working with the gathered section uppermost will allow you to check that the ripples are being stitched evenly as you work the seam.

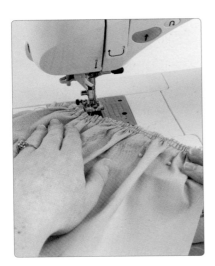

2 Using your fingertips, ease the fabric along the stitched lines to create neat, even ripples, and knot the ends of the gathering threads to secure them.

4 Using a straight machine stitch, sew along the seam to join the two sections. The lines of gathering stitches will be positioned inside the seam allowance and the stitching will permanently fix the gathers in the fabric. Press the seam allowance towards the flat fabric to finish.

Measuring for gathers

When joining a flat section and a gathered section it's important that the latter is pulled in so that it's the same length as the corresponding flat piece before it's stitched in place. The best way to ensure accuracy is to lay out the flat section on a smooth surface like a tabletop, and place the section to be gathered on top of it; this way you can pull on the gather threads gradually to draw up the fabric so that it's the correct length to be secured to the flat piece.

Pleats

Pleats are surprisingly quick to create and can be used to add volume and movement to a wide range of projects. They're particularly popular in dressmaking.

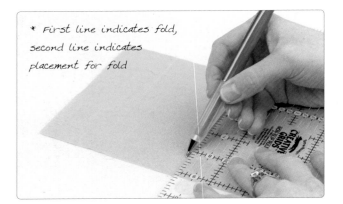

First line indicates fold, second line indicates placement for fold

1 Working on the right side of the fabric, use a ruler and chalk or erasable marker to draw the lines that will mark out the placement of the pleats. If you're sewing with a dressmakers' pattern these sections will be indicated on the pattern piece. Here I've worked with the space between each pleat, measuring twice the amount of the fabric of the pleat itself to keep it neat.

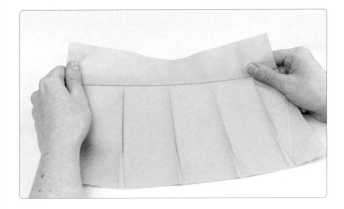

3 Work a line of tacking stitches along the length of each pleat to hold it in place. Make sure that the tacking stitches go through all the layers of the fabric – this will hold them securely while you complete the construction of the project.

2 Starting at one side, begin folding the fabric over so that the line which indicates the fold aligns with the line that marks the pleat's position. Pin the fold and press into place.

Laura's top tip

When making pleats you can use two colours of chalk, one to mark out the line where the pleat will sit and the other to mark the fold line. This makes aligning them for pressing and stitching quick and easy.

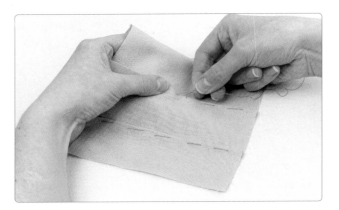

4 The pleated section will usually be secured at one end: for example, when dressmaking this would be stitched to the waistband on a skirt. Once the pleated section has been secured press the pleats carefully on the right side and then the wrong side of the fabric to set them in place. Position the iron on one section, holding it for a few seconds before lifting, then move to the next section and repeat – avoid sliding the iron around over the surface, as this will distort the pleats! Once fully pressed on each side the tacking stitches can be removed.

Centred pleats

A single pleat can be created to sit in the centre of a project. This is a common feature on the front of skirts and the back of tops and blouses.

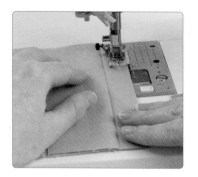

1 Working on the right side of the fabric, find the centre point and mark it with a pin. Using a ruler and chalk or an erasable marker, draw out the position lines and the fold lines for each pleat. Use the centre pin marker as a guide to get the pleats equally spaced from the centre.

3 With larger pleats, as here, the section can be secured on the wrong side, which will help keep the finished pleat tidy. Working on the wrong side of the fabric using a straight machine stitch and working to the fold, sew along the length of the pleat that will sit innermost, to secure it. Repeat for the other side.

2 Using the lines as a guide, fold in the pleats, ensuring that both pleats fold in towards the centre. Pin in place and tack to secure.

4 Once the pleated section has been secured within the project, press the sections of the pleat, holding the iron over a section for a few seconds before lifting and pressing the next. Then remove the tacks from the finished piece.

Inverted centred pleat

Using a similar method to the centred pleat, the process can be reversed to create a pleat that sits with the centre section outermost.

Working from a marked centre point on the right side of the fabric, draw out the fold and placements lines on either side of the pleat section. Fold the fabric using the lines as a guide – make the fold so that the pleat is facing away from the centre section and tack. Repeat for the second side. The unseen inner section of the pleat can be stitched on the wrong side for neatness. Press the pleat fully to secure it in position on the finished project.

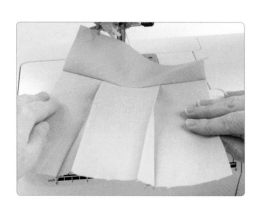

Corners, trims & edges

A few little details that can be worked into your sewing projects will really increase their wow factor. Simple seams can be transformed by the addition of a few key haberdashery items that will give your projects a unique style that you'll be really proud of.

Mitred corners

Corners will feature in a number of projects, and achieving a crisp point will give it a professional finish. A mitre is created by carefully folding the edges of the fabric to the inside and stitching them in place.

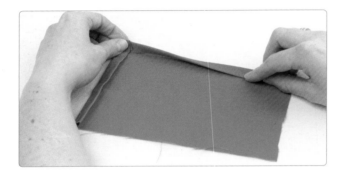

1 With the wrong side of the fabric facing upwards, fold over 1cm (0.4in) along each edge and press. Open out and then fold over 2cm (0.79in) and press again. This will create a border of two ironed crease lines around the project that will act as guides.

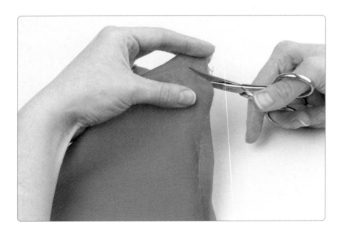

2 Where these two lines of ironed border meet at the corners there will be a small square. Snip off the corners of fabric diagonally across the centre of the square. Repeat to trim off the tips of all of the corners. Doing this will reduce the bulk.

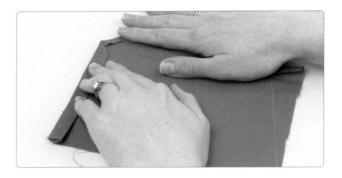

3 Press the flat section at the corners of the project over by 5mm (0.19in), then refold the fabric to the outermost border crease. The flat section will sit underneath the side of the border section.

4 Fold the fabric to the second crease line on the border and pin to secure. The project will have a neat border of fabric the whole way round, and the corners will have two angled sections that meet in a point. Carefully press each section. Sew the border to the project's main fabric with hand slip stitches. At the corners work up the diagonal intersection towards the tip with slip stitches, to secure the sections together. Continue slip stitching around the project until the whole border is secure.

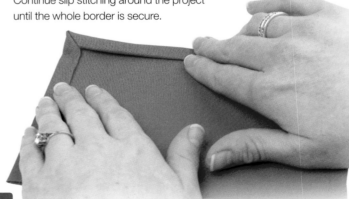

Adding bias tape

Bias tape or binding is a strip of triple-folded fabric that's used to finish off raw edges. The tape is carefully folded and stitched in place with the raw edges of the fabric concealed inside it. It can be used as a quick finish for necklines and armholes on garments, or as the finishing touch on the edges of a quilt.

1 Open the bias strip out fully and, with the right side facing the wrong side of the project, align the raw edge of the bias tape with the raw edge of the project. Allow additional tape to ease around curves or to add mitred corners.

2 With a straight stitch, sew along the length of the bias tape to secure it to the project. Keep the stitches as close to the fold line in the bias tape as possible. Continue until the whole length is secured.

3 Turn the project over to the right side and fold the bias tape over the raw edges. Using the fold in the bias tape as a guide, fold the raw edge of the bias tape under; the raw edge of the project will sit up inside the bias tape at the central crease. Pin in place along the project.

4 Working with hand slip stitches, join the bias tape along the right side of the project to secure it in place. When completed the stitching on either side won't be visible, and the edges of the bias tape will be level on both sides, creating a border.

Making bias tape

1 Cut a strip of fabric diagonally across the grain of the fabric, which is called the bias. The width of the strip can be made to suit your preference, but it will need to be four times as wide as one face of the finished strip.

2 With the wrong side of the bias strip facing upwards, fold it in half, aligning the two long raw edges, and press to create a centre crease.

3 Open out the strip, refold one of the long edges inwards to align with the centre crease and press. Repeat with the second long edge. Refold the entire length of bias tape along the centre line and press firmly.

Mitred corner with bias tape

Getting a crisp mitred corner with bias binding isn't as tricky as it might seem. The key is to follow a few simple folding steps at each corner when pinning the bias into place, so that when it's stitched and turned to the right side neat mitres will appear at the corners.

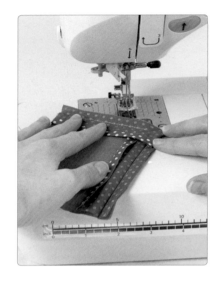

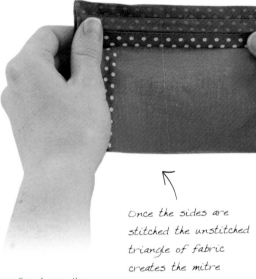

Once the sides are stitched the unstitched triangle of fabric creates the mitre

1 Pin the bias along the straight edge. When 5mm (0.19in) from the corner, fold the bias upwards above the project to create a 45° angle.

3 Sew around the binding along the crease line. Leave the corners unstitched and press the triangle so that it lies centrally in the corner; then resume sewing the next side.

2 Holding the point of the corner gently in place, refold the bias tape so that it aligns with the next straight edge. A small triangle of fabric will be created over the corner. Repeat for the remaining sides and corners, pinning the binding and corners in place as you work.

4 For the front of the project, fold the binding in place so that the raw edges of the fabric are inside the binding and the raw edges of the bias tape are tucked under. Pin in place. At the corners carefully tuck the excess triangle of fabric inside the binding and pin it in place before securing with hand slip stitches.

5 Once slip stitched in place the bias is held securely and the stitches aren't visible on either side of the project.

Creating a piping seam

Adding a length of piping to a seam will add a decorative feature to a project. This is often used in dressmaking to add interest to waistbands. The piping is made first then stitched into position as the seam is worked. When the project is turned through to the right side the piping will sit across the section where the fabrics are joined.

1 With the right side outermost, fold a piece of bias tape around a length of cord. Select a straight machine stitch and sew along the length as close to the cord as possible. Using a zip foot will help you to get the stitches really close to the cord.

2 With the fabrics to be joined placed right sides together and the piping sandwiched in between, align the raw edges of the fabrics and the bias tape and pin in place. With a straight machine stitch, sew along the section, working the stitches along the edge of the cord.

3 To prevent the cord from slipping as you stitch you can work a line of tacking stitches along the length of the seam allowance to secure it. Press the seam allowance to one side to neaten and turn through.

Adding a ribbon ruffle

Work two lines of gather stitches along one long edge of a piece of ribbon, pull up to gather the ribbon to the length of the seam and knot to secure. Place the fabrics to be joined with their right sides together. Sandwich the length of ribbon in between them, ensuring that the raw edges of the ribbon and the fabrics are aligned. As satin ribbon can be slippery, tack the pieces together before sewing. Using a straight machine stitch, join the two pieces of fabric together, ensuring that the ribbon is secured by the stitches. Remove the tacking stitches, press the seam to one side and turn through to the right side.

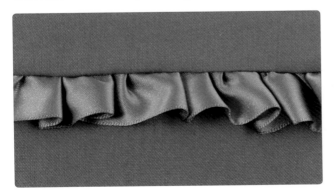

Mix and match trims

The basic principle for adding trimming into a seam is the same, so look for new items to add different decorative features to your seams.

Pompom

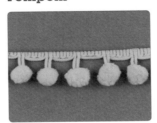

Ric Rac

Layered ribbon

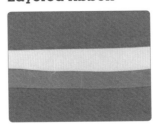

Vintage lace

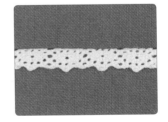

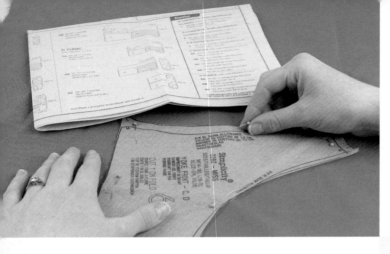

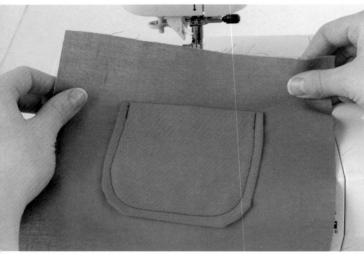
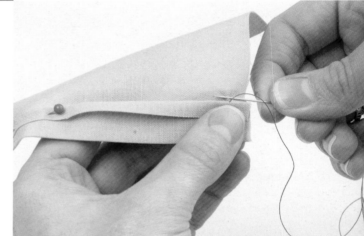

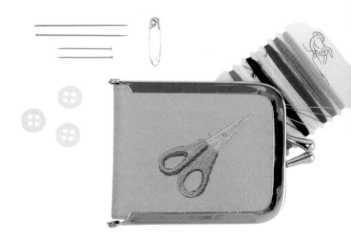

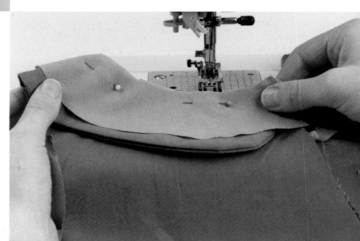

Chapter 4

Dressmaking

Creating your own clothing from scratch is one of the most satisfying forms of sewing – nothing quite beats the feeling of stepping out in a handmade dress, except perhaps replying to a compliment by saying, 'Thank you, I made it myself!' The first time you unfold a dressmakers' pattern you'd be forgiven for feeling a little overwhelmed, but once you discover the basic elements of the pattern and the sewing techniques needed to assemble the different parts there'll be no stopping you!

Taking measurements

It's all too tempting to dive right in and start cutting and stitching, but begin with some essential preparations to get you off to a flying start. A tape measure teamed with a notepad and pencil are the foundations for all dressmaking projects.

Before you begin making any garment the first thing you'll need to do is to take accurate body measurements. While you'll probably know the dress size that you wear when buying clothing from a High Street store, selecting your own pattern requires a little more careful consideration. Skipping over this stage might seem like it will save time so that you can get right on with the sewing, but it will lead to garments that don't fit properly or aren't comfortable to wear – which is really frustrating when you've taken the time to make them.

Laura's top tip

It's important to take your measurements every time you start a new project to help you get the right size and fit for your body. The size that you select from the pattern will also determine the fabric amounts you'll require to make the specific garment. I keep a record of my measurements in a notebook, and each time I measure it means that I can compare them easily to size charts; it also means that I have them to hand if I'm out shopping and come across a pattern or fabric I want to buy – it saves trying to take measurements while standing in the shop, and prevents buying the wrong amount of fabric.

Body measurements

There are a few key areas that you'll need to measure. Use a long fabric tape measure and note the measurements down so that you can use them to refer to the sizing guide on your pattern. However, before you start recording your measurements begin by removing your shoes, and wear well-fitting underwear and comfortable fitted clothing – you don't want to be wearing something that's too restrictive, as this will change your body shape, but you do need the tape measure to lie flat against your body. Better still, take your measurements in just your undies. Some measurements are a little tricky to take by yourself, so you may need a friend to help you (a very good one, if you're in your undies).

When you pass the tape measure around your body, you don't want to hold it too tight or too slack, as this won't give you a true measurement. Try to always keep the tape measure level at the front and back of your body for greater accuracy.

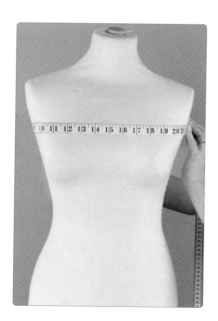

Chest
Circle the tape measure around your upper torso. Keep your arms down by your side and place the tape measure round your upper body so that it reaches the crease of your armpit.

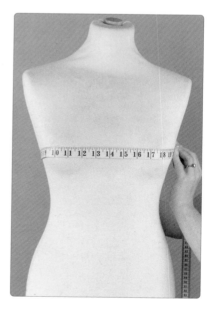

Bust
Wearing a well-fitting bra, loop the tape measure around the fullest part of your bust to take the measurement.

Choosing a pattern size

A dressmakers' pattern will include a sizing chart. This is a list of all the sizes that can be made using that specific pattern. Each size will have a list of measurements for the different parts of the body, so use your list of body measurements to select the right size to make.

Of course, very few of us have body measurements that match exactly to the bust, waist and hip measurements on a sizing chart. This doesn't mean that the pattern won't work for you, it simply means that you may need to make some adjustments. Always pick the size that fits your largest measurement – for example, if your bust measurement matches the bust measurement on the pattern chart for a size 12, but your waist and hips fall within the size 10 measurements, select your garment in dress size 12, because it's much easier to take a pattern in than it is to let it out. You'll need to keep your body measurements to hand for when you're cutting the pattern pieces; this will enable you to make adjustments to the relevant sections before cutting them from the fabric.

Additional measurements

Some patterns, particularly those for trousers, jackets and shirts, will require a few more measurements.

Collar
Loop the tape measure around the base of your neck. Don't wrap this too tight – pull it to fit as you'd want the collar on a shirt to fit. You'll want to be able to move your head without it pinching.

Shoulder
Place the tape measure at the base of your neck and lay it out over the shoulder. Take the measurement at the point where the arm and the shoulder meet in the socket.

Sleeve
Full arm length can be measured by putting your hand on your hip and letting the tape measure run from the point where the arm and the shoulder meet in the socket and over the bend at the elbow. The measurement is taken at the wrist bone.

Leg
You'll need to know both your inside and outside leg measurements to make well-fitting trousers. The outside leg measurement is taken by holding the tape measure at your natural waist and letting it run down the outside of your leg. The measurement is taken at the ankle bone. To take the inside leg measurement, stand with your feet slightly apart and hold the tape measure to your crotch. The measurement is taken at the ankle bone on the inside of your leg.

Height
With bare feet, stand straight with your back against a wall. Keep your shoulders relaxed and hold your head so that you're looking directly in front of you. Using a ruler flat against the top of your head, make a small mark on the wall at this point. Measure from this mark to record your height.

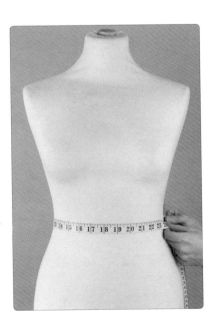

Waist
This measurement needs to be taken at the narrowest part of your torso. Be careful not to pull this too tight as it will result in finished clothes that pinch and are uncomfortable to wear.

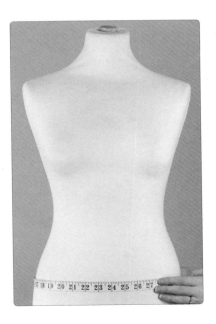

Hips
The tape measure needs to rest around the widest part of your hips. Depending on your body shape this will be around 15–20cm (6–8in) below your natural waist.

Patterns

At first glance dressmakers' patterns look complicated and confusing, but they feature a selection of symbols that make understanding the pattern easier. You'll find that you soon become accustomed to the different icons, and will be flying around a pattern in no time.

Choosing a pattern

There are many different dressmakers' patterns available, ranging from household brands to small indie designers, but whatever the brand or pattern they'll all have been designed to work in a similar way. As you create more garments and use a range of different patterns you might find that one pattern house or designer has garments that fit you better than another, or that the instructions given by some seem easier to follow; but this is all down to personal preference, and many dressmakers are happy to work from any brand of pattern.

The pattern will usually be housed in an envelope. This not only has pictures of the design – or designs – that you can make using the pattern, but also gives a lot of additional information about the pattern itself and the construction of the garment.

The majority of patterns will be multi-sized. This means that the patterns included can be made in different sizes depending on the line followed when cutting each piece. When a design is offered in a wide range of sizes – for example, from size 4 to size 22 – the design will be presented in two separate size blocks, so one pattern envelope will be for sizes 4–12 and the other for sizes 14–22.

Multiple design patterns may also include colour illustrations to show the full range of items that the pack contains.

Photographs are used to show examples of the garment in made-up form. On patterns that can be used to create several different garments, or garments with variations, there may be a couple of photographs showing these items being worn.

Some envelopes will include the number of pattern pieces that are printed on the pattern sheets. This is a good indication of how complex the construction is – for example, if the pattern only offers a couple of variations on a design yet it has a very high number of pattern pieces, this would suggest that there are lots of different components, like facings, linings, intricate bodices, that will make putting the garment together more time-consuming for a beginner.

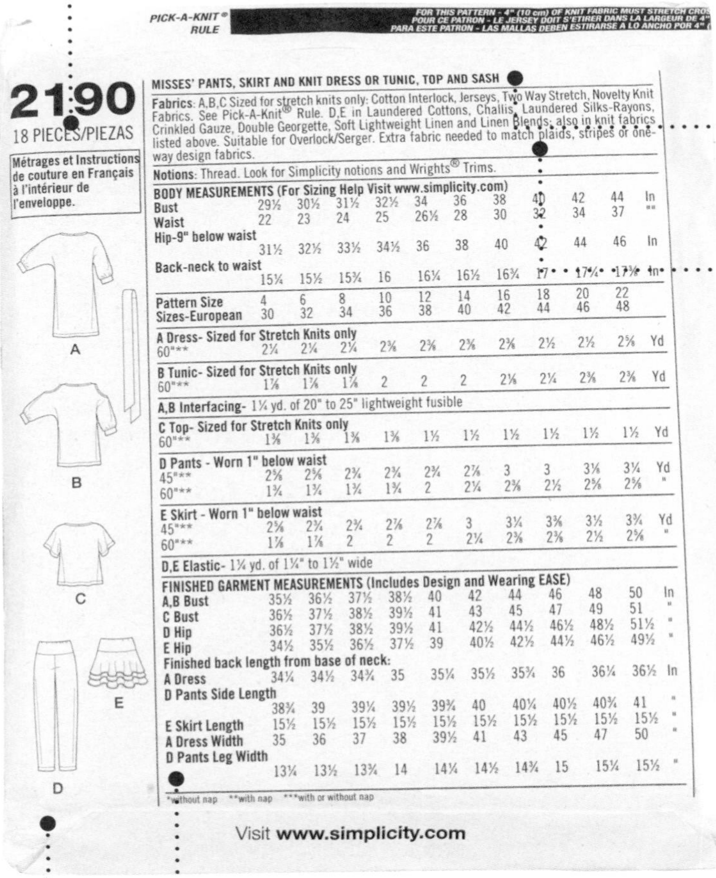
PICK-A-KNIT® RULE
FOR THIS PATTERN - 4" (10 cm) OF KNIT FABRIC MUST STRETCH CROS
POUR CE PATRON - LE JERSEY DOIT S'ETIRER DANS LA LARGEUR DE 4"
PARA ESTE PATRON - LAS MALLAS DEBEN ESTIRARSE A LO ANCHO POR 4"
2190
18 PIECES/PIEZAS
Métrages et Instructions de couture en Français à l'intérieur de l'enveloppe.
A
B
C
D
E
Visit www.simplicity.com

MISSES' PANTS, SKIRT AND KNIT DRESS OR TUNIC, TOP AND SASH

Fabrics: A,B,C Sized for stretch knits only: Cotton Interlock, Jerseys, Two Way Stretch, Novelty Knit Fabrics. See Pick-A-Knit® Rule. D,E in Laundered Cottons, Challis, Laundered Silks-Rayons, Crinkled Gauze, Double Georgette, Soft Lightweight Linen and Linen Blends; also in knit fabrics listed above. Suitable for Overlock/Serger. Extra fabric needed to match plaids, stripes or one-way design fabrics.

Notions: Thread. Look for Simplicity notions and Wrights® Trims.

BODY MEASUREMENTS (For Sizing Help Visit www.simplicity.com)											
Bust	29½	30½	31½	32½	34	36	38	40	42	44	In
Waist	22	23	24	25	26½	28	30	32	34	37	"
Hip-9" below waist	31½	32½	33½	34½	36	38	40	42	44	46	In
Back-neck to waist	15¼	15½	15¾	16	16¼	16½	16¾	17	17¼	17⅜	In
Pattern Size	4	6	8	10	12	14	16	18	20	22	
Sizes-European	30	32	34	36	38	40	42	44	46	48	
A Dress- Sized for Stretch Knits only 60"**	2¼	2¼	2¼	2⅜	2⅜	2⅜	2⅜	2½	2½	2⅝	Yd
B Tunic- Sized for Stretch Knits only 60"**	1⅞	1⅞	1⅞	2	2	2	2⅛	2¼	2⅜	2⅜	Yd
A,B Interfacing- 1¼ yd. of 20" to 25" lightweight fusible											
C Top- Sized for Stretch Knits only 60"**	1⅜	1⅜	1⅜	1⅜	1½	1½	1½	1½	1½	1½	Yd
D Pants - Worn 1" below waist 45"**	2⅝	2⅝	2¾	2¾	2¾	2⅞	3	3	3⅛	3¼	Yd
60"**	1¾	1¾	1¾	1¾	2	2¼	2⅜	2½	2⅝	2⅝	"
E Skirt - Worn 1" below waist 45"**	2⅝	2¾	2¾	2⅞	2⅞	3	3¼	3⅜	3½	3¾	Yd
60"**	1⅞	1⅞	2	2	2	2¼	2⅜	2⅜	2½	2⅝	"
D,E Elastic- 1¼ yd. of 1¼" to 1½" wide											
FINISHED GARMENT MEASUREMENTS (Includes Design and Wearing EASE)											
A,B Bust	35½	36½	37½	38½	40	42	44	46	48	50	In
C Bust	36½	37½	38½	39½	41	43	45	47	49	51	"
D Hip	36½	37½	38½	39½	41	42½	44½	46½	48½	51½	"
E Hip	34½	35½	36½	37½	39	40½	42½	44½	46½	49½	"
Finished back length from base of neck:											
A Dress	34¼	34½	34¾	35	35¼	35½	35¾	36	36¼	36½	In
D Pants Side Length	38¾	39	39¼	39½	39¾	40	40¼	40½	40¾	41	"
E Skirt Length	15½	15½	15½	15½	15½	15½	15½	15½	15½	15½	"
A Dress Width	35	36	37	38	39½	41	43	45	47	50	"
D Pants Leg Width	13¼	13½	13¾	14	14¼	14½	14¾	15	15¼	15½	"

*without nap **with nap ***with or without nap

Laura's top tip

Once you've made a pattern you can keep the pattern pieces safe by folding them up neatly and packaging them back inside the envelope together with the instructions. This way, if you want to make the garment again – perhaps in a different fabric or another colour – the pieces will be cut out ready to use.

A description of the different garments that can be made will help you to understand how the garments are constructed and give you an idea of the techniques used.

Many garments will require more than just fabrics to make them. Any items such as zips, boning or buttons will be listed.

Inside the pattern envelope

When you open the envelope you'll find several sheets of thin tissue paper on which are printed the pieces that will be used in making the garment; the number of sheets of tissue will depend on the number of pattern pieces required. There will also be a few sheets of printed instructions. These will tell you how to prepare the fabric and how to identify and cut the pieces. They'll also contain all the crucial information you'll need to make up the pattern, and in many cases will include handy illustrated guides to help you through various stages of construction.

A sizing chart is usually included on the back of the envelope. This will allow you to see the measurements that each size in the pack will be once it's worked up. Compare this to your own body measurements to pick your size.

2262
Simplicity
DRESS C OR TUNIC D
POCKETS AND SIDE SEAMS C

A selection of line drawings of different angles (known as 'views') of each garment shows how each one is constructed. You'll be able to see where features like fastenings and darts are positioned.

Pattern markings

The pattern uses a variety of different symbols on each piece that explain how the piece is to be used. They relate to the way the pattern is positioned on the fabric, how it's cut from the fabric, and how the pieces fit together. Each piece will have a number and a description, and the instruction sheet will include a reference section to help you identify the pattern pieces that you'll need to select for the design you want to make. It'll also include a written instruction of how the piece needs to be cut from the fabric and how many times you'll need to use it.

Multi-sized patterns

For patterns that offer a range of sizes for one design, each pattern piece will include a number of different cutting lines. These will be shown as a configuration of different length lines, lines with dots or lines with dashes. A key will be included in the information sheets to help you identify which style of line you need to follow in order to cut pieces to the right size for your project.

Cutting Lines

Preparing the pattern

In much the same way as you'll have prepared your fabrics by laundering and pressing them, there are a few quick steps that you'll need to take before you begin working on a pattern. For example, running a cool iron over the pattern sheets before you begin to cut them will smooth out all the folds and make the cutting both easier and neater. Also, look over the pattern information sheets and identify the names and numbers of the pieces you'll need for your chosen design. If the pattern has many different pieces, use a highlighter pen to mark the pieces that you'll need. You can also use the highlighter to draw round the cutting line for your own size – this is particularly useful in areas where the pattern lines seem to meet, as it will stop you from getting confused and cutting along the wrong one.

Pattern symbols

While there might be slight variations in the design of these symbols from pattern house to pattern house, the following icons are always used to convey set information about the usage of the pattern piece:

Grain line
This line is used to set the orientation of the pattern piece on the fabric. The length of the arrow is placed along the grain in the fabric.

Placement arrow
This arrow indicates that the pattern piece needs to be positioned on the fold in the fabric. The arrowheads are used to align the piece to the fabric.

Lengthen or Shorten Here

Adjustment lines
Many patterns will include markers to indicate where to make adjustments for length. They're most often seen on trousers and skirts.

Dots
These are used to indicate the position of zips, the points of darts, or buttonholes and buttons.

Notches
This icon is used as a marker that will help you align different pieces during construction. The notches on one section will match up to the notches on the corresponding section so that you can get the alignments just right.

Cutting the pattern

Once you've identified all the pattern pieces you need to make the garment, you'll have to cut around the pattern pieces. Place the pattern on a smooth flat surface and, using paper scissors, carefully cut the pattern piece following the correct line for your size.

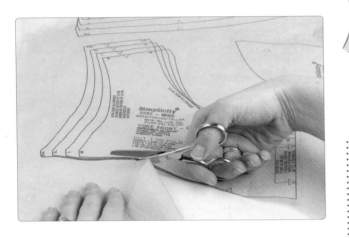

Positioning on the fabric

The way in which the fabric is folded for cutting is very important. The information sheets include illustrations called 'cutting lays' that not only show how to fold the fabric, but also how to position the pieces on it for cutting. The information sheet will often give a couple of examples of cutting lays, so be sure to select the right one for the width of fabric that you're working with. Some pattern pieces will be positioned on the grain of the fabric, and when cutting these you'll end up with two identical pieces where you've cut through the folded fabric. Other pieces will have an arrow that indicates they need to be positioned on the fold of the fabric for cutting. This creates one large piece, with the fold in the fabric being the middle point of the piece.

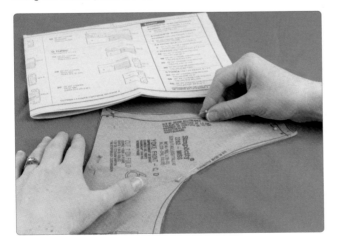

Transferring markings

After all the pattern pieces have been cut out, use tailor's chalk to transfer any markings – such as notches, darts or the position of buttons and zips – on to the wrong side of the pattern piece fabric. Having these marked out will help when you make up the garment.

Neatening the edges

It's important to neaten all the raw edges of the fabric, as although they're on the inside of the garment, fraying ends will feel uncomfortable, and may eventually unravel completely. Many people will work an overcasting stitch or use an overlocker to finish the edges once each seam has been worked. Alternatively you can work round each pattern piece with a zigzag stitch, worked close to the edge, before the pieces are placed together. Which you choose is entirely up to you – as you make more garments you'll soon find out which is the best method for you.

Using tissue paper

Dressmakers' patterns are printed on lightweight tissue paper to make them easier to use, since when the pattern piece is cut out and placed over the fabric you can see through it to the material beneath. Not only is this helpful in locating the grain of the fabric, it's also useful when working with print fabrics, as it allows you to carefully arrange the pattern elements so that the motifs are positioned in the most pleasing manner on each piece.

Altering patterns

Bodies come in all different shapes and sizes, so there may be times when you'll need to make some adjustments to the pattern pieces to get the best fit for your garment. The most common alterations are shortening and lengthening pattern pieces and making changes to the bust, waist and hips.

Shortening pieces

Many pattern pieces will include specific printed lines to show you where you can make adjustments to make the piece longer or shorter. These are positioned in such a way that they won't affect the shaping of the garment. To shorten the garment, draw a line above the adjustment line that matches the required amount – for example, if you need to lose 3cm (1.18in) from the length this new line would be 3cm (1.18in) above the adjustment line. Fold the paper over so that the adjustment line and the line you've just drawn match up. Use a length of tape to hold the fold in place.

Making a toile

To get the perfect fit, it's often recommended that you make a toile in calico before making the garment in your chosen fabric. Think of a toile as a practice version of your final garment. You'll be able to check the fit and make any adjustments to the pattern pieces before you begin working on the finished piece. This is a great idea, especially if you're making an outfit for a special occasion and want the fit to be perfect, or if you're using fabrics that are extremely expensive and mistakes would be costly.

Laura's top tip

Stand in front of a mirror and hold the cut pattern pieces up against your body. This will give you a rough idea of how the finished garment will sit – for example, the sleeves might be too long, or the skirt might be too short. The more you work with dressmakers' patterns the more familiar you'll become with your body shape, and making alterations will gradually become easier and more successful.

Lengthening pieces

To lengthen a pattern piece, cut through the adjustment line and, using a ruler, carefully move the pieces so that the gap between them is the required amount. To fill the gap between the two sections, slice a length from an edge of the paper where there are no pattern pieces (you may need to cut two or three smaller pieces and join them together), place it over the gap and tape the join to make one larger pattern piece.

In cases where the pattern is fitted, such as tapered-legged trousers, there may be two sets of adjustment lines. Here you should divide by two the amount that you need to alter the garment by and apply that measurement to each section.

Bust alterations

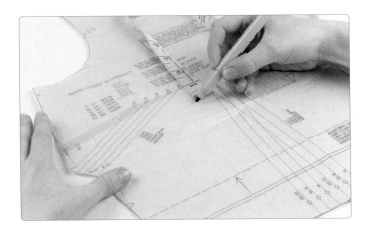

Darts are commonly used to provide shaping around the bust, and can be raised or lowered to suit your body shape. A dart should sit along the side of the bust and the tip should be level with the fullest part – holding the paper pattern piece up to your body will help you see if the dart needs to be raised or lowered.

Whether you're raising or lowering the dart the technique will be the same. Measure from the point at the end of the dart, working upwards to raise the dart and downwards to lower it. Make a mark where the new dart will end. Use a ruler to draw in the new stitching lines connecting the original starting point for the dart and the new end point.

Waist alterations

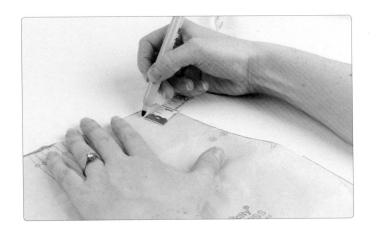

The waist section can be altered by either adding or subtracting the required amount. To keep the alterations even and neat on the pattern you'll need to see how many pattern pieces are used to form the waist section and divide the required amount evenly between the different pieces. For example, if the skirt has four seam lines, the amount the pattern needs to be altered by should be divided by four. Whether increasing or reducing the sizing at the waist, use a ruler to mark out the amount the pattern is to be altered by at the upper section of the waist. You'll need to draw a new cutting line for the pattern piece that joins the previous side seam to the new waist section. Draw along the line that's already present, then slowly extend the line upwards until it meets with the new point at the waistband.

Hip alterations

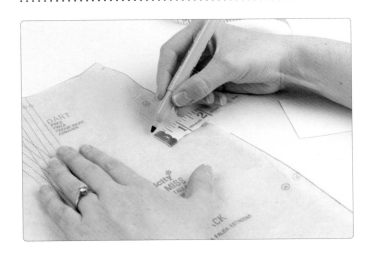

The hip sections can be altered in a very similar way to the waist sections. To keep the alterations neat, the required amount to be added or subtracted should be divided by the number of seam lines. At the hip section, use a ruler to mark out the amount that the section needs to be altered by; some patterns will include lines to indicate where the hip line is on the pattern – this is specifically for use when adjusting it.

Once the point has been marked the new cutting line needs to be drawn in. Work from the original point of the waist in a smooth line, following the previous line until it joins with the new hip marker. On some garments, such as fitted skirts, you may want to continue the line for the new hip marker to follow the remaining length of the seam. This will give a more flattering and neat finish, as the seam won't change after your alteration.

Darts

Darts are used in dressmaking to add shaping to a garment, to hold the fabric in position and tailor it to the curves of the body. They're most commonly used in women's garments, and you'll often see them along bustlines and waistlines.

Creating a dart

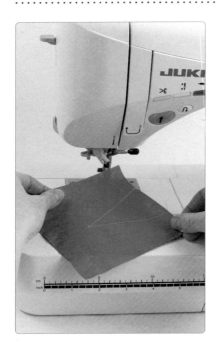

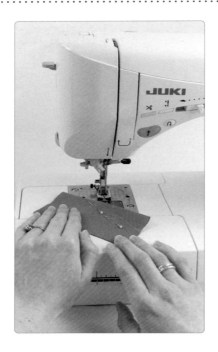

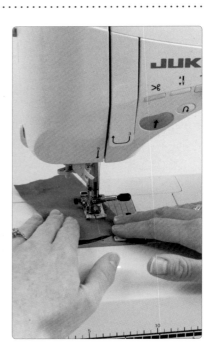

1 Using the marking on the pattern paper as a guide, mark out the start and end points of the dart with chalk.

2 Fold the fabric so that the right sides are together. The marker for the point of the dart will sit on the crease and the markers for the end points will be level. Pin the fabric in place.

3 Use chalk and a ruler to draw a line connecting the outer marker up to the marker for the point. This will be the stitching line.

Locating a dart

The section where a dart should be worked will be marked out on the pattern – it will look like a long 'V' shape, created from two lines joining to a point on an inner section of the fabric. It's important to remember that the two lines of a dart are used to indicate where the fabric is to be folded – you mustn't cut along them!

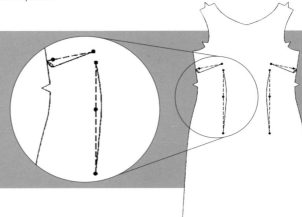

Simplicity Patterns

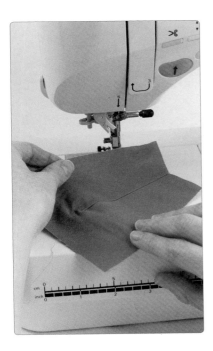

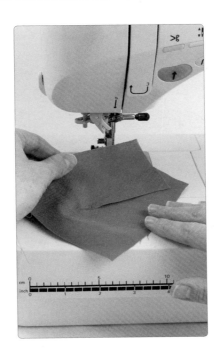

Laura's top tip

The direction in which you press the dart will have an effect on the appearance of the finished piece. For most garments the darts will be symmetrical, so you'll need to make sure that you follow the same principle for pressing them on one side of the garment as you do the other.

As a basic rule, darts along the bustline should be pressed down, away from the bust, so that the small piece of fabric doesn't hitch up against the bust.

Other darts, positioned along the front and back of the garment to give shaping to the waist and hips, should be pressed away from the garment's centre front or centre back. This means that you'll be pressing the dart towards the nearest side seam on that section of material.

Remember to fully press your darts before you join sections of fabric together.

4 With a straight machine stitch, start at the point of the dart and work 2cm (0.79in) of stitching, then set the machine to reverse and carefully work back over the same line of stitching. This will secure the stitches and also reinforce the point of the dart. Continue sewing along the chalk line to complete the dart. Work a few reverse stitches at the end of the line to secure the threads.

5 The completed dart will have a small stitched-in triangle of fabric on the wrong side, and a neat join with no visible stitches on the right side.

Finishing the dart

Once a dart has been stitched it's important to press it to achieve a neat and professional finish. Essentially the dart is pressed on the wrong side of the project.

1 First, with the fabric folded right sides together, press and hold the iron over the line of stitches to set them. The dart then needs to be pressed over to one side so that it lays flat on the side of the garment.

2 Once the stitches have been set, open up the fabric and place with the wrong side facing upwards. Using the tip of the iron, carefully press the fabric of the dart over to one side. Starting at the point of the dart, work slowly and carefully up the length of the dart until the folded fabric lies flush to one side.

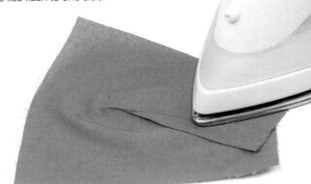

Double-pointed darts

These darts are used when the area to be shaped is longer. They're often featured in dresses – two might be positioned parallel on the back of a bodice, for instance, to provide shaping along the back section of the waist.

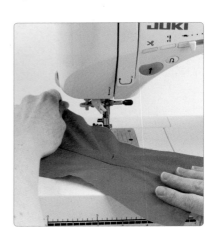

1 Using the markings on the pattern paper as a guide, mark out the start, wider middle section and end points of the dart with chalk.

3 With a straight machine stitch, start at one point of the dart and work 2cm (0.79in) of stitching, then set the machine to reverse and work back over the same line. Continue sewing along the chalk line towards the second point to complete the dart. Work in reverse stitch for 2cm (0.79in) to secure the point of the dart.

5 The completed dart will have a small stitched-in diamond of fabric on the wrong side, and a neat join with no visible stitching on the right side.

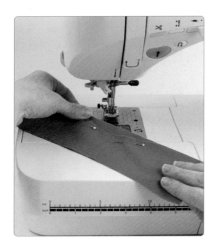

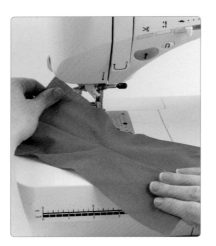

2 Fold the fabric with the right sides together – the markers for the points at either end of the dart will sit on the crease, and the markers for the wider middle sections will be level. Pin the fabric in place. Use chalk and a ruler to draw a line connecting the dart from point to point. This will be the stitching line.

4 Set the stitches of the dart by first pressing an iron over the folded fabric. Open the fabric and press the dart away from the centre of the garment. This will position it towards the side seams and provide a smooth finish when the garment is worn.

Adding shaping

A double-pointed dart is worked in a very similar way to the standard dart; however, once stitched it will create a neat diamond-shaped piece of fabric, compared to the triangle of fabric in a standard dart.

Simplicity Patterns

Necklines

Necklines come in a range of styles, from round and scoop to square and sweetheart. Adding a facing will not only give a neckline a neater appearance but will also make it more comfortable to wear.

Making a facing

1 Cut all the facing sections from the fabric and, using these pattern pieces, cut a second set of pieces from interfacing. Position the interfacing on the corresponding facing pieces and fix into place with a hot iron.

2 With the right sides together, align the short edges of the facing to create the curve of the neckline and pin in place.

3 Working with a straight machine stitch, join the sections of facing together to create a single continuous piece that'll be the same shape as the neckline.

Laura's top tip

A neckline is an area worth spending time perfecting as it's so close to your face and is often the first area people will notice.

What is a facing

A facing is a piece of fabric placed inside a garment to conceal the raw edges. It's often backed with interfacing to give added stability to the fabric. On a pattern the facing sections will be small pieces of a similar shape to the garment's neckline – they won't be the length of the entire bodice or dress. Depending on the design of the garment, the facing may cover just the front of the neckline from shoulder to shoulder, or it might cover the entire length of the neckline, front and back.

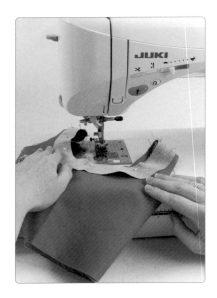

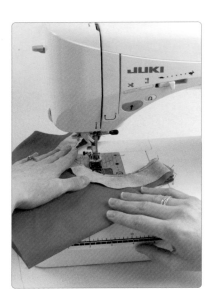

4 Press the joining seams open. You may want to work a couple of stitches over the opened seams to keep them flat, as these will lie over the shoulders. Work a line of straight hand stitches (called 'stay stitching') along the front of the neckline within the seam allowance to help prevent the curve distorting. With right sides together, align the facing along the neckline, match the shoulder seams carefully and pin in place.

6 To reduce bulk on the neckline, layer the seam allowance by trimming the allowance of the facing so that it's half the width of the allowance of the garment. Make small V-shaped cuts in the seam allowance to create a neat curve when the garment is turned through.

7 Press the seam allowance towards the facing, turn the garment through to the right side and press again to complete the neckline.

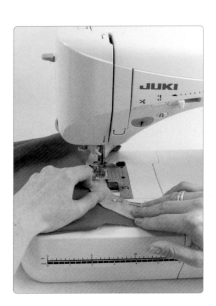

5 With a straight machine stitch, sew along the length of the neckline to secure the facing in place.

Adding top stitching

Once the facing is secured a line of top stitching can be worked along the neckline on the right side of the fabric. This stitching will be visible when the garment is worn, and can be worked up in a thread to match the garment for a discreet finish or in a contrast thread to make more of a statement. You can also work a second line of top stitching to add even more impact. Select a straight machine stitch and begin at one shoulder seam, working around the neckline. Aim to keep the stitches 5mm (0.19in) from the edge of the neckline.

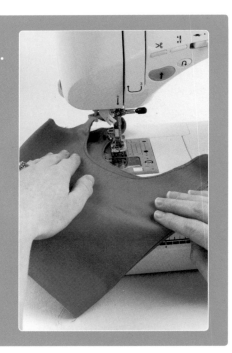

Bias tape neckline

Adding a length of bias tape is a quick and easy way to finish a neckline. You can either select a tape to match the fabric or make your own from the same fabric as the garment.

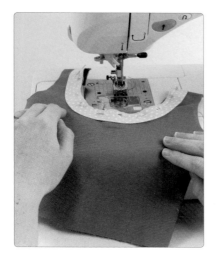

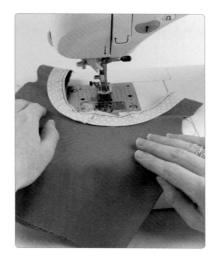

1 With the right side of the garment uppermost, place the bias tape along the neckline so that the raw edges of the tape and the garment are aligned. Pin along the length to secure it in place. Where the ends meet at the back of the neckline, trim and fold under one edge of the tape. You've now created a complete circle of bias tape.

3 Using a straight machine stitch and 5mm (0.19in) seam allowance, stitch around the neckline to secure the bias tape into position. Start at the back of the neckline and work around in a continuous circle until the whole section is secured. Set the machine to reverse stitch at the start and end of the seam to secure the stitches.

4 Fold the bias tape into the inside of the neckline and press. Pin in place to secure. Working on the right side of the neckline, using a straight machine stitch work a line of top stitching around the neckline, starting and finishing at the back of the garment. Work a couple of reverse stitches at the start and end of the seam to secure.

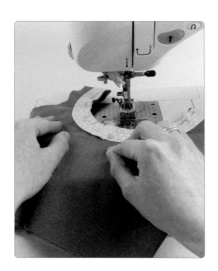

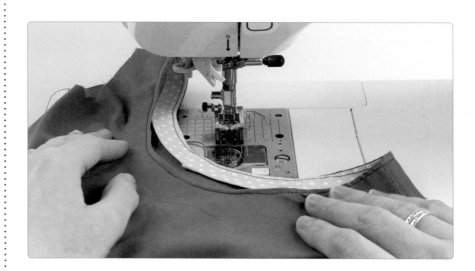

2 Fold the ends of the bias tape over where they meet at the back to conceal the raw edges and pin in place.

5 The bias tape lies neatly inside the neckline.

Collars

A collar provides a really smart finishing touch to a garment. It needs to be carefully constructed and secured to the neckline to achieve a symmetrical and professional finish.

Creating a flat collar

A flat collar is made with the same fabric for the top and the bottom. The top piece is interfaced to give the finished collar more stability.

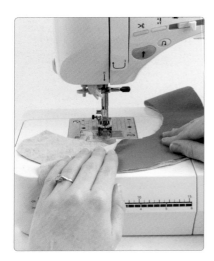

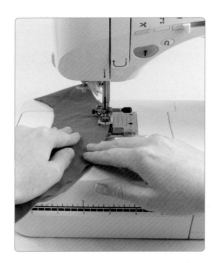

1 Cut the pattern pieces for the flat collar from the main fabric and use these to cut a piece from interfacing. Affix the interfacing to the wrong side of one of the collar pieces. This section will be the upper part of the collar on the finished garment.

2 Place the collar pieces together with the right sides facing and pin to hold in place. Work along the length of the collar using a straight machine stitch, starting at one curve and ending at the other. Work a few reverse stitches to secure the threads. The inner section of the collar, which will run along the neckline, is left unstitched.

3 To reduce bulk, trim the seam allowance on the back part of the collar – the section without interfacing – so that it's half the width of the remaining allowance. Clip around the curve of the collar, making small V-shaped cuts to make it easier to turn through. Press the seam allowance towards the back section of the collar and turn through.

Different collars

There are a number of different styles, from a stand collar, which is a short band that sits upwards of the neckline, to a shawl collar, which curves around the neck and drapes along the front of the garment. A standard collar or a flat collar is a pretty, feminine design, and the principles for applying it can be used to create other styles.

Affixing a collar

Most collars will have a facing, or at least a partial facing, on the inside to conceal all the raw edges. The collar will be sandwiched between the garment and the facing so that when the latter is turned through to the inside the collar will be positioned neatly on the neckline and all the seams will be hidden.

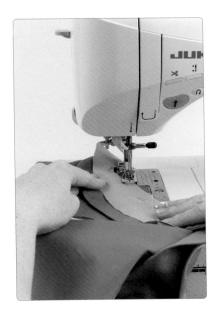

1 With the garment right side facing upwards, place the collar uppermost on the neckline, carefully aligning the raw edges; the section of collar that's interfaced will be uppermost. Once in position pin neatly in place. The facing section will usually be secured to the front of the bodice. Place the facing on top of the collar, aligning the raw edges of the neckline and bodice, and pin in place.

2 Working with a straight machine stitch, sew along the length of the neckline. Work carefully to ensure that the facing, collar and neckline of the bodice are secured together. Use the reverse function on the machine to secure the stitches at the start and end of the seam. Press the seam allowance towards the facing, push the facing through to the inside of the garment and press along the length of the collar.

3 Working on the inside of the facing, sew a line of straight machine stitches to secure the seam allowance to the facing. This will help to hold the collar in position. Press the length of the collar on the right side to finish.

Stitching a collar

When affixing a collar to a neckline the stitching needs to be strong and secure so a short, straight machine stitch is ideal. If the many layers of the garment, collar and the facing feel like a lot of components to work with try tacking them together first before finally joining them with a sewing machine.

Laura's top tip

Taking the time to carefully press the collar at every stage will help to give a neat finish to the completed garment. I also find that pressing the seam allowances fully before working the line of under-stitching helps to hold them in place. Under-stitching can be a bit fiddly when you're working on collars, as it feels as though you don't have much space to stitch. Try to keep the line of under-stitching around 2mm (0.08in) from the original seam line, and work slowly to move the fabric through the machine. As you're working on a curve it's often easier to use one hand to guide the fabric through the machine and the other hand to hold the upper section of the collar open and slightly away from the machine. This will help you to see exactly where you're sewing.

Waistbands

Being able to add a waistband to your sewing projects will allow you to create a more diverse range of garments, including trousers and skirts. The flat waistband and the gathered waistband are two of the most common styles.

Affixing a flat waistband

A flat waistband is commonly seen on trousers and tailored skirts. This is a straight piece of material that's secured around the waist section of the garment, and interfacing is often added to give this section more structure when the garment is completed.

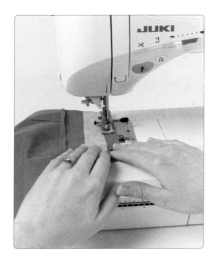

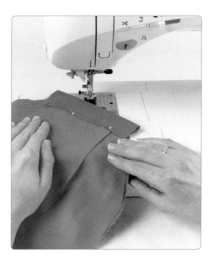

1 Fuse a piece of interfacing on to the wrong side of the waistband section. With the right sides of the garment and the waistband facing, align the raw edges of the waistband with the raw edges along the upper (waist) section of the garment. The waistband will lie downwards over the front of the garment. Pin it in place, ensuring that the waistband is centred over the garment so that there is equal fabric at either side of the fastening. With a straight machine stitch and taking a 1.5cm (0.6in) seam allowance, work along the length of the waistband to secure it to the main garment. Ensure that the sections over the fastening are left unstitched.

2 Press the waistband strip over the top of the garment, and press it in half to create the waistband. The interfaced section will lie neatly inside the fold.

3 Press the raw edges of the waistband under, and pin in place. Carefully slip stitch the inside of the waistband in place against the garment or the lining to finish.

Finishing touches

If your garment has a fastening, the fitted waistband will overlap the edges left open for a zip or buttons. These will need to be neatened and completed. Once the fastening has been inserted, fold in the raw edges of the waistband and slip stitch into place, allowing one side of the waistband to lie over the top of the other. Here you'll be able to add a hook and eye or button closure to complete the fastening.

Elastic waistband

Elastic waistbands are often featured on casual garments and frequently on children's clothing, as they're quick and easy to create. A channel is stitched into the waist section of the garment, through which a length of elastic is threaded. Once secured this creates a stretchy waist that doesn't require any additional fastening.

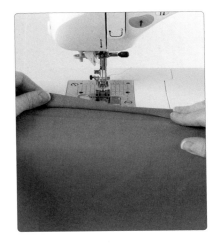

1 With the wrong side of the garment uppermost, work along the upper (waist) section of the garment to fold 2.5cm (1in) of fabric over to the wrong side. Press neatly into place.

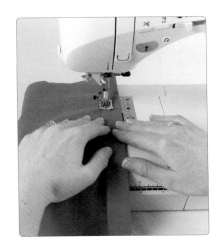

3 Using a straight machine stitch, work along the lower edge of the fold, aligning the stitching 5mm (0.19in) from the lower folded edge.

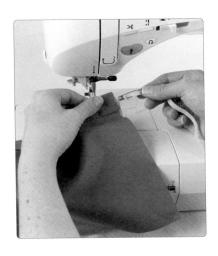

5 Trim the elastic to the desired length and tie a safety pin to one end. Use the safety pin to feed it through the channel in the fabric. When the elastic has been passed through, pull both ends free from the casing, overlap the ends and use the safety pin to hold in place. Hand sew together to secure the elastic.

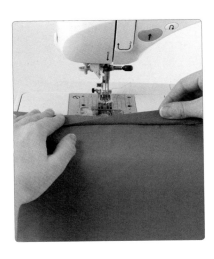

2 Repeat to fold the fabric over by a further 2.5cm (1in) to create a double fold. Press neatly and pin in place.

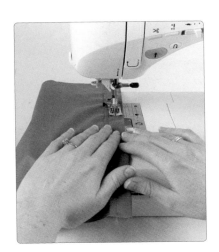

4 Again using a straight machine stitch, work along the upper section of the fold, approximately 5mm (0.19in) from the upper folded edge. Once completed the two rows of sewing will create a channel or casing.

6 Tuck the raw edges of the casing inside the channel and place the garment with right side facing to join the seam of the garment. Once the garment is seamed, carefully hand slip stitch the two ends of the casing together to complete the waistband.

Sleeves & armholes

Many garments require the addition of sleeves or the finishing of armholes, and once you've learnt the basic techniques you'll be creating fabulous shirts, dresses and jackets in no time.

Affixing a set-in sleeve

A set-in sleeve is joined to the shoulder of the garment by one continuous circular seam that sits at the shoulder.

1 Fold the sleeve in half with the right sides facing, align the long raw edges and pin in place. With a straight machine stitch, sew along the length of the sleeve to join the edges and form a tube. This will be the underarm seam. Work a few reverse stitches at the start and end of the sewing line to secure the stitches.

2 With the wrong side of the garment outermost, slide the sleeve in through the armhole. The right side of the sleeve and the right side of the garment will be touching on the inside. Align the underarm sleeve seam with the side seam on the garment and pin around the opening to secure it in place.

3 Using a straight machine stitch, sew around the armhole to join the sleeve to the garment. Work with the sleeve section uppermost and the garment fabric towards the needle plate of the machine. Start and finish the seam at the underarm section and work a couple of reverse stitches at the beginning and end to secure the threads.

Sleeve styles

When you're creating clothing you'll often need to work in sleeves. These are often created separately to the body of the garment and are fixed into it once the shoulder section has been worked. There are a number of sleeve styles, from short to long, flared to puffed. The two main types are the raglan and the set-in.

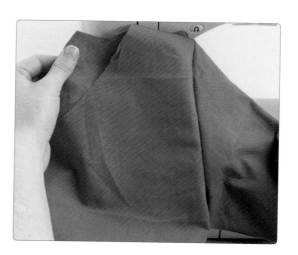

4 Trim the seam allowance and press down inside the sleeve. Turn the garment through to the right side and draw the sleeve through to the right side to finish.

Affixing a raglan sleeve

A raglan sleeve is joined using straight seams that are worked towards the neckline, the underarm section of the sleeve being joined by a continuous line of stitching that then runs down into the side seam of the bodice.

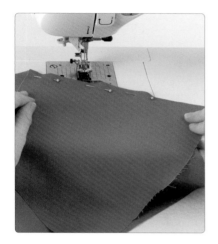

1 With the right sides facing, match the notches to align the sleeve to the neckline edge of the front bodice. Pin in place.

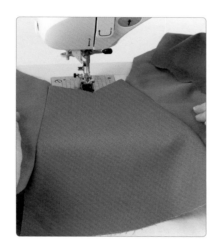

3 Repeat to attach the back section of the bodice to the sleeve using the same method. The sleeve will now be joined to the bodice with two diagonal seams running towards the neckline. The upper section of the sleeve will sit over the shoulder.

5 Working with a straight machine stitch, begin at the lower section of the garment and work up the length of the side seam, sew around the underarm of the garment and down the length of the sleeve to create the underarm seam. Work a few reverse stitches at the start and end to secure the threads.

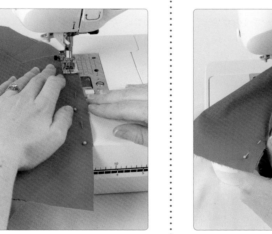

2 Using a straight machine stitch, join the two sections together starting at the neckline and working up toward the armhole. Work a few reverse stitches at the beginning and end to secure the threads.

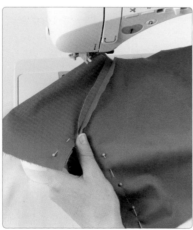

4 With the right sides facing, align the side seams on the front and back bodice and pin in place. Align the underarm seam of the sleeves and pin in place.

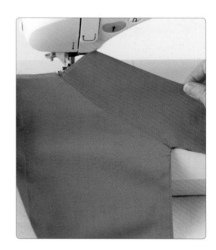

6 Press the underarm seam of the sleeve and the side seam of the bodice open and turn through.

Bias tape armhole

Similarly to binding a neckline, a length of bias tape can be used to make a quick and neat finish to an armhole. This can be made up from the same fabric as the garment for a coordinated look or can be a bought, ready-to-use tape in a contrasting colour or print for a more dramatic finish.

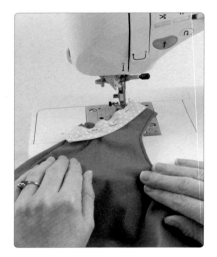

1 With the right side of the garment uppermost, place the bias tape along the armhole so that the raw edges of the tape and the garment are aligned. Pin along the length to secure in place. Where the two ends of tape meet at the base of the armhole, above the side seam, trim and fold under one edge of the tape. You've now got a complete circle of bias tape. Fold the ends of the tape over where they meet at the underarm section of the armhole to conceal the raw edges, and pin in place.

2 Using a straight machine stitch and 5mm (0.19in) seam allowance, stitch around the armhole to secure the bias tape into position. Start at the underarm section and work around in a continuous circle until the whole section is secured. Set the machine to reverse stitch at the start and end of the seam to secure the stitches.

3 Fold the bias tape into the inside of the armhole and press. Pin in place to secure.

Laura's top tip

When sewing small, tight sections of garments, like sleeves, you can remove the free arm of your sewing machine. This is the piece of outer casing that surrounds the needle plate and forms the sewing area. Doing this will give you a smaller area to sew on and it's much easier than trying to manoeuvre small sections of fabric over a large sewing area.

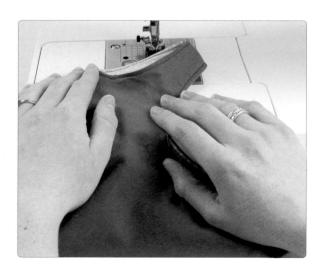

4 Working on the right side of the armhole with a straight machine stitch, work a line of top stitching around the armhole, starting and finishing at the underarm section of the garment. A second line of top stitching can be worked to create a more prominent finish. Work a couple of reverse stitches at the start and end of the seam to secure.

Pockets

These practical additions to a garment can be positioned in the seam for a discreet finish or secured to the main fabric for more impact. The fabric of the pocket is often backed with interfacing to give added strength and stability.

Creating a patch pocket

A patch pocket is made from a separate piece of fabric and can be lined or unlined. It's secured to the front of the garment with neat top stitching. The wrong side of the pocket is interfaced to give it added stability against the garment.

1 Cut out the patch pocket, and using the same pattern piece cut out a second pocket piece from interfacing. Secure the interfacing to the wrong side of the fabric with an iron. Work along the top of the pocket with an overstitch or zigzag stitch close to the raw edge to neaten.

2 Using a ruler and chalk, mark the fold line along the top edge of the pocket, usually a couple of centimetres down from the flat top. Fold the fabric over to the right side and press. With a straight machine stitch, work a line of stitches from the top of the pocket to the base of the pocket flap on each side, using a 1.5cm (0.6in) seam allowance.

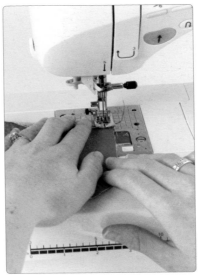

3 Work a small section of hand gather stitches around the two rounded corners of the base of the pocket, and pull the thread to gather up slightly.

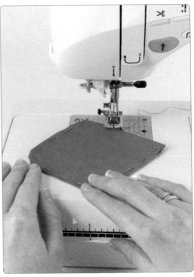

4 Clip the corners of the seam allowance at either side of the pocket flap to reduce bulk, and turn through. Press the pocket fully, ensuring that a 1.5cm (0.6in) seam allowance is pressed in towards the centre of the pocket. Tack around the outer edge of the pocket to hold in shape.

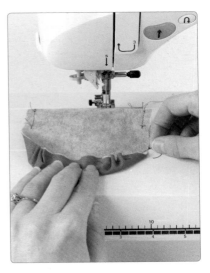

Affixing a patch pocket

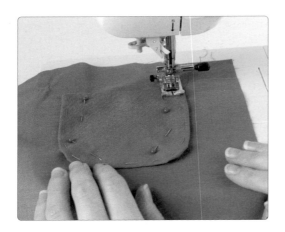

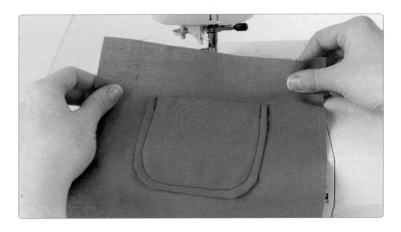

1 With the garment and pocket right sides facing upwards, position the pocket on the fabric and pin to secure.

2 With a straight machine stitch and using a 1cm (0.4in) seam allowance, sew the pocket to the fabric. Begin at one pocket flap and work around the pocket to end at the other side of the flap. For added strength to the upper section, work 2cm (0.79in) of reverse stitching at the start and end of the seam. These reinforced stitches will be at both ends of the pocket flap and will prevent the pocket from pulling on the fabric of the garment as it's used.

Creating an in-seam pocket

Some patterns are designed with the in-seam pocket cut in one consecutive piece of fabric with the garment. These will be worked as the side seams are stitched. However, if a dress or skirt has side seams it's possible for you to add an in-seam pocket by simply creating the pocket sections and sewing them into the seam before it's joined.

These pockets will lie against the body and aren't interfaced, allowing them to sit more discreetly inside the garment

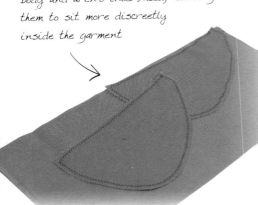

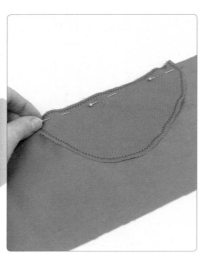

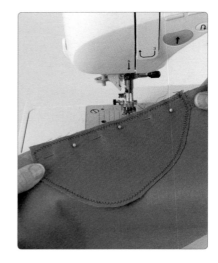

1 Cut the pocket pieces from the fabric (you'll need two pieces for each pocket), and work around each piece with a zigzag stitch to neaten the raw edges.

2 Mark the placement for the pockets at the side seam on the front and back sections of the skirt fabric. Ensure that they're level. With the right sides of the skirt and the pocket facing, align one pocket piece to the marker on the front section of the fabric – the flat edge of the pocket will line up with the outer edge of the skirt fabric – and pin in place. Repeat to position and pin the second half of the pocket on the other side of the garment.

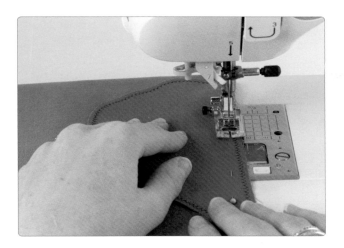

3 Working on one half of the pocket and then the other, use a straight machine stitch to join the flat edge of the pocket to the side of the garment using a 1cm (0.4in) seam allowance. Leave 1.5cm (0.6in) unstitched at the top and bottom of the pocket. Work a few reverse stitches at the start and end of the seam to secure the threads. Repeat to secure the flat edge of the second half of the pocket to the skirt seam.

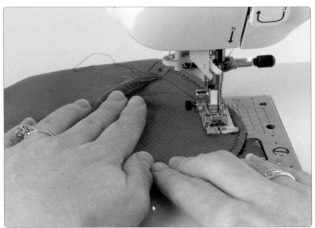

4 Press the seam allowance for each pocket towards the pocket. With right sides together, place the front and the back of the garment so that the raw edges of the side seam are aligned, fold out the pocket sections to match the right sides of the two halves, and pin around to secure into place. Using a straight machine stitch and starting at the top of the side seam, work down the seam, following around the curve of the pocket and finishing at the bottom of the seam. Work a couple of reverse stitches at the start and end to secure the stitches. Press the side seams open.

Laura's top tip

Adding in-seam pockets is a quick and easy way to adapt a garment. If the sewing pattern you're working from doesn't include pockets, use a finished or ready-made garment as a template to create the pocket shapes. To do this, turn a garment with in-seam pockets inside out, place the pocket on to a piece of paper and draw round it. Add an extra 2cm (0.79in) along the straight edge to accommodate the seams. Place on folded fabric to cut in pairs for each pocket. Insert into your project before working the side seams.

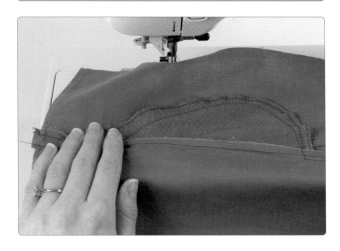

5 Turn the project through to the right side and carefully press the opening of the pocket so that it sits neatly along the seam. Press one side of the pocket, then turn to press the second side to finish.

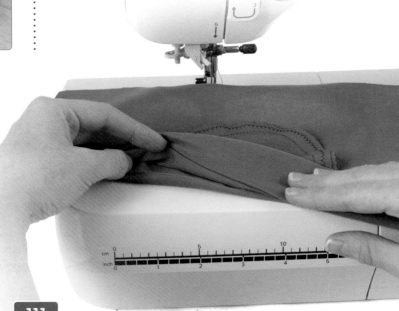

Linings

In many garments a second layer of fabric is added to the design. This lining sits on the inside of the garment and not only makes the garment feel more comfortable but will also help it to hang better.

Adding a lining

Skirts often feature a lining, but if your pattern doesn't it's simple to add one. You'll need to remember that if the skirt has a zip fastening the section of lining that lies underneath it shouldn't be seamed. Leaving a gap in the lining will allow you to get the skirt on and off. To neaten the edges of the lining at the gap simply fold the raw edges under by 5mm (0.19in), then again by a further 5mm and stitch in place with a straight machine stitch.

1 Once you've cut all the required pieces for the skirt use the pattern to cut the same pieces from the lining fabric.

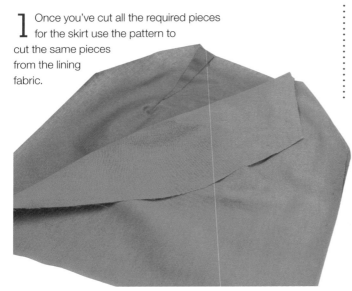

3 With the wrong side of the skirt and the wrong side of the lining facing upwards, position the lining over the skirt and align the upper edges. Pin in place to secure. Working with a straight machine stitch, sew along the length of the waist section, working inside the seam allowance. Work a few reverse stitches at the start and end of the seam to secure the threads.

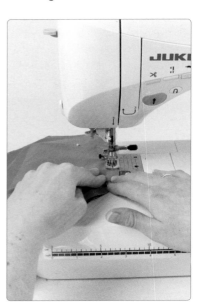

2 If the skirt has darts along the waistline, use the pattern piece to mark out the position on the lining fabric. It isn't necessary to sew the darts in place on the lining fabric, but pin them into position and press in the same direction as for the corresponding skirt section.

4 The lining will be held firmly in place while the waistband is secured.

Hemming the lining

As the lining sits underneath the skirt you'll not need to worry about working with a hemming stitch, as this won't be seen when the garment is worn.

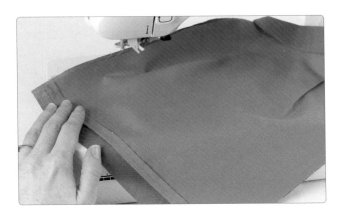

1 Create a double hem on the lining by folding 1.5cm (0.6in) to the wrong side and pressing, then folding another 1.5cm (0.6in) to the wrong side and pressing again. Pin around the hemline to hold in place.

2 Use a straight machine stitch around the base of the lining to secure the hem. Work a few reverse stitches at the start and the end of the seam to secure the threads. The hem on the lining should always be slightly higher than the hem of the finished skirt, so it's usually best to hem the skirt before hemming the lining.

Adding lining to a bodice

Adding a lining to a bodice will give the garment a more professional finish, and it will feel much nicer against the body. The lining is made up with the same pattern pieces as the bodice and is carefully stitched into place around the neckline and armholes.

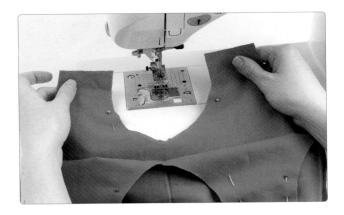

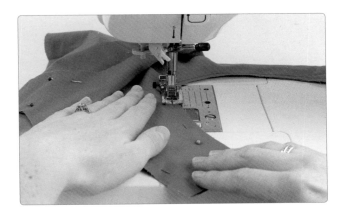

1 Working with the same pattern pieces as for the bodice, cut the bodice pieces from lining fabric. Make the lining up in the same way as the bodice, leaving the shoulder seams unstitched. To create a really neat finish, replicate any bodice dart placements on the lining fabric. Turn the bodice so that the right side is outermost and the lining so that the wrong side is outermost. Slide the lining over the bodice so that the right sides of both parts are facing.

2 Pin the two parts together along the neckline and under the armholes. Leave the upper sections and the shoulder seams aligned but unpinned. With a straight machine stitch, join the bodice to the lining along the armhole section, leaving 1.5cm (0.6in) unstitched at either end for the shoulder seam. Repeat for the second armhole to secure that section in the same way.

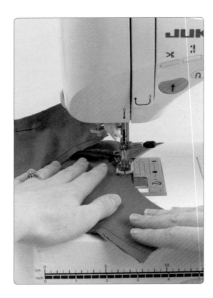

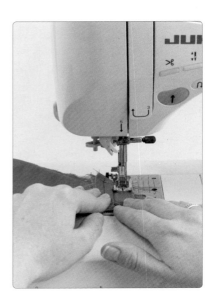

3 Using a straight machine stitch, sew along the neckline to join the bodice to the lining, again leaving 1.5cm (0.6in) unstitched at either end for the shoulder seam. Repeat for the second neckline seam. Carefully clip the curves along both necklines and the armholes.

5 Fold the lining section of the shoulder seam out of the way and pin the shoulder section of the bodice in place. Join with a straight machine stitch. Repeat for the second bodice shoulder seam.

6 Move the fabric of the bodice to the side and align the shoulder seam for the lining. Carefully pin in place and join with a straight machine stitch. Repeat for the second lining shoulder seam.

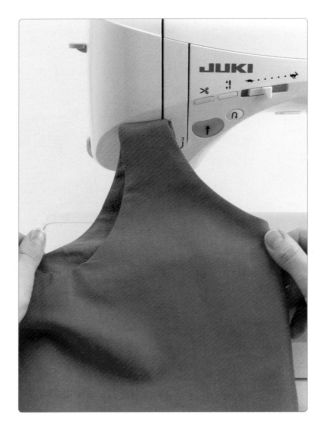

7 Place your hand inside the bodice and pull through to the right side. Carefully press the lining into the bodice to finish.

Lining fabrics come in a wide range of colours and styles. As it sits directly next to the skin a soft cotton lining fabric is a good choice, as it's both comfortable and breathable

4 Working on one side at a time, feed one half of the shoulder section through the other by passing your hand between the bodice and the lining. The fabrics will lie so that the right sides of the bodice are facing and the right sides of the lining are facing.

Hems

Neat and carefully stitched hems are essential to a great-looking finished garment, whether it's smart trousers or a casual sundress. This is usually the final stage of making a garment as you will need to slip it on to get the perfect length.

One of the final stages in dressmaking is hemming the garment. Whether it's trousers, a skirt or dress, or even a shirt or top, the lower section of the garment will need to be given a neat finish. This is done by carefully folding a measured section of the fabric to the wrong side of the garment and securing it with tidy, or sometimes nearly invisible, stitches. Hems can be finished either by hand or machine – some stitchers prefer the control that hand sewing allows them, others like the speed of machine sewing. Although it can be a rather slow process, hemming a garment by hand will certainly enable you to work very carefully and make the stitches as discreet as possible.

Measuring a hem length

Getting the hem the same length all the way round can be a tricky job, and if it's uneven it will really spoil the look of your finished garment. If you're able to enlist the help of a friend this can make the process of achieving an even hem a lot quicker and easier. Begin by putting on the finished garment and, without shoes, stand straight. Your friend will need to measure the point where the hem will be worked. Using a tape measure with one end on the floor, work around the garment inserting pins at the same height to mark the point to which the skirt or trouser legs will reach. Remove the garment and, using the pins as a guide, fold the fabric to the wrong side the whole way round. The marker pins should be sitting directly on the fold of the garment. Pin around the hem to hold it in position and press the whole section in preparation for stitching.

Hem stitch

The main function of this stitch, as its name suggests, is to secure hems. It's worked with the wrong side of the garment uppermost, and should only leave small stitches on the surface of the right side.

1 Secure the thread with a knot and draw the needle through the fabric from the wrong side to the right side. On the upper section of fabric, make a small stitch to secure and bring the needle back to the surface at the point where this stitch ends.

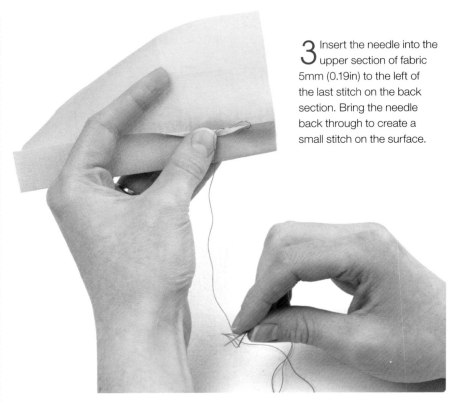

3 Insert the needle into the upper section of fabric 5mm (0.19in) to the left of the last stitch on the back section. Bring the needle back through to create a small stitch on the surface.

2 Insert the needle into the back section of fabric in line with the raw edge of the fabric 5mm (0.19in) to the left of the stitch on the upper section. Bring the needle back through to the surface to make a small stitch.

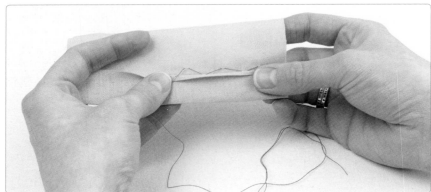

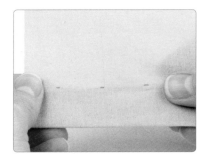

4 Continue working from right to left until the whole hem is complete. To finish, pass the needle from front to back of the upper section of fabric and secure with a neat knot.

If you work small stitches, only catching a few fibres each time, they'll only be slightly visible on the right side of the garment

Blind hem stitch

This is used when working hems where you want the finished garment to have very little sign of stitching visible on the outer surface.

1 Secure the thread with a knot and draw the needle through the fabric from the wrong side to the right side. On the upper section of fabric, make a small stitch to secure and bring the needle back to the wrong side at the point where this stitch ends.

2 Fold over the upper section of the hem allowance by 1cm (0.4in). With the tip of the needle catch two fibres from the back section of fabric and carefully draw the thread through to create a very small stitch. Repeat to make a second small stitch 4mm (0.16in) to the left on the same section of fabric.

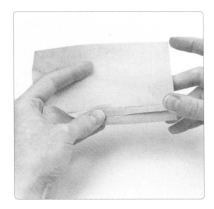

3 Working back into the folded section of the hem allowance, make a scond small stitch to add strength. Repeat to make a second small stitch 4mm (0.16in) to the left on the back section of fabric, catching only a couple of threads.

4 Continue working from right to left until the whole hem is complete. To finish, pass the needle from front to back of the upper section of fabric and secure with a neat knot. When worked with a colour-matched thread the tiny stitches are almost invisible on the right side of the fabric.

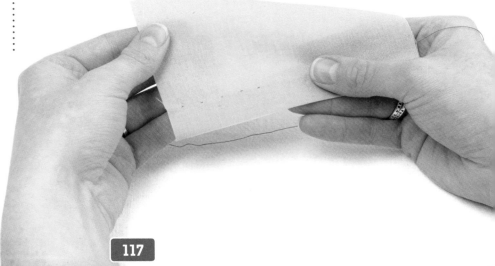

Laura's top tip

There's nothing more frustrating than a dropped hem. If one part of the stitching on the hemline comes loose, sooner or later the whole section will come undone and you'll be left with a large mending project on your hands. When I work hems I secure the stitching in sections as I work; this way if a section of the hem does start to come undone, the whole hemline doesn't unravel. To do this, every 5–10cm (2–4in) fasten the thread to the fabric in the hem allowance. I usually work a couple of wrap knots (page 52) as they are quick and secure to make. Remember not to cut the thread after you have fastened it to the hemline, simply continue hemming for another 5–10cm (2–4in) and repeat the knots to secure the next section. By securing the hem in sections like this, you should never be faced with an entire hemline to re-stitch. You can also work the knots at more regular intervals, perhaps at the back of trouser hems, as this section often catches on heels and can break easily.

Machine-finished hems

Depending on the stitches and functions available on your machine
there are a number of hemming and finishing stitches that you can use.

Blind hem stitch

To create this finish you'll need to work with a blind hem foot and
select a blind hem stitch. This setting on your machine will work
with a combination of zigzag and straight stitches to secure the
hem in place. The stitches that are visible on the right side of the
work will be very small. Try to colour-match your thread to the
fabric in natural light to help disguise the finished stitches.

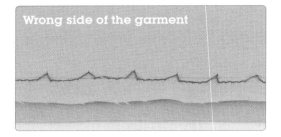

Wrong side of the garment

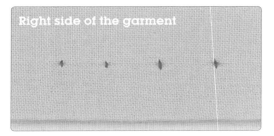

Right side of the garment

Rolled hem

A rolled hem, which is a thin hem often seen at the lower
edges of tops, is most commonly used on lightweight
fabrics like cotton. It's created using a rolled hem foot,
which, when attached to the machine, carefully rolls the
fabric as it passes through the foot, allowing the needle
to sew through a small neat fold in the fabric.

*A rolled hem can be used
with a straight stitch
or a zigzag stitch*

Double fold hem

There are times when a hemline won't be visible from the right side when the garment is being worn, for example skirt and dress linings.
On such occasions you can work a simple double fold hem, as it can be worked with straight stitches since they won't be seen.

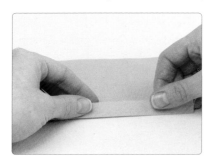

1 With the wrong side of the
fabric facing upwards, fold
1.5cm (0.6in) over to the wrong
side and press.

2 Make a second 1.5cm fold
and press again. Pin along
the length to hold in position.

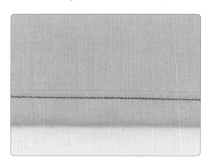

3 Working with a straight machine
stitch, sew along the length to
secure the hem in position. Work a few
reverse stitches at the start and end of
the stitching to secure the threads.

Mending

Breathe a new lease of life into your clothes with a little make do and mend!
With a few emergency supplies and a couple of quick sewing tricks you'll be
able to make repairs whether you're home or away.

Not only can your sewing skills be used to create
wonderful new handmade garments, they can also be
used to repair damaged items that previously you'd have thrown
away. They'll also enable you to pick up vintage finds and mend
or restore them to their former glory, so that you can enjoy
wearing them. Embrace the make do and mend philosophy!

A mini mending kit

A travel-size mending kit is a great way of keeping the essentials
of SOS sewing to hand, ready for when you need them most.
These dainty little sets can be bought from most
haberdashery stores and can be stowed away
in your closet or tucked into your travel bag
so that you're able to quickly and easily
make all kinds of sewing repairs.

Create your own SOS kit

Small scissors

A small pair of scissors with sharp-pointed
blades. Ideal for trimming thread ends and
snipping away frayed fabric.

Threads

Multi-coloured woven thread
bands are available from most haberdashery
stores, or you can create your own version by
winding lengths of a few common colours of
thread around a piece of card.

Sharps

Make up a mini pincushion with
a couple of hand sewing needles,
a few pins and a pair
of safety pins.

Snaps, buttons
and fastenings

A medley of different fastenings will come in
handy. They might not always be the right
items for your repair, but they'll certainly
see you through until you can replace the
fastening properly.

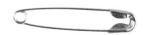

Hemming tape

Fusible tape is a quick-fix for dropped
hems. It can be quickly applied and will
hold the hem in place until you're able
to re-stitch it properly.

Dropped hem

A dropped hem isn't only irritating, it can also look very untidy. Ideally, when the stitches on a hem come loose you need to pin it back into position, press it and rework a line of hemming stitches. However, if you don't have time to work a full repair you can use a length of hemming tape to secure it.

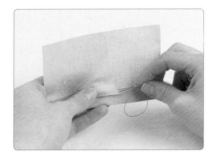

Find the loose end of the hemming thread at the point where the hem dropped and thread it on to a needle. You may need to carefully unpick a couple of stitches to give you enough length. Work a few small stitches into the seam allowance and repeat on the other side of the dropped hem. This will secure the remaining section of the hem. Cut a piece of hemming tape 5mm (0.19in) shorter than the length of the dropped hem. Place this inside the dropped section and fold the hem over the tape. Use an iron to affix the dropped section in place.

Laura's top tip

Sometimes you won't have the time to sew a quick repair or might not have an iron handy to affix hemming tape to a dropped hem or popped seam. A small safety pin is the perfect solution! These can be used to fix a wide range of repairs and as the safety pin clips up neatly you won't be in danger of pricking yourself as you wear the garment!

Split seam

Seams in high-stress areas can be prone to splitting, and when the stitches do come undone they can sometimes reveal a rip or fraying of the fabric. A small length of fusible hemming tape and a line of stitches can rejoin the seam and help to keep it secure for many wears to come.

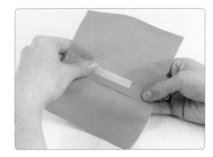

Press the ripped section of the seam flat and trim a piece of hemming tape to cover the length of the rip. Fuse it into place with an iron. Following the original seam line, work along the length of the ripped seam using neat back stitch.

Gaping buttonhole

Over time, and with continued wear, buttonholes can start to gape and can lead to the button popping open. This can be repaired with a few small stitches at the top and bottom on the buttonhole to reinforce it.

With a matching thread, secure on the wrong side of the buttonhole and bring through to the right side of the upper section. Work a few straight stitches over the end of the buttonhole and repeat at the other end. This will hold together the fabric on each side of the buttonhole and help it to sit a little tighter around the button.

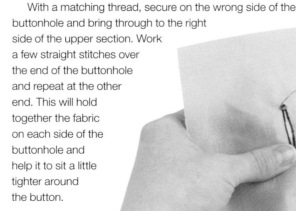

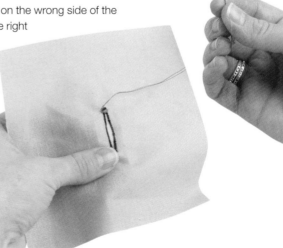

Broken zip

When a zip breaks you'll often have to take it out and replace it completely. However, it's always worth trying to repair it first. If a few teeth have become distorted or broken at the lower end of the zip it's usually possible to repair it.

If the zip pull has come loose on one side of the zip, carefully ease it back on to the teeth and pull the zip up to fasten it. With the thread fastened on the wrong side of the zip, bring the needle up slightly above the damaged zip teeth. Working with small straight stitches, sew over the width of the teeth to join and create a new base for the zip.

Repairing underwire

When the underwire of a bra pops out of its casing it isn't just untidy, it can also be extremely painful. With repeated wear and laundering underwiring or boning can come free from its channel. It may be a sign that the garment has simply seen better days, but in some cases it might be possible to repair it.

Feed the wire or boning back inside the section that it came from. Insert the tip of a tube of fabric glue into the hole and squeeze out a small blob. Move the wire around until you're happy with the placement and then allow the glue to dry. Once the glue has set, work small straight stitches around the area where the wire protruded to secure the casing in place.

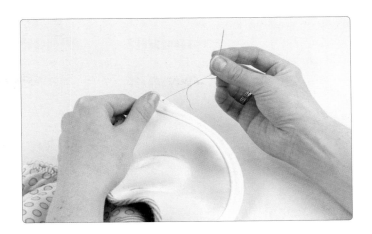

Sewing a tear

Depending on the size and position of the rip there are a few different ways in which it can be repaired.

Sewing on a patch

For large prominent rips you'll need to place a patch over the tear and sew it into place. If you're able to, use a matching or coordinating piece of fabric. This is a great way to repair a rip in a pair of jeans.

Place the patch over the rip, fold under the raw edges and pin into place. Sew the patch using small straight stitches that are worked over the edge of the patch on to the main fabric of the garment. For a more secure finish work around the patch using a zigzag stitch setting on your sewing machine.

Adding an internal patch

On small rips you can add a small patch to the wrong side and carefully stitch over the rip to rejoin the two pieces. Trim away any frayed edges from around the rip. Fuse a small piece of hemming tape, or pin a small piece of matching fabric, to the wrong side of the rip. Working with a matching thread, stitch around the rip with small straight stitches. Once the entire rip has been bordered off with stitches, sew across the rip, working backwards and forwards in neat, even zigzag stitches until the length of the rip is covered.

Cover with an appliqué patch

If the rip is in a very prominent place on a garment you can use a pretty sew-on patch – available from most haberdashery stores – or create your own appliqué motif to cover the hole.

Darning

On some fabrics, particularly knits, it's possible to join a small tear with very little sign on the surface. Using a thread that matches the fabric, work a line of stitching around the rip. Carefully work across the rip, in a similar manner to slip stiching, picking up sections of fabric at either side of the tear. This will gradually pull the fabrics together and seal the hole.

Laura's top tip

Of course, it isn't always possible to repair a rip or a tear without there being some sign of the damage. But if it's a much-loved garment that you can't bring yourself to part with, why not try up-cycling it into something else – a badly torn bodice could be cut away from a dress and a new waistband added to create a wonderful new skirt, for instance. Or you could customise it, for example by creating a large hand-embroidered monogram patch to stitch over a rip in your favourite cardigan. If all else fails, why not consider recycling it? If you love the garment that much but it isn't possible to repair it, try using pieces of the fabric to make something completely new, such as a handbag, or cut scraps to add to an heirloom quilt. Think creatively and see what you can achieve with a little make do and mend.

Chapter 5 ·

Home furnishing

Many people will invest in their first sewing machine with a view to making their own curtains and blinds. Stitching your own drapes and soft furnishings will allow you to add a very unique and personal touch to your own home. It will also enable you to select fabric designs and colours of your choice – not to mention avoiding the expense of costly made-to-measure services. These key techniques for cushions, curtains, blinds and bedding will allow you to add a fresh new look to your interiors in no time.

Curtains & blinds

Made-to-measure curtains can be costly, so learning to make
your own will not only save you money, but will allow you to
create the interiors you've always dreamed of.

Drapes, blinds and window dressings come in a wide range of styles, from traditional heading-tape style to the classic cafe curtain. Making curtains may seem like an extremely large project, but in actual fact they're created with only a few simple seams and a couple of different techniques. The most important aspect of curtain making is to take correct measurements – rushing at this stage can result in unsightly curtains that are either too short, too long, too wide or too narrow.

The measurements that you'll need to create your curtains will depend on the type of window dressing that you want to make. No matter what type of curtain or blind you're making it's always wise to use a retractable metal tape measure (available in DIY stores) – while your fabric measure may well be long enough for the task, the fact that it's soft makes it harder to hold flush to the window to get exact measurements. Break down the measurements into two stages: begin with the width of the curtain, and then move on to the length.

Measuring width

Net and voile curtains

These are often fitted close to the window in a recess, so the measurement needs to be taken along the internal section of the window. The easiest and most discreet way to hang them is by securing them with curtain wire that's fitted into the recess by screws at either side. Position the tape measure to take the measurement across the top of the window, inside the recess. Multiply this measurement by two – or even three – in order to calculate the width of the curtain, as this will give the nets lots of lovely drape.

Track and pole curtains

This style of curtain will be secured above the window on either a track (for curtains with heading tape) or a pole (for curtains with fitted rings or tabs). The measurements of these windows need to be taken on the wall surrounding the window – or the recess, if it sits in one.

The track or pole will run along the top of the window and will usually be 10cm (4in) longer than the window, so that there's space for the lengths of curtain fabric when they're drawn back. It will also sit around 10cm above the window. If a track or pole is present you can use this as a guide for your measurements.

Take the measurement along the centre of the curtain track or pole – or the position this will be in if you're adding one. If you're making traditional curtains with heading tape you'll need to multiply this measurement by two. This will give you the width of the entire curtain. If you're making tab top or ring fixture curtains you may not want as much material as is needed when making the gathers for heading tape curtains, so multiply this measurement by between one and a half and two to get the width of the entire curtain.

Calculating fabric amounts

Once you have the measurements for your window you'll be able to work out the amount of fabric that you'll need to make each curtain. To the length of the curtain you'll need to add 5cm (2in) to accommodate the upper edge and 15cm (6in) to accommodate the hem. For the width you'll need to add 2.5cm (1in) to each side for the seam allowance.

If you pick a fabric with large prints, or the width of the window is greater than the width of your chosen fabric, you'll need to buy more fabric to allow for joining pieces and matching prints. It's always wise to take the full window measurement into the fabric store when buying curtain material, just in case you need to do any additional calculations.

Measuring length

Net and voile curtains

As these will sit in the recess of the window, you'll need to measure from the top of the window to the windowsill. A curtain wire should sit between 5cm (2in) and 10cm (4in) from the top of the recess – the lower it sits from the top of the recess, the larger the space for ruffles at the top of the curtain. Position the tape measure at the centre of the curtain wire, or the position where the curtain wire will be secured, and take the measurement at the windowsill. When finished these curtains will need to just skim the surface of the sill – this is achieved when hemming them.

Track and pole curtains

As these are secured to a track or a pole that's affixed flush to the wall you can decide whether you'd like the curtains to fall to the floor (full length) or level with the windowsill.

For curtains that will run on a pole, place the tape measure at the bottom of the pole and take the measurement to wherever you'd like the curtains to reach.

For curtains that will be secured to a track, place the tape measure in line with the top of the track and take the measurement where you'd like the curtains to reach.

If you're making tab top cafe-style curtains you'll need to measure from the top of the pole and deduct the length of the tabs from the curtain length to ensure that the finished curtains hang exactly where you want them to. To calculate the length of the tabs, bend the tape measure around the curtain pole so that the end is level with where the top of the curtains will run. Taking the measurement here will give you the length of the tabs – note this measurement down for later. Deduct half of this length from the length of the curtains to take into consideration the addition of the tabs when affixed.

Adding lining

The addition of a curtain lining will transform flimsy fabrics into luxurious drapes, and will also help to keep light out and warmth in. The amount of lining is calculated by adding 5cm (2in) for the top section and 15cm (6in) for the lower hem to the finished length. The width of the lining fabric needs to be between 2 and 5cm (0.79 and 2in) narrower than the curtain material, so that when it's seamed the lining fabric won't roll to the front of the curtains when they're hung. If your window requires two or more curtain panels you'll need to repeat the steps for each panel.

Making heading tape curtains

These traditional-style drapes are created by securing a strip of heading tape to the upper section. Small plastic hooks are fed into the tape, allowing them to be hung on a track.

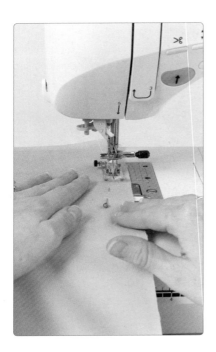

Heading tape

Heading tape is a strip of woven banding that's secured to the upper section of the curtains. This band is woven with cords which, when pulled up, create gathers in the curtain. Small plastic hooks are fed into the special sections woven into the band of the tape and these are then clipped on to the track to secure the curtains. The length of heading tape will need to be the same measurement as the width of each finished curtain panel plus an additional 5cm (2in).

1 Begin by taking accurate measurements for your window and cutting the main fabric and the lining to the required lengths. With right sides together, pin the lining and main fabric along one side and, with a straight machine stitch, join the two sections together with a 2.5cm (1in) seam allowance.

With right sides facing, align the main fabric raw edges with the lining on the second side and pin into place. As the lining is narrower than the main fabric there will be excess main fabric to the left-hand side of the seam line – ensure that this is smoothed out of the way when stitching. Press the seam allowances open and turn the curtain through to the right side. Move the lining panel so that it sits centrally on the back of the main fabric. There will be a section of main fabric bordering the lining on each side. Carefully press the seams in place, keeping the borders neat.

2 Along the upper edge of the curtain fold over 4cm (1.6in) on to the lining side and press. Fold the raw edges under and press again. Place the heading tape along the length of the curtain, aligning it with the lower edge of the folded section with 2.5cm (1in) of tape overlapping at each edge. Pull the cords free from the band so that they hang from the outer edge of the curtain. Fold the raw edges of the heading tape inside the upper section of folded-over curtain on each side, and pin in place along the length of the curtain. With a straight machine stitch, join the heading tape to the curtain, first along the upper section then along the lower section of the tape.

3 Knot the cords at one end of the heading tape and pull the other ends gently, easing the fabric along the cords to create gathers. Once the curtains are gathered to the desired amount, knot the cord ends, insert the plastic hooks at regular intervals and carefully hang the curtain. The lower section of the curtain should sit around 10cm (4in) lower than the desired length. Fold the curtain fabric towards the lining and pin in place for the desired hem length.

4 Once the hem has been pinned into position, remove from the track and press the hem in place. Trim the lining fabric so that it sits just inside the bottom crease for the hem – this will reduce bulk. Trim off as necessary and turn 1.5–2cm (0.6–0.79in) of the folded hem to the inside to conceal any raw edges. Work across the length of the hem with a hand hemming stitch to secure. Carefully tuck the ends of the cord into the loops on the top of the heading tape and hang the finished curtains.

Laura's top tip

Taking the time to hang curtains before hemming them is a sure way to check that they fit the window exactly as you want them to, and allows you to make any adjustments while they're in position. Make the most of the large hemming allowance to make sure that the lower section is neat and tidy. To ensure that they're happy with the final hem some stitchers prefer to hang their curtains for a few days before pinning. This allows any wrinkles in the fabric to drop out and relax into position before they sew the hem in place.

Tab top curtains

Often called cafe curtains, these are quick and easy to make even for beginners. They're affixed to the curtain pole with fabric strips that are secured to the top of the curtain and then slid on to the pole so that they can be moved back and forth to open and close.

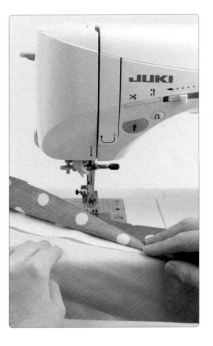

Tab spacing

As the curtain panels aren't as gathered as those featuring heading tape they can be made from less fabric, which means that they're easier and cheaper to make. The tabs at the top should be a minimum of 5cm (2in) wide when finished and can be positioned around 10cm (4in) apart. Add 2cm (0.79in) to the length of the tabs, which is calculated from the measurement of the top of the curtain around the pole. Remember to add 1.5cm (0.6in) to each side for seam allowance.

1 Begin by taking accurate measurements for your window and cutting the main fabric and lining to the required lengths. With right sides together, pin the lining and main fabric along one side and, with a straight machine stitch, join the two sections together, taking a 2.5cm (1in) seam allowance. With right sides facing, align the raw edges of the main fabric with the lining on the second side and pin into place. The lining is narrower than the main fabric, so ensure the excess fabric is kept clear from the needle while sewing. Press the seam allowances open and turn the curtain through to the right side. Move the lining panel so that it sits centrally on the back of the main fabric. There will be a section of main fabric bordering the lining on each side. Carefully press the seams in place, keeping the borders even.

2 Working along the top edge of the curtain, fold over 4cm (1.6in) towards the lining and press. Fold the raw edges under and press again. Cut a length of medium-weight interfacing to the dimensions of the folded section and pin in place between the curtain and the upper folded section. Join the section along its entire length using hand slip stitches.

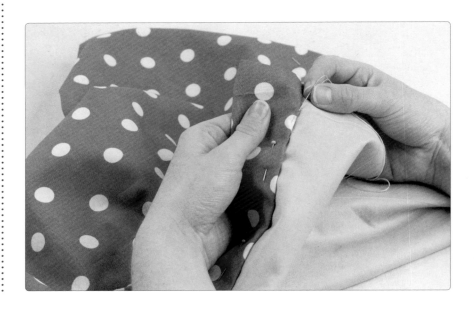

3 Using the measurements for the finished upper panel, calculate the number of tabs required, ensuring that they're spaced evenly along the length with a tab at either end of the material. If the finished width for each tab is 5cm (2in) you'll need to cut strips that are double the width plus 3cm (1.18in) for seam allowance. Cut the required number of tab strips.

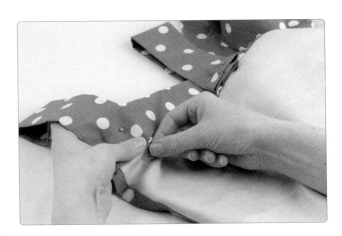

5 Fold under 1cm (0.4in) on each end of the tabs and pin into position along the top of the curtain. Check the spacing and position of the tabs before hand slip stitching them into place. Work on the front of the tabs first then turn the curtain to work on the back until all the tabs are secured.

4 For each strip cut a piece of medium-weight interfacing 4.5cm (1.8in) wide and the same length as the strip. Working on one tab at a time, fold the strip in half with the right sides facing, align the long edges and join with a straight stitch. Press the seams open and turn the tab through to the right side. Position the seam so that it lies down the centre back of the tab. Insert the interfacing into the tube and press again.

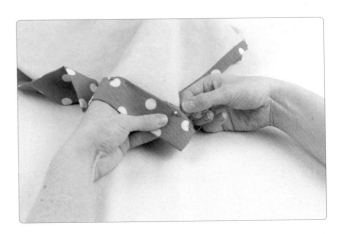

6 Slip the tabs over the curtain pole and hang the curtain to pin the hem in place. Hand sew the hem to finish.

Tab top curtains are quick and easy to make – ideal for beginners!

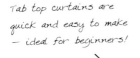

Net and voile curtains

Nets and voiles are perhaps some of the quickest curtains to make. Their lightweight fabrics are ideal for letting in light while also preserving some privacy. Net fabrics are available in a wide range of colours and designs, so you can pick something that suits your interiors.

1 Using the measurements you've taken, cut the nets to the desired dimensions. Fold the upper section over by 5cm (2in) and press. Fold the raw edges under by 1cm (0.4in) and finger-press and pin in place. Using a straight machine stitch, work along the lower edge of the folds to secure the section in place.

3 Slide the curtain on to the wire, evenly distributing the ruffles, and hang in the window. Work along the lower length, turning the fabric to the wrong side to create a hem that sits 2mm (0.08in) above the windowsill. Trim to create a 1cm (0.4in) double hem and work along the length of the hem with a straight stitch to finish.

Laura's top tip

The ruffles that sit above the curtain wire can be made larger or smaller by changing the amount of upper section fabric that's folded over: the less fabric that's folded the smaller the ruffles, while folding a lot will create a more dramatic ruffled effect. If you want to make larger ruffles you'll need to increase the length of fabric you cut to accommodate the larger folds at the top. Remember, no matter what size ruffles you prefer you'll always need to create a channel that's around 2cm (0.8in) wide through which to feed the curtain wire.

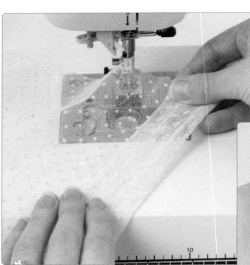

Coloured threads show the two lines of stitching that create the casing through which the curtain wire is fed.

2 Repeat with a second line of stitching at least 2cm (0.79in) above the first. These lines of stitching will form the casing through which the curtain wire will be fed.

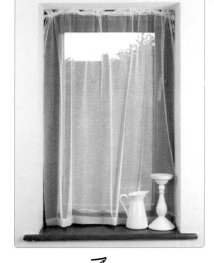

Nets can be hung alone or teamed with curtains or blinds

Blinds

The addition of fabric blinds is a fuss-free and easy way to refresh a room. They can also be hung on doors with large windows for another colourful makeover. A roll-up blind is both quick to make and secure. You can create them to either sit inside a recess close to the window or on the wall around a window.

1 With the right sides facing, align the raw edges of the main fabric and the lining and pin in place. Join with a straight machine stitch to secure. Repeat on the second side. The main fabric will need to be kept away from the needle while the second seam is stitched. With a straight machine stitch sew the lower hem with a 2.5cm (1in) seam allowance.

3 Cut two lengths of ribbon twice the length of the fabric blind. Fold each piece in half and place the fold over the top of the blind so that half of the ribbon falls to the back and the other half to the front. Position the ribbon ties around 10–15cm (4–6in) from the outer edges and pin. Work a line of stitching across the upper section of the blind to secure it and the ribbon ties.

2 Press the side seams open and turn through to the right side. Move the panel of lining fabric so that it sits centrally on the back of the blind and press. With a straight machine stitch, sew a line 3cm (1.18in) from the lower edge. Turn over 5cm (2in) at the top of the blind and press. Refold a further 1cm (0.4in) to conceal the raw edges.

4 Secure one length of adhesive Velcro fastening tape to the top section of the blind and another to the blind track and secure the blind in place. To give the bottom of the blind more substance a small wooden baton the width of the blind can be inserted to sit within the channel of the hem. Hand sew the hem in place to finish.

Measuring blinds

When measuring for a blind you must first decide whether you want it to sit inside a recess or flush on the wall. The process for taking measurements is much the same as for measuring curtains. Measure the width of the blind – this will be either the width of the recess or the width of the wall surrounding the window – then add an additional 5cm (2in) at either side. The length is measured from the top of the recess to the bottom, or from the upper position of the blind to the bottom of the sill for blinds that rest against the wall.

Calculating fabric amounts for blinds

Once you've taken the measurements for your window you'll be able to work out the amount of fabric that you'll require. To the length of the blind you'll need to add 5cm (2in) to accommodate the upper section and 2.5cm (1in) for the hem. For the width add 7.5cm (3in) to each side to account for the seam allowance and create a border on the back to prevent the lining fabric rolling round to the front. Remember, if you're using patterned fabric you may have to buy more than your measurements suggest in order to match up any motifs. The back of the fabric blind is made using either a contrast fabric or curtain lining. Selecting a lining will help to block out the light and give the blind added stability. Cut the lining fabric so that it's 2.5cm (1in) narrower on each side than the main fabric.

Cushions

These simple soft furnishings can be made in any colour, fabric or size that you wish, and make a superb addition to almost any room in your home. These two common methods can be scaled up or down to make a cushion of any size.

Cushions can be constructed in a wide range of different ways, and can include a zip or button closure or even use folds of fabric to encase the internal pad. A basic cushion can be adapted and customised to create a variety of designs to suit your interiors, or can be kept simple to show off fabulous fabrics.

Zip closure cushion

Most cushion covers will be made so that the internal cushion pad can be easily removed for laundering or replacing. This basic cushion uses a zip closure that sits along one edge, and the design can be scaled up or down to suit your preferred cushion pad.

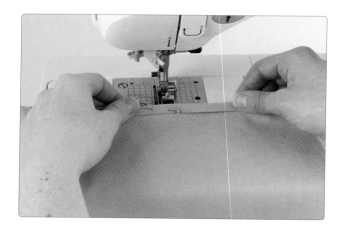

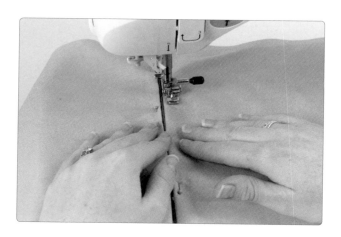

1 Trim your fabric to create two squares that are 4cm (2.8in) larger than the cushion pad on each side. This is to accommodate the seams and also the bulk of the cushion pad. With the wrong side uppermost, fold one side over by 1cm (0.4in) and pin in place. Fold again to make a double fold. Repeat to create an identical double fold on one side of the other square of fabric.

2 Take a zip the same length as the cushion and position it so that it runs along the folded edge of the fabric, with the teeth of the zip and the right side of the fabric uppermost. Pin in place. Repeat to pin the second side of the zip to the folded edge on the other piece of fabric. Once pinned in place the zip teeth should sit between the folded edges of each piece of fabric. Make sure that these folds are touching over the teeth, as this will help to conceal the zip. There'll be a small amount of fabric at either end of the zip – this will form the seam allowance for the side seams. Secure the zip in place down one side with a straight machine stitch. Repeat for the second side of the zip.

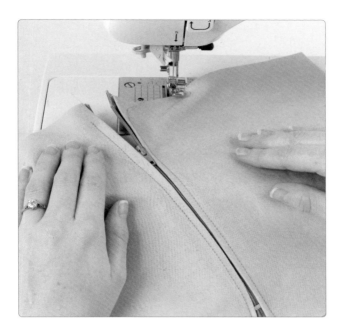

3 The two fabric squares will be joined together by the zip that runs centrally between them. The edges of the folded fabric will cover and help to conceal the zip when the right sides are uppermost. Open the zip partway, as this will allow the cushion to be turned through once the seams are stitched.

Laura's top tip

Cushions are a quick and easy way to brighten up tired interiors. You may want to pick a contrasting colour to your room or perhaps a dramatic bold print. If you're working with fabrics that have large and striking motifs you'll need to ensure the fabric is cut and folded in such a way that the design is centred on the front of the cushion. The best way to do this is, before cutting the fabric, place it around the cushion with the right side outermost. This will show you the section of fabric that'll be visible on the front of the cushion when it's complete. Try moving the fabric around until you're happy with the placement of the design. Use pins or tailor's chalk to mark out the position of the pad and use this in turn to arrange the lines for cutting and sewing the fabric. As these cushions are made with two separate pieces of fabric you can mix and match prints and plain fabrics, which will create cushions that are reversible and can be flipped over to give quick change to your interiors whenever the mood takes you.

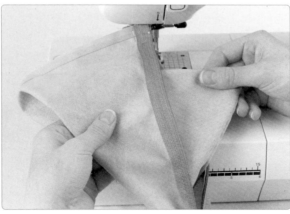

5 Carefully clip the corners and, through the open section of the zip, turn the cushion through.

6 Carefully push out all the corners and press neatly to finish.

4 With the right sides of the conjoined fabric squares facing, align the three remaining raw edges and pin in place. Working with a 1.5cm (0.6in) seam allowance, begin at one end of the zip and, with a straight machine stitch, work down the side and along the bottom and second side to join the remaining edges of the cushion.

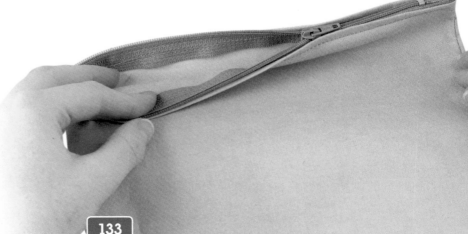

Envelope cushion

This is one of the quickest and easiest home furnishing items you can make. Rather than adding a fastening to secure the cushion cover, a length of fabric is folded around the cushion with an overlap at the back. This holds the cushion pad in place without the need for zips or buttons.

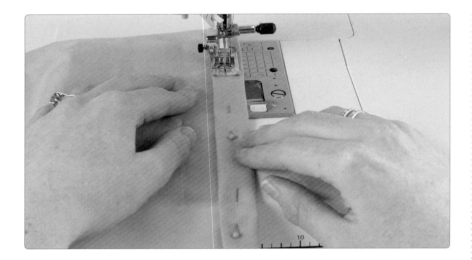

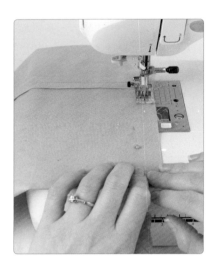

1 Measure a length of fabric that's three times the length of the cushion pad and the same width as the cushion pad. Before cutting the fabric you'll need to add 4cm (1.6in) to all sides for the seam allowances. Then cut the fabric, and with the wrong side uppermost, fold one of the shorter edges over by 1.5cm (0.6in) and again by 1.5cm (0.6in) and pin in place. Repeat with the opposite short edge. With a straight machine stitch sew a hem on each of the short edges.

3 With a straight machine stitch and using a 1.5cm (0.6in) seam allowance, work along each side of the cushion in turn to join the two side seams.

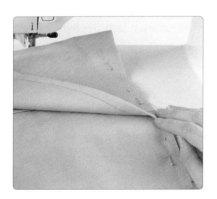

4 Carefully clip and press the seam allowance, then turn the cushion cover through to the right side through the overlapped section.

5 Press the cushion cover neatly and insert the pad through the overlapped section at the back.

2 Using the cushion pad placed in the centre of the fabric fold the two shorter ends over the back of the cushion, using pins to mark the position of the folds and the side seams of the cushion. Remove the pad and refold the fabric with right sides together: the two hemmed edges will overlap on the centre back. Pin the sides of the cushion along the two side seams.

Blankets & throws

Soft furnishings aren't only a great way to add a flash of colour or a new style to your home, they're also fabulous for keeping you cosy on long winter evenings. Blankets, throws and comforters are great for draping over the back of a couch or armchair or adding to the end of the bed to give your home a warm and welcoming feel.

Blankets

Flannel and brushed cotton are the ideal options for blankets, as they're lightweight but will keep you incredibly warm. They're also available in a wide range of colours and prints perfect for guest rooms, children's bedrooms or even your own room. You can make the blanket any size you want and finish it with your own choice of edging.

Supersized blankets

If you want to make an extremely large blanket you can always buy two or three lengths of fabric and join them across the width, first by tacking them and then by working a zigzag stitch over the join. Run a length of ribbon over the seam and top stitch down each side to secure. You could even join together squares of different designs to create a chequerboard effect.

Fancy edges

Work around the entire length with blanket stitch. Pick a contrasting coloured embroidery thread for a more striking effect. Or alternatively, press a length of ribbon in half, align the long sides, pin and stitch securely around the edge of the blanket – the soft silky texture of satin ribbon is a hit with small children!

Ribbon bound edge

Blanket stitch edge

Comforter

This thick padded blanket is often added on top of a bedspread to give extra warmth in the winter. It can be made to any size you like. Whether you want it large enough to cover the entire bed, or just a strip to run along the bottom to keep your feet cosy, the construction is the same whatever dimensions you make it.

1 Using the measurements of your bed or desired comforter size, cut a piece each of cotton, thick wadding and fleece, adding 2cm (0.79in) for seam allowance on all sides.

2 Pin the wadding to the wrong side of the fleece and tack it in place. Treat this as one piece of fabric for the remainder of the construction.

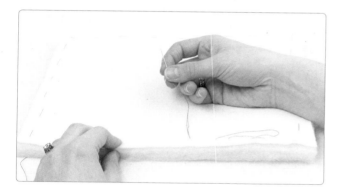

3 With the right sides facing, place the cotton fabric over the fleece and pin in place.

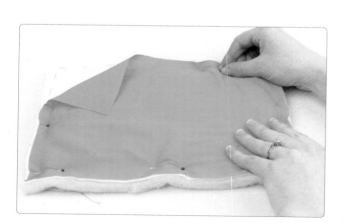

4 Working with a 1.5cm (0.6in) seam allowance, sew around the edge of the comforter, leaving a gap partway down one side that's large enough to turn the whole blanket through.

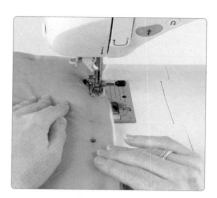

5 Carefully working around the comforter, remove the tack stitches from the wadding and the fleece and trim down the wadding in the seam allowance close to the stitches, being careful not to cut through the threads. Turn the entire comforter to the right side through the gap in the side seam, making sure the corners are fully pushed out. The wadding will now be sandwiched in the middle.

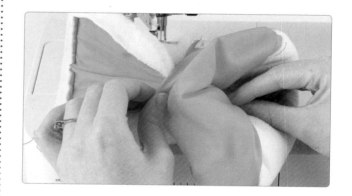

6 Fold under the raw edges along the gap in the seam and join with neat hand slip stitches.

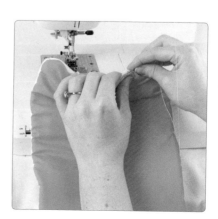

7 With the comforter cotton side facing upwards, use a ruler and chalk to draw guide lines for stitching. Begin by marking out a border around the entire comforter 1.5cm (0.6in) from the edge. Then draw diagonal lines along the length of the comforter spaced 10cm (4in) apart. Turn the comforter and repeat to add intersecting lines, also spaced 10cm (4in) apart.

8 Complete the comforter by sewing across the lines using a straight machine stitch. Start with the lines in the centre first, then move to the lines to the left, then to the right, alternating each side until the surface is stitched. Ease out any creases as you start working a new stitching line and be sure to start and stop the stitching before you reach the line for the border. Finish by sewing around the lines marked out for the border.

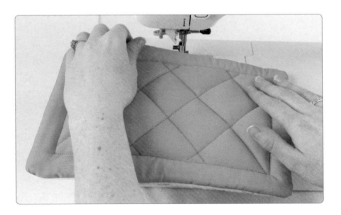

Throws

Whether you keep one on your favourite armchair or at the end of the bed, the addition of a new throw is a fast and simple way to update soft furnishings.

Fleece fabrics are a great option for throws as they're soft, warm and available in a wide range of colours. You can make a throw any size that you wish. Although fleece doesn't fray, cut edges may curl up slightly, so be sure to take that into consideration when you calculate your amounts. A simple rectangle of fleece might not look very special, but with a few finishing techniques you'll be able to give your throw a fantastic makeover.

1 **Add a fringe**
With a ruler and chalk draw a line 5cm (2in) in from the raw edge on each of the two shorter sides of the throw. Work along the line to draw horizontal lines from the raw edge to the marked line 1.5cm (0.6in) apart. With a sharp pair of scissors, work along one end of the throw, then the other, carefully cutting along the lines until both edges have fringes.

2 **Make a knotted fringe**
You can add interest by tying a single knot in alternate lengths of fringing, pulling the knot so that it sits two-thirds of the way down the fringe.

Quilting

This heirloom craft might look like a large-scale project, but you can make a quilt to any size you wish, and as it's created by working small sections at a time you can pick it up and put it down whenever you like. You'll very soon find yourself creating wonderful and unique bedcovers!

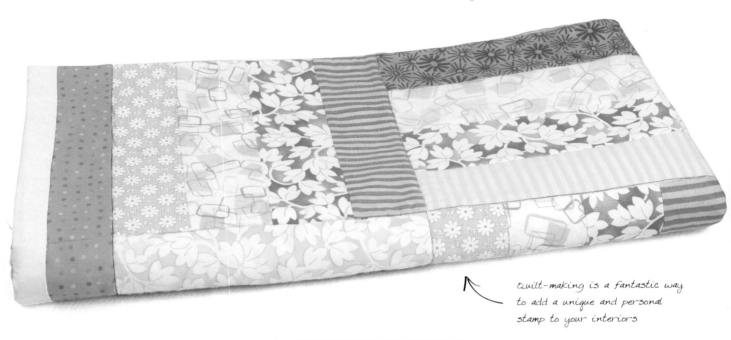

Quilt-making is a fantastic way to add a unique and personal stamp to your interiors

While quilts look like an extremely large project, it's important to remember that each one is made up of a series of elements called 'quilt blocks', which are stitched together to create the quilt's colourful upper section. Depending on the design of the quilt this can be made using blocks of one design or numerous different blocks of the same size but various colours or patterns.

This crib-sized quilt is made using a pre-cut fabric roll. These fabric bundles are great for beginners, as they reduce the amount of measuring, cutting and trimming that you'll need to do in the early stages of the project, allowing you to get on and try out the technique. Sew together the strips and trim them to create 16 blocks measuring 21.5cm (8.5in) each. These are then sewn together to create the quilt top, which is finished with a plain backing fabric folded over to the front to create a neat border.

Seam allowance

Quilting most commonly uses imperial measurements, and the dimensions given on quilting patterns are therefore often given only in inches; so if you aren't used to working in imperial you'll need to be careful when converting the figures. Unlike dressmaking and the majority of other sewing projects, which are worked with a 1.5cm (0.6in) seam allowance, quilts are sewn using a 6mm (0.25in) seam allowance.

Remember to check your conversions before you begin your project. Ensuring that you maintain the correct seam allowances throughout will help you to create a series of quilt blocks that fit neatly together.

Common quilting conversions

Use this imperial to metric table to help you convert the measurements most commonly found in quilting:

Imperial	Metric
0.25in	6mm
0.50in	1.3cm
2in	5cm
4in	10cm
6in	15cm
10in	25.5cm

Making a quilt

1 Cutting the fabric

Using a pre-cut roll, select 16 different coordinating strips. Alternatively from a selection of print cotton cut 16 strips measuring 6.4cm (2.5in) wide by 112cm (44in) long. Select four strips for the borders, or cut four additional 6.4cm by 112cm strips.

2 Join two strips

Begin by arranging the 16 strips into four separate piles. Each batch will create a block. Ensure that you're happy with the arrangement of the prints within each batch – swap them about until you're happy with the placement. Working with one pile at a time, begin to join the strips together. With right sides facing, place two of the strips together with the raw edges of the long sides aligned. With a 6mm (0.25in) seam allowance and a straight machine stitch, work along the length to join the two strips together.

3 Join a third strip

In the same manner, place a third strip over the long edge of one of the two joined strips so that the right sides are facing. With a straight machine stitch and a 6mm (0.25in) seam allowance, join the third strip.

4 Join the final strip

Place the fourth and final strip from the batch on to the last strip added with right sides facing. With a straight machine stitch and a 6mm (0.25in) seam allowance, join the fourth strip. Repeat the process for the other three batches of fabric, joining each of the four strips in turn. This will create four large strips each made up of four strips of fabric seamed together.

5 Trim to create blocks

Working with each stitched strip in turn, press the strips so that the seam allowances are all flat and in the same direction. With a rotary cutter, mat and ruler, take each sewn strip in turn and carefully trim into four 22cm (8.5in) squares. These squares are the quilt blocks.

6 Position the blocks

Once the four strips have been trimmed into 16 blocks, arrange them into four rows of four to create the quilt top. These can be placed in sequential order, or can be mixed randomly until you're happy with the overall design. As the blocks are square they can be rotated so that the strips making up each block run horizontally or vertically. In this quilt the blocks have been alternated between horizontal and vertical.

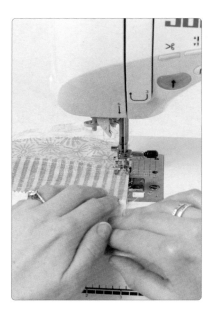

7 **Join the blocks to create rows**
Work on one row of four blocks at a time. Beginning with the block on the left-hand side, place the next block on top of this with right sides facing aligning the raw edges. Work with a straight machine stitch and a 6mm (0.25in) seam allowance to join the two blocks together.

8 **Complete the row**
Complete the row by placing the third block in the sequence, with right sides facing, on the right-hand block of the pair just joined, and sew together with a 6mm (0.25in) seam allowance. Finally, in the same manner join the fourth and final block, to create a row of four joined blocks.

9 **Create the remaining rows**
Working each row in turn, join the blocks together with a 6mm (0.25in) seam allowance to create three more rows. Work from the left-hand block and always add the next block to be joined to the right-hand side of the row. Press the seams flat on all the rows of blocks.

Laura's top tip

Pressing the seams when quilting is a crucial part of the construction process, as it makes each section neater and makes it much easier to piece multiple blocks together. Try to get into the habit of pressing each seam once you've stitched it. Press the seams carefully, working the iron from the right side of the fabric to give a crisp finish to the front of the quilt.

As a general rule, if you're working with a range of coloured fabrics try to press the seam allowance so that it sits under the darker of any two adjoining fabrics, as this will help to prevent it from showing through to the surface on lighter fabrics. On quilts with bold fabrics, such as this one, where seam allowances won't show through on the right side of the finished quilt, press all the seam allowances in the same direction. To make the process a bit quicker, set up your ironing board next to your sewing machine. If your iron is always handy you will be less likely to skip this important stage.

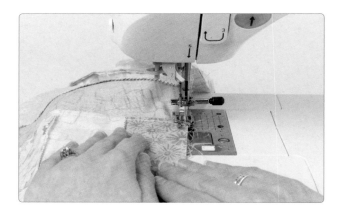

10 **Join the rows together**
Lay the rows flat in the order that you want them to appear on the finished quilt. Working from the bottom row, place the row above it on top with right sides facing. Getting each of the blocks to align on the two rows as they're joined will give the quilt a neat finish. The best way to do this is to carefully align the two rows so that the intersection of the joined blocks from the row above matches with the two adjoining blocks of the row below. Once you've lined this up, work a couple of stitches over this section inside the 6mm (0.25in) seam allowance. Remove the quilt from the machine and check the section.

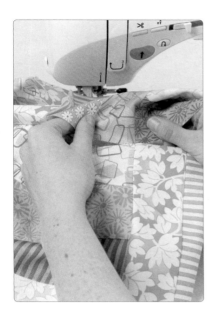

11 **Check the placement**
Once opened the blocks from the adjoining rows should match perfectly, held in place by the couple of stitches within the seam allowance. If you're happy with this placement, repeat across the row, matching the blocks from the adjoining rows and working a few stitches to secure them.

12 **Join the rows**
When the sections are all neatly aligned, work with a straight machine stitch and a 6mm (0.25in) seam allowance to join the two rows together. Once complete, repeat this process to join the remaining two rows, until all four are stitched together.

13 **Press all seams**
Once the four rows have been stitched together, press the seams in the same direction and trim the edges so that they're all straight and the section is square.

14 **Add a border**
Decide which part of the quilt is the top and which is the bottom. Working on the two side sections first, place a 6.4cm (2.5in) by 112cm (44in) strip with right sides facing along one side of the quilt. Stitch in place with a straight machine stitch, using a 6mm (0.25in) seam allowance. Repeat for the other side of the quilt. Once the side border pieces are in place, press the seams in the same direction and carefully trim the ends of the borders level with the top and bottom of the quilt. Place a border strip over the top edge of the quilt with right sides of the border and quilt facing, and sew in place with a straight machine stitch and a 6mm (0.25in) seam. Repeat to add the bottom border, pressing the seams and trimming the excess border fabrics to complete the quilt top.

Construct the quilt

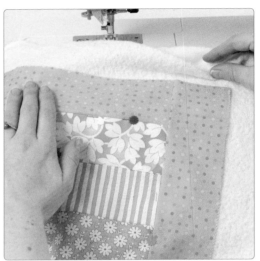

1 Layer the quilt

A quilt is made up of three layers: quilt top, wadding and backing fabric. Begin by placing the backing on a flat surface with the wrong side uppermost. Position the wadding on the backing and then the quilt top on the wadding, right side uppermost. Work across the quilt, carefully securing the layers of fabric together with long quilting pins. Using a rotary cutter, mat and ruler, trim the wadding and the backing so that they're 10cm (4in) larger than the quilt top on all sides.

Laura's top tip

How you choose to quilt your project is entirely up to you. It can be quilted by hand, using hand quilting thread to sew neat running stitches across the project while it's held in a large hoop; or you can use your machine, working along the seam lines (a technique known as stitch-in-the-ditch) or using free-motion stitching for more creative designs. If you're working on an extremely large quilt it's possible to get the project quilted for you, since some patchwork and quilting shops offer a long-arm quilting service, which makes use of a specialist quilting machine and a large frame to quilt big areas. Some shops even offer workshops and classes so that you can learn to long-arm quilt your own large-scale projects.

Quilt sizes

Of course, you can make a quilt in any size that you wish, but here are a few common quilt sizes that you can use as a guide when designing your own projects.

Crib	91.5cm x 91.5cm (36in x 36in)
Baby quilt	91.5cm x 137cm (36in x 54in)
Single	147cm x 228.5cm (58in x 90in)
Double	183cm x 228.5cm (72in x 90in)
Queen	228.5cm x 275cm (90in x 108in)
King	275cm x 275cm (108in x 108in)

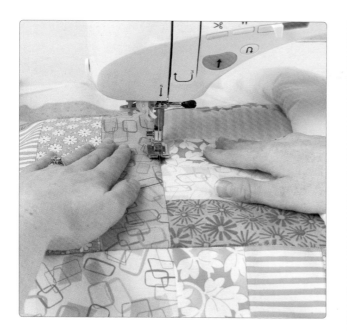

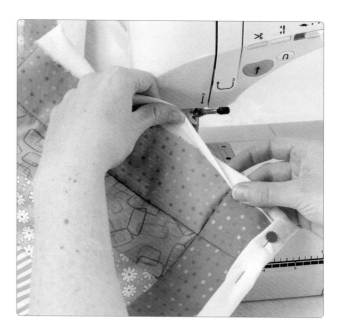

2 Begin quilting

Select an appropriate machine foot, edge stitching for stitch-in-the-ditch quilting or free-motion for more creative designs. Roll the quilt in towards the middle from both sides, leaving the centre section flat. Begin sewing along the centre section. The stitches will work through all three layers of fabric. Once the centre section is complete gradually work outwards, stitching across the entire surface of the project. Carefully smooth out any creases and wrinkles in the fabric towards the outer edges before you stitch, for a neat finish.

3 Create the binding

The edges of the quilt are finished with binding, which conceals the raw edges of all three layers. With a rotary mat cutter and ruler, trim the quilt wadding in line with the quilt top, being careful to fold the backing fabric out of the way of the blade so as not to slice through it. Press the backing fabric and carefully fold it in half and then in half again, so that it sits on the front of the quilt top and conceals the raw edges. Pin in place. Fold the corners of the backing fabric to create mitres on each corner.

Bias tape edging

Quilts can also be edged using bias tape – either handmade from your quilting fabric or ready-made. To secure this, trim both the wadding and the quilt backing in line with the quilt top. Working on the back of the quilt, open out a length of bias tape and pin around the quilt, aligning the raw edges of the backing with the raw edges of the tape. Ensure there's enough bias tape on the corners to create mitres. With a straight machine stitch, work along the line of the fold to secure the tape in place. Turn the quilt over so that the right side is uppermost and fold the bias tape over the raw edges. Following the remaining fold in the bias tape, tuck the raw edges under and pin in place. Work with neat hand slip stitches around the quilt to secure the binding in place on the quilt top.

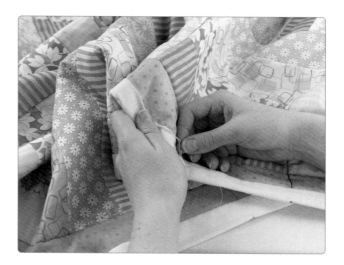

4 Sew the binding

Carefully work around the edges of the quilt using hand slip stitches to secure the binding in place. Snip away any thread ends and press the quilt neatly to finish.

Chapter 6

Embellishing & customising

While stitching is a fundamentally practical skill, it's also incredibly creative – which is one of the main attractions for me. When you're making something, you're creating a piece of clothing or a home decor item that's unique and one-of-a-kind. That's the beauty of handmade projects. But you can also use a few clever sewing techniques to add a personal touch to almost anything. You can transform any shop-bought fabric item, from cardigans to cushions, by adding a handful of pretty buttons, a smattering of sequins or lashings of ribbons. Try out these simple customising techniques and let your imagination run wild!

Embroidery

Needlework is a fantastic way to add a personal touch and a flash of colour to your projects. Try your hand at this selection of pretty embroidery stitches and discover a world of creative possibilities.

Hand embroidery is a very satisfying pastime. You begin with a few basic stitches that, once mastered, enable you to create a wide range of beautiful designs. With a little practice you'll learn to keep each element of your stitching even, which is the key to elegant embroidery. What's more it's a deceptively simple craft. Work with colourful stranded or perle cottons and a combination of a few basic stitches to add motifs and designs on to any fabric or project.

Transferring a motif

There are a number of different ways in which you can transfer a motif on to your fabric. The simplest is to place the motif under your fabric and trace over it with either an air-erasable or water-soluble pen, or an embroidery pencil. Just secure your fabric in a frame with the motif in the centre and you're ready to stitch!

Stem stitch

This stitch is great for outlining. The stitches are worked with a slight overlap, creating a pretty scrolling effect.

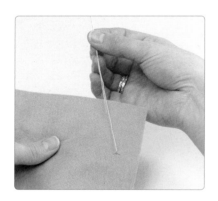

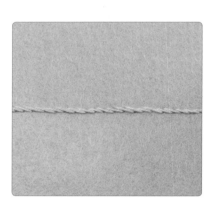

1 Secure the thread with a knot and draw the needle through the fabric from the wrong side to the right side at the point where you want to start a line of stitching. Put the needle back through the fabric to make the first stitch.

2 Bring the needle back up to the right side of the fabric so that it's halfway along the top of the first stitch. Aim to push the tip of the needle directly up through the middle point of the stitch, being careful to slide the threads of the first stitch away from the tip of the needle.

3 Pass the needle back down to complete the stitch so that it ends in front of the first stitch, spaced evenly along the stitching line. Continue working along the stitching line, ensuring that every new stitch comes through to the surface at the halfway point of the previous stitch and sits snugly above it.

Chain

This pretty stitch can be used to edge and outline designs or can be curled around to make motifs on its own.

1 Secure the thread with a knot and draw the needle through the fabric from the wrong side to the right side. Put the needle back through the fabric 4mm (0.16in) above where you began, but don't pull the thread all the way through. Leave a short loop of thread on the surface.

2 Bring the needle back up about 5mm (0.19in) in front of the last stitch, and pull the thread up through the loop.

3 Put the needle back through the fabric, catching the loop and leaving a new loop through which to pull the needle on your next stitch. Continue working along to create a length of chain stitches.

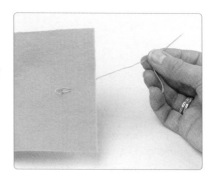

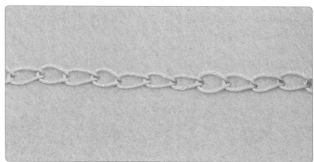

Lazy daisy

This is also known as a detached chain stitch, as it uses elements of the chain stitch worked to create a flower.

1 Secure the thread with a knot and draw the needle through the fabric from the wrong side to the right side.

2 Put the needle back through the fabric 4mm (0.16in) above where you began, but don't pull the thread all the way through. Leave a short loop of thread on the surface.

3 Bring the needle back up about 5mm (0.19in) in front of the last stitch, and pull the thread up through the loop.

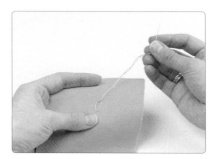

4 Pass the needle back down at the other side of the loop. Pull the thread through to secure the loop into position. Work a few lazy daisy stitches in clusters from a central point to make a pretty flower, or use them on their own as pretty petal shapes.

Satin stitch

If you have an area of a project that you'd like to fill you can use long straight stitches to 'colour in' the section.

1 Secure the thread with a knot and draw the needle through the fabric from the wrong side to the right side at the start point of the section you'd like to fill.

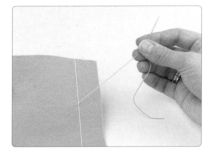

2 Moving across to the second side of the section to be filled, pass the needle back down through to the wrong side, creating a long straight stitch that covers the length of the section.

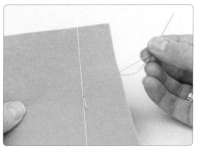

3 Bring the needle back to the right side on the start of the first stitch, carry the thread over the section to be filled and pass it back down on the opposite side.

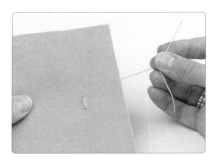

4 Continue working in straight stitches until the entire area is covered.

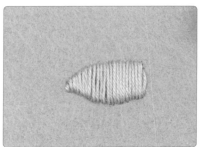

French knot

This decorative little knot can be used on its own to add little dots to the surface of the fabric, or it can be worked repeatedly to fill large sections with colour and texture.

1 Secure the thread with a knot and draw the needle through the fabric from the wrong side to the right side at the point where you'd like the knot to be.

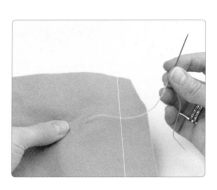

2 With the needle held almost flush to the project, take the emerging thread and wrap it twice around the needle.

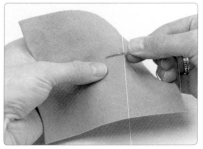

3 Holding the length of thread taut with your fingertips, pass the needle back through to the wrong side. Try to pass the needle through as close as possible to where the thread came through.

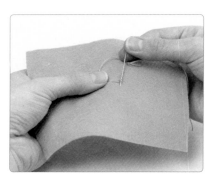

4 Draw the thread down through the fabric and the French knot will tighten and sit neatly on the surface of the project.

Cross stitch

As the name suggests, this comprises of two stitches that cross in the centre. They can be worked in blocks of colours to create large designs – as in cross stitch or tapestry – or can be used to outline and edge designs.

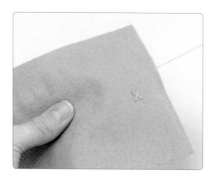

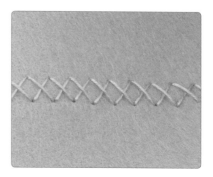

1 Secure the thread with a knot and draw the needle through the fabric from the wrong side to the right side. Push the needle through the fabric 5mm (0.19in) up and to the right of the entry point and draw the thread through.

2 Push the needle through from the wrong side to the right side of the fabric directly below the top of the last stitch. Draw it across the previous stitch and pass through the fabric at the top left-hand side of that stitch to complete.

3 Continue working to create the desired number of cross stitches. It doesn't really matter whether you work the left-to-right slanting section of the stitch first or the right-to-left, but always work in the same order – this way the top stitches will always point in the same direction.

Short & long stitch

A variation of satin stitch. Its name is derived from its combination of different-length stitches worked in the same way across the area to be filled.

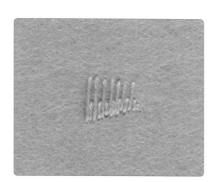

Seed stitch

Small straight stitches that can be worked individually or in lines to add interest and colour to an area without filling it completely.

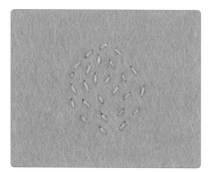

Seed stitch can be worked in a scattered or more uniform fashion by bringing the needle up and down through the fabric to make a collection of small straight stitches. If you want to work lines of seed stitch weave the needle back and forth through the fabric before drawing the thread through; this quickly creates a lot of little stitches.

Finishing embroidery

When sewing an embroidery project you should aim to keep the back of the work as neat as possible. Using thread lengths no longer than the length of your forearm will help prevent you from getting in a tangle. Each time you finish working with a length of thread, or change to a different colour, turn the work over and create a small knot and trim the ends.

Once the complete design has been stitched, place a soft towel on the surface of your ironing board and lay the project on top so that the wrong side of the design is upwards. Carefully press it: place the iron on one section at a time and hold for a few seconds before lifting and moving to the next section. Working slowly in sections will help to neaten the stitches and will prevent them from becoming distorted.

Appliqué

Overlaying fabric shapes secured with machine or hand stitches is a simple yet effective way to embellish your fabrics. This technique can be used in a wide variety of projects from customising clothes to updating soft furnishings.

Creating an appliqué motif

1 Draw around your appliqué motif or create a freehand design on your chosen fabric, and using an iron carefully affix interfacing to the wrong side of the design. If you're using double-sided interfacing you can draw the design on the paper backing, secure the interfacing to the fabric and use these lines as a guide for cutting the motif. Carefully cut out the design from the fabric and trim away any excess interfacing.

Beginner-friendly

Appliqué is a fabric motif that's cut from one material and carefully secured to another. The motif can be added to almost anything, and you can pick a size, colour and design to suit your project. This decorative technique can be used on a whole range of projects. Using double-sided interfacing will help to secure the motif on the project prior to sewing, making the creation of fantastic designs a quick and easy process.

Hand appliqué is a great introduction to this technique as you can work carefully and slowly around the design to get the stitches exactly as you want them. Start out with simple shapes so that you can master getting the stitches even and neat, then move on to more complex and intricate designs.

2 Position the motif on the surface of your project. Once you're happy with the placement, remove the backing paper from the interfacing to reveal the second adhesive side and press into place.

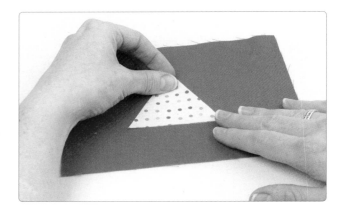

3 The appliqué motif can be finished either by hand or with a sewing machine.

Hand appliqué

1 Secure the fabric fused with the appliqué motif in an embroidery hoop so that the motif is central and the fabric is taut around the design. This will make sewing the decorative details much neater.

2 Using a selection of embroidery threads, begin working around the outline of the design using an outlining stitch. You can choose from back stitch, stem stitch, running stitch, chain stitch or even a row of cross stitches. Work carefully just inside the fabric of the motif, keeping the stitches neat and even.

3 Once the outline of the design has been stitched, work in any details of the motif using colourful embroidery threads. Try adding clusters of seed stitches or French knots.

Finishing an appliqué

If you're adding an appliqué motif to a piece of clothing the wrong side of the project will need to be finished. This will stop the threads from the appliqué tickling or being uncomfortable if it's worn next to the skin.

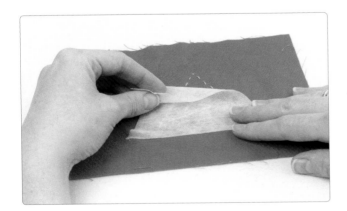

1 Turn the finished appliqué project through so that the wrong side is uppermost, and trim away any stray thread ends. Cut a piece of interfacing (this only needs to have adhesive on one side) to the size and shape of the motif.

2 Place a soft towel on the surface of the ironing board to protect the stitches, and position the project so that the wrong side of the appliqué is upwards. Carefully affix the interfacing to the back of the design. Pay particular attention to ensuring that the edges of the interfacing are securely fixed.

Machine appliqué

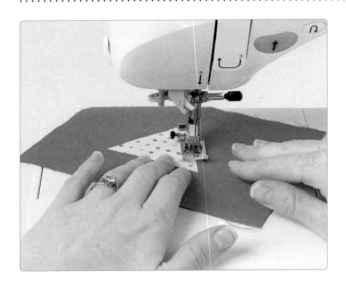

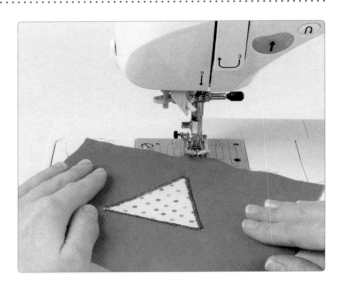

1 Place the fabric with the fused appliqué design on the sewing area of your machine, with the right side of the design facing upwards. Position the needle to begin at the start point. It's easier if you can work around the entire design in one consecutive line of stitching, though with more complex designs this may not be possible.

2 Select a zigzag stitch with a 1.5mm (0.06in) width and a 1mm (0.04in) length and slowly and carefully begin working around the design. Work a couple of reverse stitches to secure the threads. The stitches should be positioned partly on the appliqué motif and partly on the fabric of the project. Try to keep the stitching even. Once you've stitched the whole way around the design, work a couple of reverse stitches to secure the thread, and trim away any thread ends to finish.

Decorative machine stitches

While machine appliqué is often worked using the zigzag stitch setting on your machine, you can try out a selection of different decorative stitches if your machine has them. If you're experimenting with other decorative stitches look for styles where the needle will move to the left and the right while stitching, as this will allow you to position the stitches so that they sit on both the motif and the project fabric. Try a few different styles on a scrap of fabric before you start working on your project.

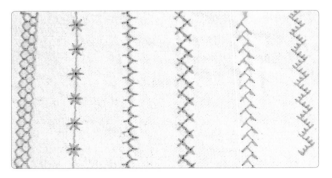

Laura's top tip

It's all too tempting to set your machine to a high speed and try to race round the design, especially if the shape looks rather simple. The trick to a really neat finish is to aim to have the line where the motif and the main fabric join positioned halfway through the stitch. The best way to achieve this is to work with a slow to medium speed, carefully moving the fabric under the needle. If the design that you're working on is rather complex it can be a little tricky to manoeuvre the fabric to get the stitches in the right position. Sometimes it's wise to have a practice run before you start working on your finished piece. To do this I use the appliqué motif as a template and draw out the shape on to scrap fabric using chalk. This gives me a line to work around so that I can familiarise myself with the way I need to move the fabric before I start the project.

Reverse appliqué

As it sounds, the motif is cut from the upper fabric, allowing the fabric below to show through the design.

1 With an erasable marker, draw out your design on the right side of the fabric.

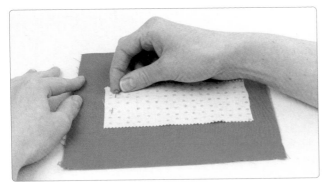

2 Pin a section of contrasting fabric, 2cm (0.79in) larger than the motif on all sides, to the wrong side of the fabric. The main fabric and the contrast fabric will both have their wrong sides uppermost. Secure with a narrow border of fusible interfacing.

3 Secure the motif into an embroidery hoop and with coloured embroidery thread begin to work around the outline of your motif. You can choose from back stitch, stem stitch, running stitch and chain stitch; if you want to sew this with a machine, select a straight stitch or even a narrow zigzag stitch to work around the outline.

Laura's top tip

Using fusible interfacing that's adhesive on both sides will secure the motif in place on the surface of the fabric. This way it will be held steady while you work around the design with hand or machine stitches to complete the appliqué. Working with pieces of colourful felt is a good way to get started with this technique, as it's both easy to cut and sew and has the benefit that it won't fray.

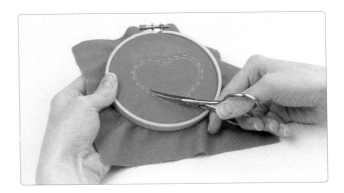

4 Once the outline of the motif has been stitched, using a small pair of scissors with sharp pointed blades carefully trim the top fabric around the stitches. Work as close as you can to the stitches on the upper fabric, being particularly careful not to snip the threads or the fabric below.

5 Once the cut section has been removed the reverse appliqué is revealed.

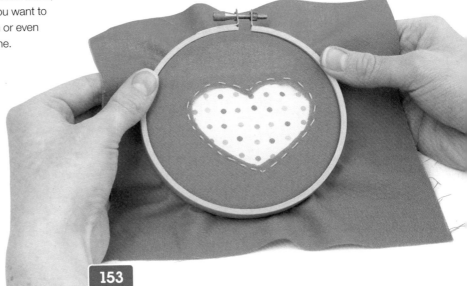

Adding sparkle

Whether you're making a party dress or creating festive decorations, adding some bling to your projects is a great way to give your makes a little lift. A collection of beads, sequins and gems will add the wow factor to your makes.

Sewing on sequins

Sequins are shiny discs, often faceted, that reflect light and add a bit of glam to a project.

Secure a single sequin

With the thread secured at the back of the work, draw the thread to the right side of the project at the point where you want the sequin to be positioned. Thread the sequin on to the needle and lay it flat on the surface of the fabric. Pass the needle back through to the wrong side of the project so that the thread lies just at the outer edge of the sequin to hold it in place, and fasten off.

Secure a sequin with a bead

With the thread secured at the back of the work, draw the thread to the right side of the project at the point where you'd like the sequin to be positioned. Thread the sequin on to the needle and lay it flat on the surface of the fabric. Thread a bead slightly larger than the hole in the centre of the sequin on to the thread and slide down towards the sequin. Insert the needle back through the hole in the centre of the sequin, drawing down the bead to hold the sequin in position and secure the thread on the back of the project.

Sewing a line of sequins

With the thread secured at the back of the work, draw the thread to the right side of the project at the point where you'd like the first sequin to be positioned. Thread the sequin on to the needle and position it flat on the surface of the fabric. Pass the needle back through to the wrong side of the project so that the thread enters just at the outer edge of the sequin. Position the second sequin so that it overlaps the first sequin slightly and the hole in the centre sits just past the edge of the first sequin. Bring the needle through to the right side and through the hole in the centre of the second sequin. Pass the needle back through to the wrong side at the outer edge of the sequin and repeat to secure a line of sequins.

Creating costumes

Sequins are commonly used on dance and theatre costumes, as the many facets of the sequin will reflect stage lights for a wonderful dramatic effect. Many dance costumes are made from stretch-knit fabrics, to allow the body movement. If you're adding sequins to a stretch knit you'll need to make sure that the line of stitches securing the sequins doesn't restrict the stretch of the fabric as the dancer moves, which could result in the threads snapping. To prevent this, try pulling the fabric out to half its full stretch and securing it in an embroidery hoop; this will provide the completed stitches with a little more give and will allow the fabric to flex.

Sewing on beads

Beads can be stitched to the surface of a project in clusters or continuous lines.

Securing a single bead

With the thread secured at the back of the work, draw the thread to the right side of the project at the point where you'd like the bead to be fixed. Thread the bead on to the needle and position flat on the surface of the fabric. Pass the needle back through to the wrong side of the project close to where the thread came through. Draw the thread through the fabric to secure the bead to the surface. Repeat the process three or four times more and fasten off.

Sewing a line of beads

With the thread secured at the back of the work, draw the thread to the right side of the project at the point where you'd like the first bead. Thread the bead on to the needle and place it flat on the surface of the fabric. Pass the needle back through to the wrong side of the project to hold the first bead. Position the second bead so that it sits close to the first bead, and bring the needle through to the right side of the fabric on the far side of the bead. Pass the needle through the bead, pushing the needle tip in the direction of the first bead. Push the needle back through to the wrong side of the project through the small space between the first and second beads. Continue working back through each bead in turn until the line is complete, then secure the thread on the back of the project.

Sew-on gems

There are various types of sew-on gems available. Some have a stone encased in a metal cup while others will have small drilled holes for a needle and thread to be passed through.

With the thread secured on the back of the project, bring the thread up to the right side of the fabric at the position where the gem will be secured. Pass the needle through the holes in the gem or the holes in the metal casing and back down through to the wrong side of the fabric. Repeat working the stitches through the holes until the gem is secured.

Stick-on gems

A quick and easy no-sew method for attaching some sparkle to your project is to use stick-on gems. These are available from most haberdashery stores, and either have peel-off backing or need to be applied by heat fixing using a special tool.

Hot-fix gems

Using the special tool, select the corresponding size applicator for the chosen gem. Plug in the tool and wait a few seconds for it to heat up. Place the gem's shiny side up, and once the tool is hot place it over the gem to pick it up. Holding the tool away from your work, wait a few seconds for the glue on the back to melt. Carefully press into position on your project and repeat until the desired area is covered.

Laura's top tip

Vintage beads, sparkles and buttons are a beautiful and unique way to customise your clothing and accessories. I always keep an eye out for vintage beads and buttons as they're often one-of-a-kind and will really transform a project. Charity shops and markets are a great place to pick up collections of old buttons, or even pick out garments with lovely embellishments that you can unpick and reuse. Start collecting your vintage treasures in a glass jar – you'll be amazed at how quickly the collection will grow, and how much it inspires you to get customising.

Fabric blooms

Your sewing stash is a treasure trove for customising; always keep remnants
of pretty fabrics and colourful ribbons for adding accents to future projects.
Mix together print and plain fabrics for really bold accessories.

Fabric yo-yo

Also known as Suffolk puffs, these little decorations are created with circles of fabric and can be made any size.

1 Draw a circle on to the wrong side of a piece of fabric and cut it out.

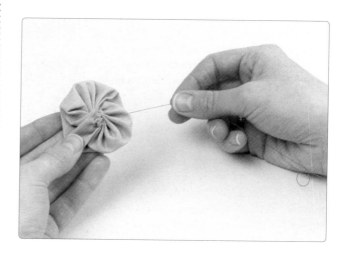

3 Draw up the threads to gather the edges of the circle until they're touching in the centre.

2 Using gather stitch, carefully hand sew around the circle 4mm (0.16in) in from the raw edge.

4 Pass the needle through the centre of the puff and fasten it on the back to finish.

Simple scrap flower

Small circular off-cuts of pretty prints can be layered together to transform them into voluminous fabric blooms.

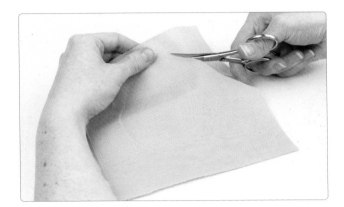

1 From a range of scrap fabrics, cut three circles, each one 2.5cm (1in) smaller than the last. Pinch and twist the centre of the smallest circle until the fabric ruffles. Work through the twisted centre section with a few hand stitches to secure in place and fasten off the thread.

2 Repeat with the middle-sized circle to create a twist at the centre, secure with a few hand stitches and fasten off the thread.

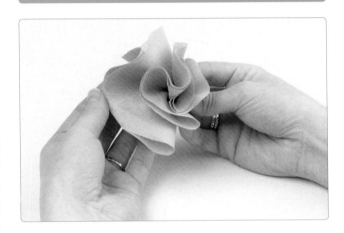

4 Pass the needle up through the centre of the middle circle, position the smaller circle in the centre and secure in place with a few hand stitches.

3 Repeat with the final (largest) circle, then pass the needle up through its centre and position the middle-sized bloom on top. Secure in place with a few hand stitches.

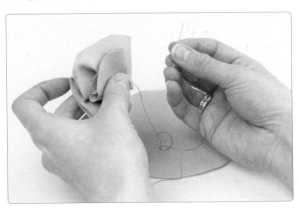

5 Pass the needle back down through the centre of each layer and fasten off at the back of the project.

Ribbon accents

Ribbon comes in a wide range of finishes, from satin and velvet to grosgrain and organza, not to mention every colour you could wish for, so you can create just the right accent for any project.

Fixed bow

Made with a loop of ribbon that's secured so that it can be added to a project without fear of it coming undone.

1 Cut a length of ribbon 10cm (4in) long and a second 5cm (2in) long. Then fold both ends of the longer section into the centre and overlap slightly.

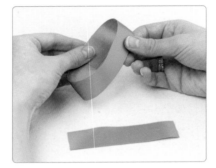

2 Press the centre of the ribbon loop to create the two rounded ends of the bow. With small hand stitches, work through the centre of the bow to secure it in place.

3 Wrap the smaller section of ribbon over the bow, overlap the ends slightly and trim to neaten. Work a few stitches through the back of the bow to secure the loop into position.

Layered fixed bow

Create a layered bow by making two loops of ribbon, positioning a larger one to the back before drawing in to make the bow and securing with a neat loop.

Neat ribbon ends

Ribbon ends can be prone to fraying, so when working with ribbons it's always wise to neaten the ends of the cut lengths before you add them to your project. Trimming the ends of the ribbon diagonally across the grain will both neaten and prevent them from fraying. With small sharp scissors, snip with either a single angled cut or two angled cuts meeting in the centre. Another option for treating ribbon ends is to heat seal the fibres by quickly passing the end of the ribbon through a candle flame to melt the fibres together. Always be very careful when heat sealing – you don't want the ribbon to catch alight! And remember that the sealed ends will remain hot for a while after the fibres have been melted together.

Ribbon corsage

Not only do these make perfect corsages or fascinators, they can also be used for wrapping extra-special gifts!

1 With a length of ribbon, fold the raw end in to the centre to create a loop. Secured with a knot, draw a thread through the ribbon and work a small stitch to join.

2 Twist the ribbon to create a second loop that will look like a figure eight. Pass the needle through and secure in the centre to make a small stitch.

3 Continue working around the centre point, folding the ribbon into figure-eight loops and securing with a small neat stitch at the centre. Add as many loops as you want.

4 Secure the last loop at the centre point. Ensure that the thread is worked through all the layers of ribbon and secure with a knot. Carefully trim the ribbon so that the end sits neatly inside the corsage.

Ribbon rosette

Off-cuts of ribbon and a button team together to make a charming vintage accent.

1 Take a 30cm (12in) length of ribbon and begin folding back and forth on itself to create a series of 1cm (0.4in) folds. With a knotted length of cotton push a needle through the centre of the fold as it's made, drawing the thread through all the layers.

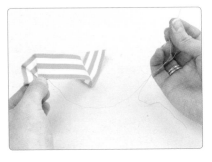

2 Pull the thread ends together and knot to make a circle. Join the two ends of ribbon with a couple of hand stitches.

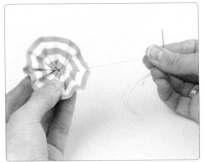

3 Layer two 10cm (4in) lengths of ribbon and fold them in half. Secure to the back of the rosette with a few neat hand stitches and snip the raw ends of the ribbon into neat swallow tails.

4 Hand-sew a button to the centre of the rosette to finish.

Additional accents

When it comes to customising, if there's something that you can sew on to a project there's nothing to stop you doing so. Items that you've stowed away in your stash can provide the inspiration for lots of new projects.

Lace trims

Lengths of pretty lace trim can be quickly and easily secured to garments to add a feminine touch to collars, cuffs, necklines and hems. Cut a length of lace trim at least twice as long as the section you want to apply it to. Work a length of gather stitches along the upper edge of the trim. Pull the threads to carefully draw up the lace to the same length as the section you want to trim and fasten with a knot. Pin the length of gathered trim along the section, distributing the gathers carefully. Work around the entire section with hand running stitch or a straight machine stitch to secure in place.

Make a lace Peter Pan collar

A Peter Pan collar is a flat, rounded collar that sits on the neckline of a garment. A length of wide lace trim can be used to give an old sweater or plain T-shirt an instant makeover.

Cut a length of wide lace trim slightly longer than the length of the neckline. Carefully trim the ends into even curves that will meet at the front. Working around the collar, pin in place along the whole neckline, ensuring that the two rounded ends sit neatly at the front. Secure in place with running stitches or a straight machine stitch. Finish with a small fixed bow at the centre, or a covered button, or both!

Layered buttons

Sewing on a smattering of pretty buttons is a great way to add colour to a project: you can mix and match different shapes and sizes, or you can create a real focal point by layering buttons, using a larger one as a base and a smaller one on top. As these are usually used for decorative effect you can simply sew them flat on to your project. But if you want to use them as functioning buttons you'll need to check that the large and small button layered together will fit through the buttonhole, and you'll need to fasten them with a thread shank (see page 74).

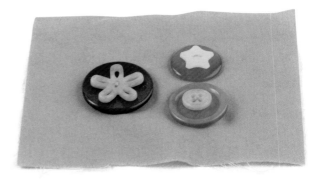

Secure the thread on the wrong side of the project with a knot and bring through to the right side at the point where you want the button positioned. Thread the larger button on to the needle so that it lays flat on the surface of the fabric. Thread the smaller button on to the needle so that it sits over the top. Push the needle back through to the wrong side, being careful that the thread passes through both buttons. Continue making stitches through both buttons until they're secure, and fasten with a knot on the back of the project.

Laura's top tip

You'll find it easier to sew on layered buttons if both the larger and smaller buttons have the same number of holes. So team two-hole buttons with two-hole buttons and four-hole buttons with four-hole buttons!

Covered buttons

Ready-to-use covered button packs are available from most haberdashery stores and contain both the button blanks and a template for cutting the fabric to the correct size. Some kits contain a little press tool to construct the button, others are formed by simply pressing the pieces together with your fingertips.

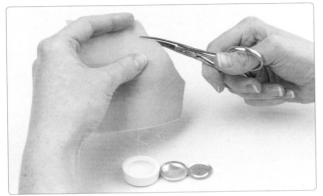

1 Use the template in the button pack to cut a circle from your chosen fabric.

2 Place the fabric circle wrong side uppermost and position the top section of the button face down in the centre of the circle.

4 Once the fabric has been tucked inside the top of the button, position the back section on the button and, with either the tool provided or your fingertips, snap it into position.

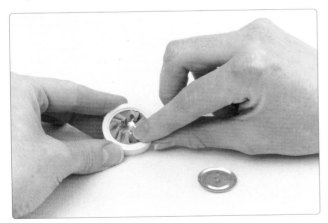

3 Work around the button, carefully folding in the edges of the fabric inside the top section. Many cover buttons will have small metal teeth running around the inside of the top section – if so press the fabric against these to help grip it in place.

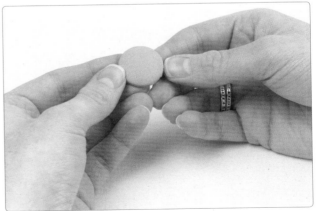

Cottons are usually the best choice for making covered buttons, as they're thick enough that the metal blank of the button won't show through but not so thick that the sections won't snap together – plus you can pick from a wide range of colours and prints!

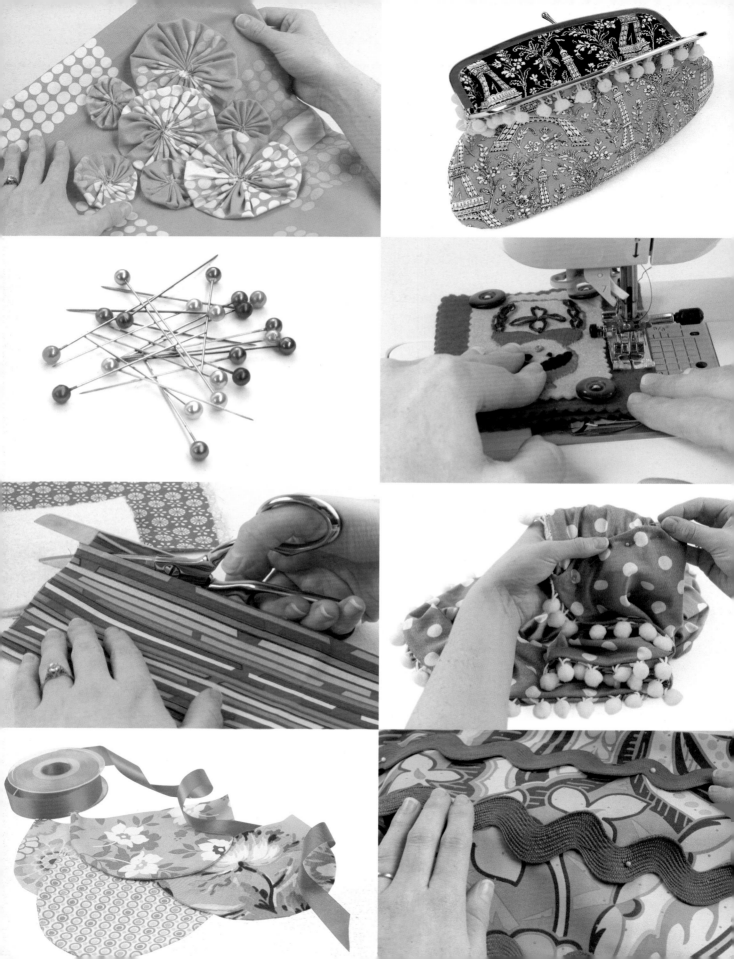

Chapter 7 ·

Projects

Getting stuck into some different sewing projects is great fun. And remember, all the projects that you work on are made up using a series of various techniques. So if at first the instructions look a little confusing, break them down step-by-step and review the multiple skills that you'll need. Even then you may not know where to start, so here are a few easy projects to get you going. Before you know it you'll be able to turn your hand to a whole host of exciting and creative designs!

Wrap scarf

This simple scarf is created by sewing a length of stretch jersey into a tube, then joining the ends to make a large ring that can be worn looped around the neck to add a dash of colour to your outfit.

Difficulty ✂️✂️✂️✂️✂️   **Total time** Allow 30 minutes per scarf

You will need...
- Jersey, 60cm x 1.5m (24in x 1.6yd) – the greater the length, the more wraps you can create with your scarf
- Pompom trim, 2m

Laura's Top Tip

Working with jersey can take a little practice to get the tension right, so test your stretch stitch on a scrap of your fabric first so that you can get the settings on your machine just right before starting on the finished project. Selecting a specialist stretch stitch on your machine will help to ensure that the threads of your stitches don't snap as the stretchy fabric moves and flexes.

1 Add trimming to the fabric
Press the jersey and place a length of trimming down one long edge. Ensure that the woven band of the trimming is aligned with the raw edge of the jersey, so that the embellishment, in this case the pompoms, are lying on the main section of the fabric. Pin in place.

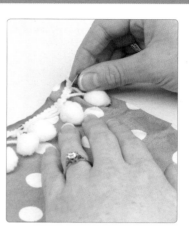

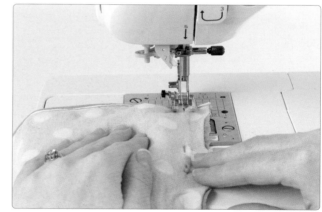

2 Join the fabric in a tube
Fold the fabric to align the two long edges with their right sides facing, the trimming tucked to the inside, and pin in place. Select a stretch machine stitch and join the two pieces together with a 1cm (0.4in) seam allowance. This line of stitching will need to pass through both the sections of fabric and the woven band of the trim. You may need to adjust the seam allowance to ensure that you don't miss the trim band or catch the pompoms in the line of sewing.

Laura's top tip

This simple design can be worked up in a number of ways to create different looks. You can create a wrap scarf that uses two different fabrics by cutting two strips to the desired length and seaming up both long sides to create a tube – you can opt to include a fancy trimming in to just one or even both of the seams – before hand stitching into a loop to finish.

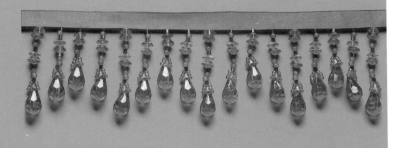

For a more elegant evening accessory, swap the stretch jersey for a more luxurious fabric like silks and satins, try inserting a beaded trim into the seams for even more glitz.

If you want to make a more cozy wrap for winter, work with sumptuous velvets or fur-style fabrics.

Working with different lengths of fabric will change the finished look too. Longer lengths of the fabric strip will create a larger wrap scarf, can be looped a around a number of times, where as shortening the lengths will create a smaller wrap that can be worn looped once around and will sit around the collar of your coat.

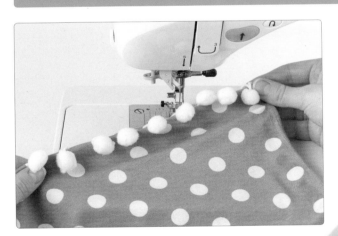

4 Join to make a loop
Fold under the raw edges at each of the shorter ends and pin in place. Work with neat hand slip stitches to join the two shorter ends together to create a loop and complete the scarf.

3 Turn the fabric tube to the right side
Once the long seam has been worked, turn the tube through to the right side, spread the fabric so that the seam runs along one side of the scarf and press. The pompoms will be poking out from the seam.

Free-motion necklace

Team up your little fabric scraps with small beads and free-motion stitching to accent the motifs on the fabric. You'll be able to create a one-of-a-kind accessory that'll be sure to turn heads.

Difficulty   **Total time** Allow 60 minutes per necklace

You will need...

- Print cotton, remnants
- Felt, for backing, 15cm x 20cm (6in x 7in) or sized to accommodate your fabric motifs
- Wadding, 15cm x 20cm (6in x 7in) or sized to accommodate your fabric motifs
- Necklace fastener
- Cord

1 **Cut fabric motifs**
Press the print cotton, select the areas that you'd like to use in the design and cut around with a 1cm (0.4in) border. Decide on the position of the fabric motifs – swap around the different elements until you're happy with the composition.

2 **Layer and stitch the fabrics**
Place the wadding on top of the felt. Transfer the print cotton motifs in your preferred arrangement to the centre of the wadding, with right sides facing uppermost. Working in a contrasting thread, tack the three layers together with long, loose hand stitches. Lower the feed dogs on your sewing machine and, working with the free-motion foot, sew around the design using the stitches to highlight and accent the motif.

3 Add beaded accents

Carefully trim around the fabric and felt to create a neat border to the motifs. With small hand stitches, sew a selection of small beads on to the surface of the necklace to enhance the motifs on the fabric.

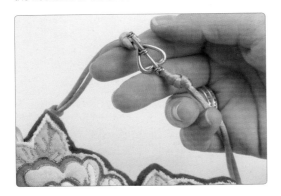

4 Secure the necklace fastening

With the cord held doubled, cut to the desired length of the necklace. Fold the cord in half again and secure a necklace fastener to the centre of one length. Repeat for the other half of the necklace fastener and length of cord. Each length can be knotted in the centre for added detail. Pin the raw ends of cord to either side of the necklace back and carefully stitch in place.

Laura's top tip

When cutting the motifs from the fabric snip out more shapes than you require. This will give you different placement options and allow you to configure the elements to your chosen design. In this necklace I've selected motifs from one print cotton; however, you can mix and match assorted prints to create your own unique finish.

Free-motion stitching

When working with free-motion sewing it's all too easy to get carried away and want to sew really fast. However, in order to get neat stitches you need to ensure that your hands are moving the fabric at a similar speed to the machine stitching. Before you begin working on your finished project, test out working free-motion stitches on some fabric scraps so that you can master the movement of your hands and select the correct speed to sew at.

5 Add a neat backing

A second layer of felt can be added to the back of the project to conceal all the stitch work. Affix with fabric glue and trim to create a neat border around the design.

Don't let remnants of your favourite prints go to waste – piece them together to make a statement necklace

No-pattern skirt

Created with only a couple of seams and an easy-to-fit elasticated waistband, you'll be impressed with how quickly you can make this chic retro garment.

Difficulty ✂✂✂✂✂ | **Total time** Allow 60 minutes per skirt

You will need...
- Print cotton, 1.5m (1.6yd)
- 8cm (3.2in) wide elastic, the length of your waist measurement plus 6cm (2.4in)
- Large sheet of paper (I like to use wide gift wrapping paper)
- Long tape measure
- Marker pen

Pick out some colourful cottons and create a fun and stylish summer skirt. Why not add your own spin to it with pretty patch pockets or a retro appliqué motif for true '50s style?

1 Draw the pattern
Using a sheet of wrapping paper, work from the corner marking dots at the required radius measurement, and join them to create an arc. Use this circle to mark out the desired length of the skirt in the same manner, and draw in the arc that will form the lower hem. Cut out the two circles. This is the pattern that you'll use to create your skirt.

Take your measurements

Using your waist measurement and the desired length of your skirt, create a small pattern that will be used to cut the fabrics. Add 5cm (2in) to your waist measurement, then divide this by 6.28 to give you the radius that will be used to create the waist section of the skirt.

My skirt has been made using the following measurement: 63.5cm waist, therefore 63.5cm + 5cm = 68.5cm ÷ 6.28 = 10.9cm radius. Or if you're working in imperial measurements, 25in waist, therefore 25in + 2in = 27in ÷ 6.28 = 4.3in radius.

Laura's top tip

If you're working with print cottons remember that the print will be reversed on the back of the garment, so pick your patterns carefully if you don't want the design inverted on the back! This classic style of skirt is a popular retro design: you can adapt it and make it your own with an appliqué motif, adding in contrasting patch pockets or even affixing a netting underskirt and as it's made using body measurements you can scale it up or down for either adults or children.

2 Cut the fabric

Fold your fabric in half, then in half again. This will create a square with one corner that has no raw edges (this is the centre of the fabric). Position the pattern on the fabric, with the small curve – the waist section – positioned at this folded corner, and pin in place. Carefully cut around both of the curves and remove the pattern piece.

3 Edge the skirt

Unpin the pattern template and open out the fabric. You'll be left with a ring of material, which is the main section of your skirt. Secure the raw edges at the waistband section by working with a zigzag stitch around the smaller circle to prevent the raw edges from fraying.

4 Create the waistband

Cut a length of wide elastic 6cm (2.4in) larger than your waist measurement. Align the two short edges of the elastic and sew together using a 2.5cm (1in) seam allowance. Press the seam open and zigzag stitch over the two edges of elastic to strengthen.

5 Affix the waistband

Pin in position around the waist section of the skirt, ensuring the fullness is evenly spaced around the band, and stitch into place with a straight stitch. You may need to stretch out the elastic so that the fabric fits smoothly around the band. Fold the elastic to the wrong side and restitch to conceal the waistband.

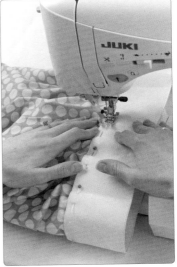

6 Hem the skirt

With a rolled hem foot, work along the lower edge of the skirt with a straight stitch to secure the raw edges and finish the skirt.

Needlebook

Working with only a few simple embroidery stitches and colourful threads you can create a fun needlebook that will be a pretty addition to your sewing box.

Difficulty ✂✂✂✂✂   **Total time** Allow 90 minutes per needle book

You will need...
- Felt, a selection of coordinated colours
- Selection of embroidery threads
- Four flat buttons
- Double-sided fusible interfacing

★ This simple design is stitched directly on to trimmed felt, making it quick and easy to make

1 Trim the fabric
Using pinking shears, cut the felt so that you have a cover measuring 10cm x 18cm (4in x 7in), the inside leaves measuring 9cm x 16cm (3.6in x 6.3in) and the front panel measuring 6cm x 8cm (2.4in x 3.2in).

2 Add the motif
Draw the motif from the template on to the piece of felt cut for the front panel and outline the design using back stitch. Work the details of the hair and collar of the design using satin stitch.

Laura's top tip
....

Transferring a motif on to felt is a little tricky, as the template can't be seen through the dense fibres in the same way as it can with lightweight fabrics like cotton. With this design, try cutting out the motif directly over the outside lines and using this to draw round on the felt. Work freehand, using the template as a guide, to draw in the remaining details inside the design.

Embroidery threads

When working with stranded embroidery threads it's possible to split the threads and work with a smaller number of strands. This will create finer stitches. For projects on thicker fabrics, like felt, using all the strands together will create thicker stitches that stand out well against the fabric.

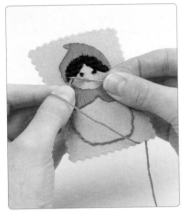

3 Embroider the features

Use black embroidery thread to make two French knots for the eyes and pink thread to make a French knot for the mouth.

4 Stitch a floral pattern

Work a lazy daisy stitch motif in the centre of the body using purple embroidery threads. Then sew a line of chain stitches along both sides of the motif to add decoration to the body.

5 Embellish with buttons

Position a flat button in place over each corner of the front panel and carefully stitch into position using coordinated thread.

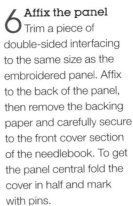

6 Affix the panel

Trim a piece of double-sided interfacing to the same size as the embroidered panel. Affix to the back of the panel, then remove the backing paper and carefully secure to the front cover section of the needlebook. To get the panel central fold the cover in half and mark with pins.

7 Construct the needlebook

Fold the cover of the needlebook in half, then fold the leaves of the needlebook in half and slide inside the cover. Secure with pins, and with a straight machine stitch sew the spine of the needlebook, ensuring that all the layers of fabric are stitched through.

8 Complete the needlebook

Insert a selection of sewing and embroidery needles into the felt leaves of the needlebook to keep them safe.

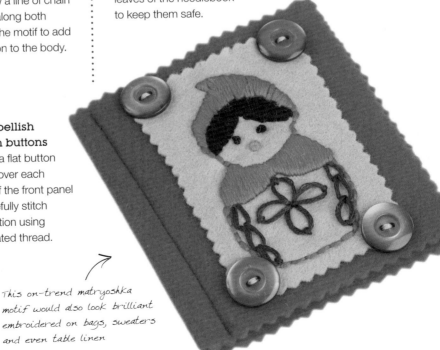

This on-trend matryoshka motif would also look brilliant embroidered on bags, sweaters and even table linen

Appliqué tech cases

These soft padded tech cases are created to specific measurements to fit your gadgets, so whether you want to make one for an eReader or a smartphone the construction is the same.

Difficulty ✂✂✂✂✂   **Total time** Allow 50 minutes per case

You will need...

- Print cotton, double the length of your gadget by the width of your gadget, plus 3cm (1.18in) extra on all sides
- Lining fabric, double the length of your gadget by the width of your gadget, plus 3cm (1.18in) extra on all sides
- Wadding, double the length of your gadget by the width of your gadget, plus 3cm (1.18in) extra on all sides
- Remnants of fabrics for appliqué
- Double-sided fusible interfacing
- Embroidery cottons

1 Measure and cut the fabrics

Take measurements of your gadget and use these to cut your fabrics. Cut out the main fabric, the lining and the wadding pieces, which are double the length by the width plus an additional 3cm (1.18in) on each side to accommodate the seams.

2 Create the motif

Trace the appliqué motif on to the double-sided interfacing. Fuse to the wrong side of a fabric remnant and cut out. Carefully peel away the backing, position on the right side of the main fabric in the desired position and affix.

An appliqué motif is worked on to the front of the sleeve before it's stitched together

Laura's top tip

The best way to get the correct placement of the motif is to fold the case in half and slide the gadget inside. With the base of the gadget pushed down towards the fold, move the device so that there's equal surplus fabric on either side and tuck this under the gadget. With the fabric folded in this way you'll be able to decide on the best position for the motif.

3 Stitch the appliqué design

Use embroidery threads to carefully work around the edge of the design and add in any details to the motif. The work can be held securely in an embroidery frame to make the sewing easier.

4 Create the outer sleeve

Fold the main fabric in half with the right sides facing, aligning the short raw edges at the top of the fabric. Repeat to fold the wadding in half, place it around the main fabric and pin in place. Working with a 1.5cm (0.6in) seam allowance, using a straight machine stitch, sew from one long side, along the bottom and finish at the top edge of the other long side to join the pieces together.

5 Turn the sleeve to the right side

Trim the seam allowances close to the line of stitching to remove bulk, being careful not to slice the threads of the stitches as you do so. Then turn the case through and press to neaten.

6 Create the lining

With right sides facing, fold the lining fabric in half, aligning the raw edges of the two short ends, and pin in place. With a straight machine stitch and a 2cm (0.79in) seam allowance, start at one long side and sew down, along the bottom of the case and ending at the top edge of the other long side.

7 Insert the lining

Slide the lining inside the main fabric sleeve. Trim away excess main fabric and wadding in line with the top of the gadget if required. Fold the lining fabric over to the main case to conceal the raw edges. Fold under the raw edges of the lining and pin in place. Secure the lining around the top of the case with a neat hand slip stitch and press.

* Give your gadgets a personalised makeover with a hand-stitched tech sleeve

Snap-frame purse

A stylish snap-frame or Parisian clutch bag can be the perfect finishing touch to your look. It's also ideal for stowing all essentials or tucking into your everyday handbag.

Difficulty ✂✂✂✂✂ **Total time** Allow 60–90 minutes

You will need...

- Print cotton, 0.5m (0.6yd)
- Lining – select either a plain or print cotton to suit your main fabric
- Medium-weight interfacing
- Pompom trimming
- Snap frame
- Fabric glue

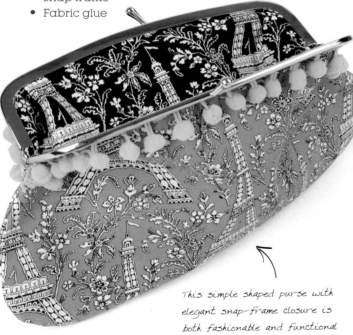

This simple shaped purse with elegant snap-frame closure is both fashionable and functional

Laura's top tip

Securing the purse into the frame can feel a little tricky, but using a strong fabric glue will ensure that it's held firmly in place. Some glues work best if they're left for a few moments to become tacky before the fabric is pressed into place – check the glue manufacturer's instructions to see what is the best option for you.

1 Cut the fabric pieces
Use the template to cut the purse shape from your fabric. You'll need to cut two shapes each from the main fabric, the lining and the interfacing, ie six pieces in total. Divide the pieces into two sets, each comprising one piece of main fabric, lining and interfacing. These will become the front and the back sections of the purse.

2 Layer the fabrics for each section
Working on one set at a time, place the interfacing on the wrong side of the main fabric shape. Align all the raw edges and treat as one single piece. With the right sides of the main fabric uppermost, place the lining fabric on top so that the right sides of the two pieces are facing, and pin in place.

3 Join the upper section of the purse
Working with a 5mm (0.19in) seam allowance and a straight machine stitch, join the sections together along the upper edge of the pieces. Repeat for the second set of fabric pieces.

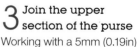

4 Turn the purse to the right side

Carefully clip the seam allowance and turn the purse through to the right side. Press the seamed upper edge neatly. You will now have two parts of the purse, both joined at the top.

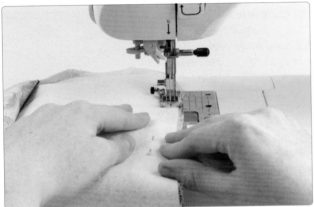

5 Join the main fabric of the purse

Open out the section of the bag and carefully place the main fabric (with interfaced backing) on to the other section of interfaced main fabric so that the right sides are facing. Align the raw edges and pin in place, ensuring that both the lining sections are pushed out of the way to the left-hand side of the project. With a 5mm (0.19in) seam allowance and a straight machine stitch, join the two sections together, starting at one end of the purse, working around the base and finishing at the other end.

6 Join the lining

Turn the purse around and match the two lining sections so that the right sides are facing. Align the raw edges and pin into place. Working with a 5mm (0.19in) seam allowance and a straight machine stitch, begin joining the lining sections together. Leave a 5cm (2in) gap in the centre of the base of the purse unstitched and continue sewing the second side.

7 Turn the purse to the right side

Carefully clip the seam allowances and pull the purse through the gap in the lining to turn through. Press the purse and hand slip stitch the opening in the lining closed before pushing the lining down inside the purse.

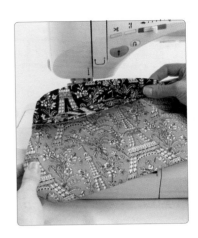

8 Add the trimming

Place the snap frame on top of the purse and carefully pinch in the fabric at the corners of the frame to create small folds. This will ensure that the purse fits neatly into the frame. Pin in position. Cut the length of pompom trim to cover the upper edge of the purse and pin in place. Sew it with a straight machine stitch, ensuring that you secure the small fabric folds at either side as you stitch. Repeat for the second side of the purse.

9 Secure the snap frame

Open the snap frame and fill one channel with fabric glue. Working with one side of the purse at a time, starting at one corner and working across the top of the purse, carefully push the fabric into the channel so that it bonds with the glue to secure it in place. Allow to dry fully before securing the second side.

Bunting

From birthday celebrations to summer garden parties, there seem to be few special occasions that can't be made a little more lovely with the addition of bunting. Mix and match your fabrics to create the perfect colour scheme for you.

Difficulty ✂✂✂✂✂ **Total time** Allow 15 minutes per flag

You will need...

- Selection of print cotton fabric remnants
- Ribbon, at least 4m (4.4yd) and 2cm (0.79in) wide
- Scissors
- Rotary cutter
- Ruler
- Pencil
- Card or paper

* This fabric decoration is a timeless classic

1 Make the template

Draw a template for the pennant on card and cut it out. The template that I've made measures 18cm (7in) along the flat base, 22cm (8.7in) down the centre line from the base to the tip, and 22.5cm (9in) down the two long edges. You can make larger or smaller flags to suit the occasion.

2 Cut the fabric

With the fabric folded in half and half again, place the template on the material and use the ruler and rotary cutter to slice the shape. You'll be able to cut up to six layers of fabric with your rotary cutter. Flip the template each time to make the most economical use of the fabric.

Size guide

Knowing how much bunting to make isn't tricky. Basically, on every 3m (3.3yd) length of ribbon you'll be able to position up to nine pennants. Decide on the length of strand that you want to make and then cut the required number of pennants to suit. Remember, you'll need to leave up to 40cm (16in) pennant-free at the start and end of each strand to create ties.

Laura's top tip

You can sew all the pennants one after another, or you can create a chain effect by allowing the machine to run on a few stitches between finishing one flag and starting the second. Continue until all the flags have been stitched – you'll end up with a string of flags. Snip the thread chain between each to separate them, then go on to create the bunting.

3 Sew a pennant

Place two cut pennants right sides together, aligning the raw edges, and pin in place. Select a straight machine stitch and, taking a 6mm (0.25in) seam allowance, sew along one long edge to the point, stop the machine to pivot the work, then sew back up the other side, leaving the base unstitched to turn through.

4 Turn the pennant to the right side

Snip away the excess fabric at the point of each flag and turn through to the right side. You might need to use the end of a pencil to ease out the tip of the flag. Press the flag. Sliding the card template inside as you press will help you to get neat, crisp seams.

5 Create the ties

Fold the length of ribbon in half aligning the long edges. Then with a straight stitch and working close to the two open edges, sew the length of ribbon together for at least 40cm (16in). You will repeat this at the end of the length of flags. This will make hanging the bunting easier.

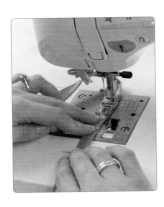

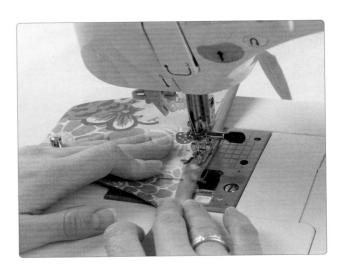

6 Assemble the bunting

Place the first pennant so that it's sandwiched between the fold in the ribbon and stitch across to join in the first flag. Sew the ribbon together to create the space between the flags. I like to leave a gap the same size as the width of a single pennant, but this can be as big or small as you like. Position the next flag between the ribbon and stitch in place. Continue until you've taken in all the flags and finish by sewing 40cm (16in) of ribbon at the end to make the second tie.

Fancy flags

Once you've made a string of bunting with standard pennants you may want to branch out. You can make a template for a rounded flag using the same width as the triangle but drawing a neat curve at its end – a soup bowl is ideal to trace around! Proceed in the same way as with the triangular pennant, sewing together two pieces with right sides facing and a 6mm (0.25in) seam allowance, then clip around the curve before turning through and pressing. These rounded flags can be stitched into place just like the triangles, or you can alternate the two different shapes.

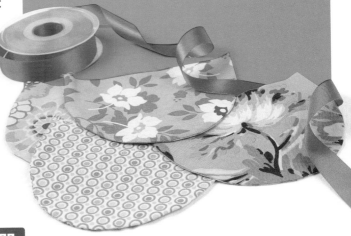

Cushion covers

Cushions are by far the most satisfying – and easiest – soft furnishing item you can make. Mix and match different techniques and bold fabrics for instant transformation of your interiors.

Difficulty ✂✂✂✂✂   **Total time** Allow 50 minutes per cover

You will need...
- Cushion pad
- Heavyweight cotton or furnishing fabric, three times the size of the cushion, plus 4cm (1.6in) on each side. The 'ripple' cushion requires five times the size of the cushion pad, while the 'bow-fronted' cushion will need an additional section of material measuring the same size as the cushion pad plus 3cm (1.18in) on all sides
- Ric rac

* Combine different techniques for statement interiors

Yo-yo cushion

A selection of different-sized yo-yos are hand sewn to the front of the completed cushion – you can make these up in a contrasting fabric, or even cover the entire cushion with them!

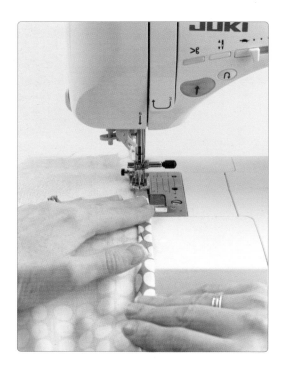

1 Hem the ends of the fabric
With the wrong side of the fabric uppermost, double fold over the raw edges by 5mm (0.19in) and pin in place. With a straight machine stitch sew along the length to create a hem. Repeat to hem the opposite short end.

2 Fold and stitch the cushion

With the right side uppermost and with the cushion pad in the centre as a guide, fold the two shorter ends over the back of the cushion, creating an overlap. Remove the cushion pad and pin the sides of the cushion in place. With a straight machine stitch and using a 1.5cm (0.6in) seam allowance, sew each side in turn to create the two side seams.

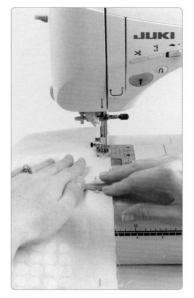

3 Turn the cushion to the right side

Once both side seams have been stitched, carefully trim any excess from the seam allowance and turn the cushion through to the right side via the opening in the back. Press neatly.

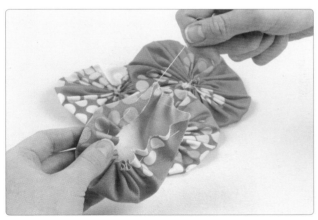

4 Create fabric yo-yos

Cut a circle of fabric and hand sew a line of gather stitching around the outer edge. Draw the threads up to gather the fabric into the centre to create a yo-yo. Fasten the threads with a few small, neat stitches at the back of the yo-yo. Repeat to create a selection of embellishments.

Laura's top tip

To ensure that the fabric is folded correctly before sewing the side seams, place it with the right side facing uppermost and position the cushion pad in the centre. Fold one end over the cushion, then the other to create the overlap. Use pins to mark the point of the fold. You can also use pins along the sides to ensure the correct placement of the side seams.

5 Embellish the cushion with yo-yos

Place the yo-yos over the front of the cushion and pin in place. With neat hand stitches, secure each yo-yo to the front of the cushion with a few small stitches in the centre. Be careful to only sew through the front of the cushion cover – slide one hand inside to make the sewing easier. Once all the yo-yos have been secured, insert the cushion pad through the opening in the back.

Ripple cushion

A section of tucks are stitched into place on the front panel of this cushion to create a rippled effect. This cushion requires more fabric than a standard envelope cushion, to accommodate the folded tucks. Ensure that the fabric can wrap around the cushion up to five times, plus the additional material to allow for the side seams.

1 Mark out the tucks
Using the cushion pad as a guide, measure out the upper section of the cushion. With a ruler and chalk carefully mark out lines for the tucks – the wider the lines, the larger the tucks will be. Using these lines as a guide, fold and press the fabric and pin into place.

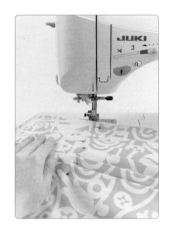

2 Sew the tucks in place
With the main fabric of the cushion folded to the left-hand side, and out of the way of the needle, select a straight machine stitch and work along the chalked lines to sew the tucks into place. Move the fabric as you work on each tuck in turn, so that you're only sewing through the fabric folded for the tuck and not the other sections of the cushion! Repeat until all the tucks have been stitched into place.

3 Create a ripple
Smooth the tucks so that they lie flat in one direction and pin along each side seam to hold into position. Measure the centre of the tucks and fold each one in the opposite direction along the centre line. Pin in place. With a straight machine stitch, work a line of stitches down the centre of the tucks to hold the ripple in place.

4 Sew the hems
With the fabric wrong side uppermost, fold over a 5mm (0.19in) double hem along the short edges and pin in place. Work along the fold with a straight machine stitch to create a hem. Repeat the fold on the opposite end of the fabric and sew to make a second hem.

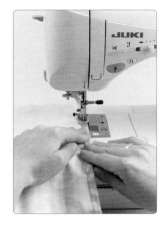

5 Construct the cushion
With the right side uppermost and with the cushion pad in the centre as a guide, fold the two shorter ends over the back of the cushion, creating an overlap. Remove the cushion pad and pin the sides of the cushion in place. With a straight machine stitch and using a 1.5cm (0.6in) seam allowance, sew each side in turn to create the two side seams. Turn through to the right side via the opening and insert the cushion pad.

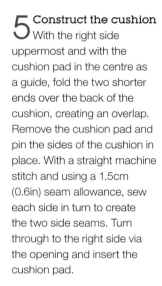

Ric rac cushion

Simply by sewing lengths of jumbo ric rac to the front panel you can transform a plain cushion into something a little more eye-catching.

1 Position the ric rac

With the right side of the cushion panel facing uppermost, mark out the front panel, using the cushion pad as a guide. Trim lengths of jumbo ric rac to the same width as the fabric and place across the width. Position the ric rac so that it runs across the cushion front, with its raw edges aligning with the raw edges of the fabric. When you're happy with the placement, pin into position.

2 Secure the ric rac

With a straight machine stitch, work along the length of the ric rac to secure it to the fabric. Repeat to sew each length of ric rac to the cushion front.

3 Create the hems

With the fabric right side uppermost, fold over a 5mm (0.19in) double hem along the short edges and pin in place. Work along the fold with a straight machine stitch to create a hem. Repeat the fold on the opposite end of the fabric and sew to make a second hem.

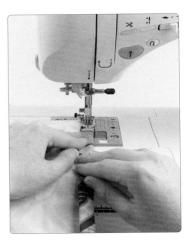

4 Construct the cushion

With the right side uppermost and with the cushion pad in the centre as a guide, fold the two shorter ends over the back of the cushion, creating an overlap. Remove the cushion pad and pin the sides of the cushion in place. With a straight machine stitch and using a 1.5cm (0.6in) seam allowance, sew each side in turn to create the two side seams. Turn through to the right side via the opening – the ric rac panel will be on the front of the finished cushion. Press neatly and insert the cushion pad through the opening.

Laura's top tip

When sewing jumbo ric rac it's possible to work a straight line down the centre of the trimming without the line of stitches straying off its edge. You do this by simply working slowly when sewing and guiding the fabric carefully through the machine. Or you can use a ruler and chalk to draw out the centre line and use this as a sewing guide.

Bow-fronted cushion

A section of fabric secured along the two side seams is gathered up to create a quick and easy bow effect.

1 Create the hems
With the fabric wrong side uppermost, fold over a 5mm (0.19in) double hem along the short edges and pin in place. Work along the fold with a straight machine stitch to form a hem. Repeat the fold on the opposite end of the fabric and sew to make a second hem.

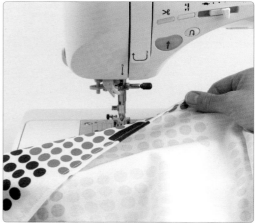

2 Prepare the bow fabric
Working with a section of fabric the same size as the cushion pad plus 3cm (1.18in) on all sides, fold under 1.5cm (0.6in) along one side and pin in place. With a straight machine stitch, sew along the fold to create a hem. Repeat to hem the opposite side.

Simple envelope cushions

All four designs are made using a simple envelope cushion construction, with the fabric folded around the cushion and secured at the side seams; the cushion pad is tucked inside the opening and doesn't require any buttons, zips or fastenings. The cushions are made with multiple techniques to create a completely different design for each finished item.

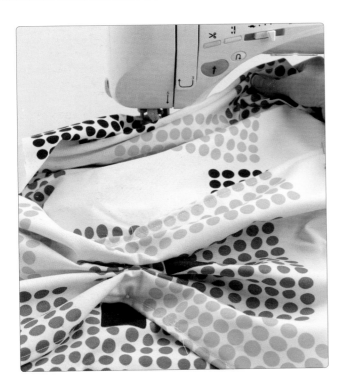

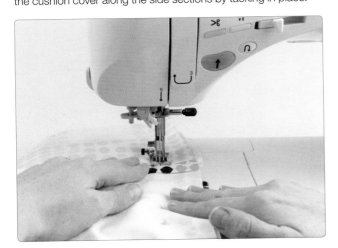

3 Secure the bow fabric

Place the smaller piece of fabric over the front section of the cushion so that the right sides of both sections are uppermost. Pinch the centre of the smaller piece to create gathers and pin in place. Secure the upper piece of fabric to the cushion cover along the side sections by tacking in place.

5 Create the centre of the bow

Cut a strip of fabric from the remnants measuring 7cm (2.8in) wide and 8cm (3.2in) long. Fold the fabric in half with right sides facing, aligning the two long edges, and pin in place. With a straight machine stitch, work along the length of the strip to join. Turn the tube through to the right side and press so that the seam lies at the centre back.

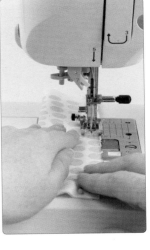

6 Complete the bow

Removing the pins from the centre of the bow, carefully wrap the fabric strip around the centre, overlapping the raw edges at the back of the bow detail. Pin in place. Hand slip stitch in place to secure and insert cushion pad through the opening in the back.

4 Construct the cushion

With the right side uppermost and with the cushion pad in the centre as a guide, fold the two shorter ends over the back of the cushion, creating an overlap. Remove the cushion pad and pin the sides of the cushion in place. With a straight machine stitch and using a 1.5cm (0.6in) seam allowance, sew each side in turn to create the two side seams. Turn through to the right side via the opening – the bow section will be on the front of the finished cushion.

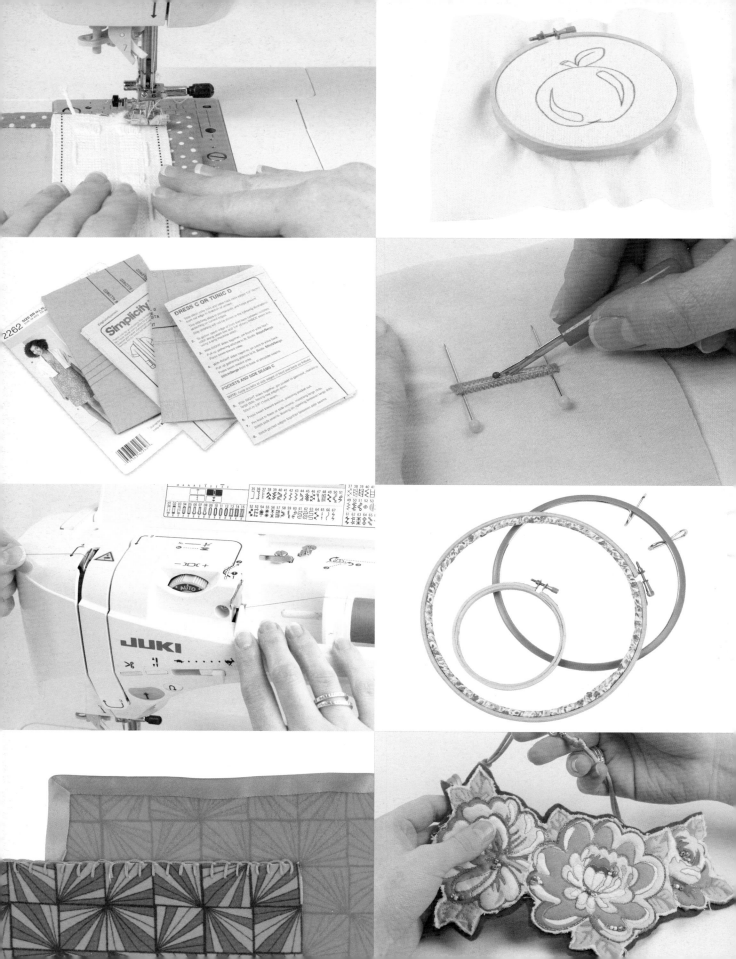

Appendix

The more you sew the more you will learn about this creative and practical hobby. Here are a few handy guides to help you get off on the right food with your sewing projects – from templates to specialist terms, essential supplies and resources.

Project templates

Use these templates to help you create the projects in this manual. They're all provided full size, so just trace them and use them as cutting and sewing guides.

Appliqué owl

- Cut one in fabric.
- Cut one in double-sided fusible interfacing.

Appliqué owl wing

- Cut two in fabric.
- Cut two in double-sided fusible interfacing.

Appliqué telephone

- Cut one in fabric.
- Cut one in double-sided fusible interfacing.

Matryoshka

- Use as a guide for embroidery.

Triangular bunting

- Cut two fabric pieces per pennant.

Rounded bunting

- Cut two fabric pieces per pennant.

Snap-frame purse

- Place on fold.
- Cut two from main fabric.
- Cut two from lining.
- Cut two from interfacing.

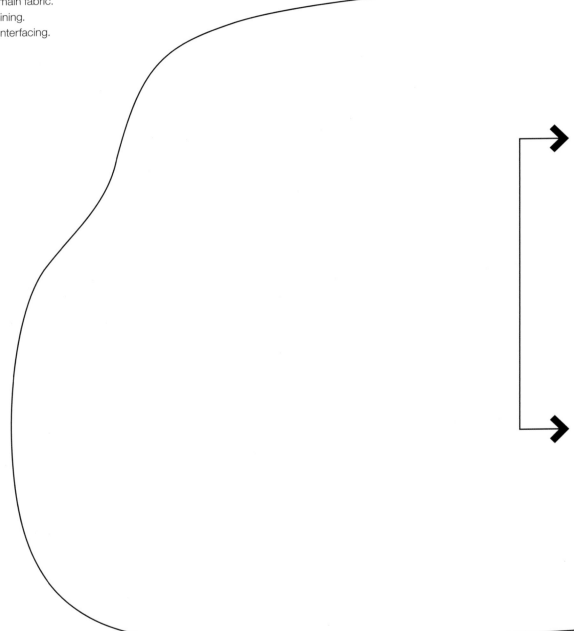

Troubleshooting

This handy guide will help you solve your sewing dilemmas

While sewing is a really rewarding pastime, you may encounter a few challenges along the way – and there's nothing more frustrating than getting partway through a project only to find that something's gone awry! Whether your stitches are puckering, threads are snapping or the instructions you're following seem to be making little sense, there's often a simple answer to your predicament. So before you throw your hands up in despair and vow never to look at a sewing machine again, grab a cup of tea and check out these common problems and handy solutions.

Getting started

Help!
I keep getting confused between the right side and the wrong side of plain fabrics. Is there an easy way to tell them apart?

Laura says...
It's easy to tell the right side from the wrong side on printed fabrics as the motif will be more vivid on the surface of the right side, but it can be a little trickier on plain fabrics. For the most part fabrics are presented on the bolt with the right side facing outwards; however, sometimes silks may be shown with the wrong side outermost to prevent it from getting snags on the surface. So until you get accustomed to identifying one from the other, you can ask the shop where you buy it to make a mark on the selvedge of the right side when they cut your requirements.

If you're working with a fabric and really can't determine which is the right side, it doesn't matter too much. Simply look it over carefully and use the surface that appeals to you most as the right side. Just remember that whichever side you pick, you must then use it as the right side throughout the entire project for a neat and consistent finish.

Help!
The instruction for my project is for fabrics without nap. What does this mean?

Laura says...
The term 'nap' is used to describe the pile of a fabric. If a fabric is described as 'with nap' this means that there'll be a visible pile, or nap, on its right side – for example, velvet and corduroy. Fabrics described as 'without nap' won't have this luxurious pile. Fabrics with a nap surface need to be handled in a different way to those without nap to ensure that the pile always looks its best on the finished item.

Help!
I pricked my finger on the needle and have got blood on my project. Can I save it?

Laura says...
Blood is a tricky stain to get out of fabrics, especially if they're light-coloured. It's best to try and remove it from the fabric while it's still wet. Try licking the tip of your finger (not the one that you've pricked!) and use your saliva to dab away the blood. If the mark still remains, use a little cold water to get rid of the residue.

If the blood has dried it will be harder to erase. Try washing the area carefully in cold water. If that fails a stain remover may need to be applied. Remember to test this on a scrap of fabric to be sure that it won't damage the material. Whenever you prick your finger, always check it to see if you've broken the skin: it's far easier to take a few moments to treat the finger than to spend time trying to remove a dried-in stain on the finished project.

Hand sewing

Help!
I've just finished sewing a cross-stitch project and now that I've taken it from the hoop the fabric looks grubby. What can I do?

Laura says...
It's not uncommon for needlework projects to look a little dirty when they're finished, especially as they may have taken a long time. The fabrics will have gathered dust along with the natural oils from your hands. With a little care it's possible to wash the finished piece. For the most part modern embroidery threads are colourfast, which means the dye from the threads won't bleed when they're washed, but you can check this by snipping a small length of thread from the skein, working a few stitches on fabric and washing it as you would the finished piece. Mix a small amount of gentle detergent in cool water and carefully lower the project in until it's fully submerged. Begin by agitating the water around the project, lifting it out regularly to check whether the fabric is clean. Use your fingertips to carefully dab away any more stubborn marks; be very careful not to scrub the surface too hard, as this could damage the neat stitches. Once clean, remove and allow the water to drip off. Don't wring out the project, as this will almost certainly damage all your hard work. Instead, place the project flat on a clean towel and fold the towel over it. Starting at the fold, carefully yet firmly roll the towel up so that the project is sandwiched inside. This will remove the excess moisture. Unroll and leave the project to dry on a clean, flat surface. Once fully dried your project will be ready for framing.

Help!
I find pushing a needle though thick fabric hurts my fingertips, but I can't seem to get a thimble to feel comfortable. Which finger should I wear a thimble on?

Laura says...
When hand sewing the needle is usually held between the thumb and first finger. The thimble is worn on either the middle or index finger of the same hand, and is used against the back of the needle to help push it through the fabric. So try sewing with it on one of these fingers and then the other, to see which is the most comfortable for you. At first it may feel a little awkward to sew while using a thimble, but you'll quickly get used to it.

Thimbles come in a range of various materials, including plastic, metal and leather. They're also available in different sizes, so be sure to select one that's not so tight that it cuts off the blood to your fingertip and not so loose that it flies off whenever you move your hand.

Help!
Whenever I need to separate embroidery threads I get into a huge knot. What's the best way to separate them?

Laura says...
To create more delicate stitches you'll often need to separate the strands from a length of embroidery cotton. The easiest way to do this is to pull a single thread free at a time – even if you require two strands don't be tempted to pull more than one, as this will create tricky tangles. Begin by cutting the embroidery thread to a workable length – usually the length of your forearm – then gently roll the cut end between your fingers until the separate strands become visible. Holding the thread vertical, pinch up one strand. Use the other hand to loosely grip the bottom of the threads, and pull the single thread until it comes free. The remaining strands may bunch up as they're pulled, and the length may spin in your hand, but simply smooth out the threads and repeat to remove another single strand until you have the required number.

Machine sewing

Help!
I keep snapping my machine needles – what am I doing wrong?

Laura says...
There are a number of different reasons why a machine needle might snap. Run through this checklist to eliminate any problems on future projects.

- Check the needle is correctly inserted. If it isn't inserted fully, or the clamp isn't secured, the needle can become dislodged by the machine's movements and become damaged or broken.

- Try re-threading the machine. This will ensure that both the spool thread and the bobbin thread are correct and not affecting the tension and damaging the needle.

- When a needle breaks, while you're replacing it with a new sharp take the time to clean out the bobbin area of your machine with the small brush provided in its maintenance kit. A build-up of lint and dust can affect the movement of the needle; there may also be small pieces of the broken needle still in there that could damage or break the new one.

Help!

Sometimes when I'm sewing I forget to remove the pins when I work. It doesn't seem to make a difference, but is this OK?

Laura says...

Always remember to remove your pins before they pass through the sewing machine. If the pin were to get caught up in the mechanism it would break the needle, and the broken tip could fall into the workings of the machine and damage it, or fly into your face and cause serious injury. When inserting pins try to put them into the project so that the sharp tips will be facing towards the machine as the line is stitched. Positioning them in this manner will make it easier to quickly slide them out while you're sewing.

Help!

Some of the fabrics I sew end up all puckered as I stitch. What can I do to stop this?

Laura says...

This is usually caused by using the wrong thread, working with an incorrect needle, or selecting the wrong tension. Be sure to check these things first. If you're certain that all your settings and selections are correct, it may be that you need to help the fabric through – some fabrics are just a little more tricky than others. To do this you need to hold the area for stitching under a little tension. This is done by placing one hand in front of the sewing line and one hand behind the machine. Hold the fabric under a gentle, even tension as you carefully guide it through. This will help to stop it from puckering, but be careful not to tug too hard in either direction as this will prevent it from feeding though the machine evenly and will create wonky stitches.

Techniques

Help!

I've just sewn in a zip and it's really tough to pull up and down. Do I have to take it out and start again?

Laura says...

Zips can be a little tricky. It's wise to check that the zip can be opened and shut easily before you sew it into a project. Try rubbing a bar of soap lightly up and down the teeth of the zip – this may give it the lubrication it needs to work properly.

Help!

I've stitched a thin tube of fabric for my project but I'm having real trouble turning it through. What do I do?

Laura says...

Tight tubes are always rather fiddly to turn through to the right side after sewing. Using a long knitting needle is great for feeding the fabric back through to the right side. Next time, before you sew the seam, stitch a piece of yarn to the top of the strip and run it along the right side of the fabric before it's folded in half to make the seam. Sew the seam with the yarn stitched at the top, ensuring there's a piece of yarn protruding from the bottom of the tube once it's been stitched. After the seam has been stitched, pull on the yarn to draw the tube through to the right side, then snip off the yarn.

Help!

When affixing fusible interfacing to my project I've managed to get some stuck to the plate of my iron. Can I remove it?

Laura says...

Getting adhesive from fusible interfacing on a hot iron plate is almost unavoidable, but it can be removed. A commercial iron plate cleaner should be used to dislodge the glue before it becomes burnt on. Try placing a pressing cloth or piece of muslin between your project and the iron to prevent too much adhesive becoming burnt to the iron plate.

Clothing and dressmaking

Help!

I bought a stash of pretty dressmaking fabrics and put them through a machine wash so they'd be ready to sew, but the ends have all frayed and look dreadful. What should I do?

Laura says...

Don't worry! It's quite common for fabrics to fray a little when they're being washed, and it's better that it happens now rather than when the finished project is laundered! The fabric isn't ruined by any means, and can easily be prepared for sewing. Begin by pressing the fabrics flat, taking your time over the raw edges so that they lie neat and flat. Using a pair of sharp dressmaking shears, work around the piece of fabric to snip away all the frayed edges. Re-press the fabric as required and fold up ready for use.

Help!

I've got a lovely vintage pattern but the dresses on the front look really small. How will I know if they're going to fit me?

Retro girls

Laura says...

Vintage designs are great to work with; they often use a range of fabulous tailoring techniques that many modern patterns omit. Body shapes and dress sizes have changed considerably over the last few decades, so ensuring that you take accurate body measurements when working with a vintage pattern is crucial. If you usually take your own measurements it might be wise to ask a friend to help, since the size needs to be as accurate as possible.

With your measurements noted, check through the sizing guide supplied with the pattern. You may be able to find a size that'll be suitable for your body – don't be put off if this isn't the dress size that you'd usually wear or make; concentrate instead on the measurements. If you find that you're between sizes you'll need to make some alterations to the pattern pieces. If you're new to pattern alteration, begin by cutting to the larger measurements, as it's easier to redraw a small pattern line than it is to create a larger one. Finally, consider making a toile of the dress from calico. Think of this as a practice run, so that you can make any final adjustments to the pattern before you start on your 'real' garment. It might sound time-consuming, but it'll be worth it for the perfect fit of your finished dress.

Help!

I'm trying to cut a pattern from silk chiffon, but every time I place the pattern pieces ready to pin, the fabric slips and doesn't line up. How do I hold these slippery fabrics steady?

Laura says...

When fabrics slip it can be very hard to pin and cut them accurately. Covering your table with a fabric like calico and ensuring that it's pinned taut all the way around will provide more grip than a regular smooth tabletop. Lay the slippery fabrics over this and begin pinning and cutting as required. Using a fabric like calico is great for the extra friction it provides to hold slippery fabrics in place, but be sure not to use any fabric that's very precious as a base, just in case you snip into it by accident.

Home furnishing

Help!

I'm trying to sew some homewares using oilcloth, but it keeps getting snagged up as it passes through the machine. How can I make it feed through more easily?

Laura says...

The water-resistant surface of oilcloth can make it stick to the machine as it passes through. Begin by selecting a smooth foot if you have one, as these are often coated with Teflon and won't stick to the surface of the fabric. Alternatively, place a strip of unwanted dressmakers' tissue paper from a pattern (you can use the offcuts surrounding the pattern pieces, or cut off the borders), or a piece of baking parchment, on top of the sewing line. This should help the machine to glide over the fabric and is transparent enough to allow you to see where you're sewing on the fabric underneath.

Help!

The curtains I've made don't seem to hang properly, even though I've taken all the correct measurements. What can I do to help them hang neatly?

Laura says...

Sometimes you'll need to add small curtain weights to the bottom hem of curtains to help them to hang neatly. This is especially good for drapes made from lightweight fabrics that move about in a breeze. Small disc-shaped weights can be bought from your local fabric store, or alternatively you can use ten-pence pieces – if you're feeling a little flush! Sew a strip of fabric along the inside hem of the curtains, and work lines of vertical stitches to create pockets to slip the weights in – remember to remove the weights before you launder the curtains to prevent them from damaging your machine or the curtains.

Help!

I've begun working free-motion stitching to quilt a project, but I can't get my stitches to look neat. How do I fix this?

Laura says...

Uneven threads are usually caused by incorrect tension. Begin by re-threading the machine. Sometimes the threads from the spool will have come loose from the tension discs inside the machine. Be sure that your machine is clean and free from any dust or lint build-up – even the smallest amount of debris can affect the way the machine works. Change your needle: working with a fresh sharp will help you to make neat stitches; if you find the needle starts to skip stitches this is a sign that the tip is starting to get dull. When you've cleaned the machine, re-threaded or replaced the needle, test out the tension by working on a small sandwich of cottons and wadding that are a similar thickness to your quilt. This way you can get the tension correct or make any further adjustments before working on the finished project.

Laura's top tip

There's a lot of specialist jargon that goes with sewing, but don't let that put you off! Turn the page for a handy glossary of stitching terms that you'll come across as you begin new and exciting sewing projects.

Glossary

Do you know your thimble from your bobbin? Unsure what's the warp and what's weft? Use this handy guide to get you on the right track!

Acrylic – Man-made fabric with a rich, dense texture.

Appliqué – A technique where a fabric motif is secured to a second piece of fabric with neat hand or machine stitching around the outer edges.

Armhole – The area of a bodice that's cut away for the arm to fit through.

Back stitch – A straight hand stitch often used to outline designs. Each stitch is worked back to the end of the previous one to create a solid line of stitches.

Back tacking – See 'reverse stitching'.

Basting – The US term for tacking. You'll often see it in quilting projects, since quilting has a strong tradition in the United States.

Bias – The section that runs through the centre of the fabric at a 45° angle to the warp and the weft. Fabric cut in this manner will have more stretch.

Bias tape – Also known as bias binding, this is a strip of fabric cut across the bias and triple folded so that the raw edges are concealed towards the centre of the strip. Frequently used in the finishing stages of projects.

Blanket stitch – A hand sewing technique worked over the raw edges of fabric to secure them and prevent fraying. Also used as a decorative feature.

Blind hem stitch – A stitch used to discreetly join the fabrics to form a hem. Can be worked by hand or with a machine.

Bobbin – A small reel on to which thread is wound before inserting into the sewing machine; with the mechanism of the sewing machine this will create the bottom section of each machine stitch.

Bodice – The upper section of a garment that covers the torso.

Bodkin – A large-eyed needle used to draw elastic through a casing or to weave ribbon through eyelets.

Bridal pins – Fine, almost headless pins that make very small holes in fabric. Also called 'satin pins'.

Buttonband – The section on a garment on which a series of button fastenings are secured.

Buttonhole – A small slit in fabric reinforced with stitches through which a button can be passed.

Buttonhole stitch – A series of strong, knotted stitches worked around the edge to secure and reinforce fabric.

Calico – A plain woven fabric, often uncoloured, frequently used to create toiles.

Casing – Two rows of stitching worked over a fold in fabric to create a tube through which elastic, for example, can be threaded. Frequently used to create waistbands.

Centred zip – A zip fastening secured to the fabric within a seam. The sections of seam allowance fold over to hide the teeth of the zip.

Chain stitch – A decorative hand stitch where loops of thread are secured to the surface of the fabric along a stitching line.

Chiffon – A lightweight, often sheer, fabric used in dressmaking.

Collar – A smart addition to a neckline, reinforced with interfacing for a tailored finish.

Colourfast – Term applied to thread or fabric that's been treated so that the dye used won't bleed when washed.

Comforter – A heavy, thick padded blanket, stitched together for extra warmth.

Concealed zip – A fastener that when it's inserted into a garment or project is nearly invisible from the right side.

Corduroy – A fabric with nap that runs in rows of pile, commonly used for making clothing.

Cotton – A natural fabric that's available in a wide range of colours and patterns, is comfortable to wear against the skin and is used in numerous of sewing projects.

Covered button – A special button blank that's covered with fabric, allowing you to create fastenings to suit your project.

Crease or crease line – A mark made in the fabric by pressing with an iron, often used to aid the construction of a project.

Cross stitch – A decorative hand stitch created by two straight stitches intersecting to form a cross. Also the name given to the needlework discipline that uses these stitches in a range of shades to create colourful designs.

Cutting lays – Illustrated diagrams provided with a dressmakers' pattern to assist in the placement of the cut pattern pieces on the fabric for correct cutting.

Cutting lines – A series of lines printed on patterns to indicate where each piece should be cut. Multi-sized patterns will feature a range of lines.

Cutting mat – Also known as a self-healing mat. Used as a base on which to cut and trim fabrics with a rotary cutter. Often marked with a grid to aid precision, it prevents the surface below becoming damaged.

Dart – A technique used to add shaping to fabrics by folding two points together to meet at a tapered end, stitched in place to create a triangle in the fabric. Commonly featured in women's garments.

Double-pointed dart – A variation on the dart, used to add long sections of shaping to a garment. Often seen on the back of a bodice around the waist. The fabric is folded to meet at two points and stitched to create a diamond shape in the fabric.

Drape – A term to describe the way that a fabric moves or behaves, used when assessing the suitability of a fabric for a project.

Dress form – Also called a dressmakers' dummy or mannequin, this is a torso-shaped form that's used to assist in dressmaking.

Dressmakers' tissue paper – Thin tissue paper printed with a series of pattern pieces that are cut and used to create a garment. The lightweight paper is easy to cut and the fabric can be seen through it, aiding the positioning of each piece.

Embroidery – A needlework discipline that uses a combination of different hand stitches to create colourful designs.

Embroidery machine – A specialist sewing machine that features a wide range of embroidery stitches and motifs.

Embroidery needle – Has a medium-length shaft and a moderately large eye to accommodate multiple strands of an embroidery thread.

Embroidery threads – Often referred to as embroidery floss, this stranded cotton is used either as multiple strands or separated into thinner strands to create colourful stitched designs.

Facing – A term used to describe the placement of fabrics in relation to each other, for example 'with right sides facing' means placing the two fabrics so that their right sides touch.

Facings – Sections of fabric stitched to lie on the inside of a garment to hide raw edges and make it more comfortable to wear.

Feed dogs – Small metal teeth that sit under the throat plate of a sewing machine and move to draw the fabric through the machine for sewing.

Felt – A thick fabric that's available in a wide range of colours. Its raw edges don't fray, making it quick and easy to work with.

Finger press – Applying pressure with your fingertips to create a temporary crease line in a project.

Flannel – A soft, warm fabric that's often used in creating bedding and blankets.

Foot – Also called a presser foot. A small attachment that's secured to the bottom of the needle clamp and lies flush with the fabric being stitched. A wide range of feet is available, each designed for a specific task.

Foot pedal – The pressure-sensitive pedal that controls the sewing machine. Greater pressure results in faster sewing.

Free-motion – A machine sewing technique where the feed dogs are lowered, allowing the fabric to be guided through the machine in any direction.

French knot – A hand embroidery technique where the thread is looped so as to create a neat knot to sit on the surface of the fabric.

French seam – A seam that's worked on the right side then the wrong side of two pieces of fabric, to provide additional strength. Often used when working with delicate fabrics.

Gathering – A row of long, straight hand or machine stitches left unfastened at one end so that the fabric can be drawn up along it to create gathers.

General-purpose needle – The type of needle most commonly used for hand sewing projects. Has a medium-length shaft, a small rounded eye and a very sharp point.

Glass head pins – These have a brightly coloured ball of glass on the head to make them easy to insert and remove from fabric.

Grading – The scaling up or down of a dressmakers' pattern to create different dress sizes.

Grain – The lines created by the threads that run the length of the fabric.

Grain line – A marking used on dressmaking patterns to indicate the position in which the pattern pieces need to be placed on the fabric in relation to its grain.

Haberdashery – The term used to describe sewing supplies, fabrics, threads and notions.

Hand wheel – The wheel positioned at the right-hand side of a sewing machine used to manually raise and lower the needle.

Handle – A term used to describe the way that a fabric feels and moves, used when assessing the suitability of a fabric for a project.

Heading tape – A woven strip secured to the top of curtains. The length is gathered up by pulling the cords woven through it to create the upper section of curtains.

Hem – The treatment of the lower edge of a garment to hide the raw edges, ensure the correct length and finish the garment.

Hemming stitch – A discreet stitch, worked by hand or machine, that's used to secure the lower section of a garment or project to create a neat hem.

Hemming tape – Fusible tape that's often used in the repair of dropped hems.

Hook and eye fasteners – Small metal fasteners that are secured to two sections of fabric, often above a zip, to complete the fastening.

In-seam pocket – A neat pocket that's inserted along the side seam line of a garment. The soft fabric of the pocket lies flush to the body.

Interfacing or interlining – Material applied to the wrong side of fabric to provide added strength and stability. Available in a wide range of weights. Some are fused in place with a hot iron, others are stitched into position.

Jersey – A stretchy knitted fabric that's often used to make clothing.

Knit fabric – A type of fabric, such as jersey, created by knitting the threads together on a machine, in a similar way to hand knitting.

Lazy daisy – Also known as detached chain stitch, this hand embroidery stitch features small loops of thread secured to the surface of the fabric, often to create floral motifs.

Lining – A piece of fabric cut to sit on the inside of a garment to make it more comfortable and to help it hang well when worn.

Long arm – A specialist quilting machine, often used with a large frame, to assist in the quilting of large-scale projects.

Magnetic snaps – Strong magnetic fasteners used to hold together two sections of fabric.

Mannequin – See 'dress form'.

Mitre – Folding in the sides of a project to create neat corners with a diagonal section towards the point where the two sides meet.

Multi-size pattern – Dressmakers' patterns often come in a range of sizes, with different styles of line to represent the sections to be cut for each size. A key is provided to identify the correct line for each size.

Nap – The pile present on the right side of some fabrics that give it a luxurious feel, for example velvet.

Neckline – The upper section of a garment that's cut away and sits around the neck. There's a wide range of shapes, styles and finishes.

Needle clamp – The section of a sewing machine that holds the needle securely for stitching.

Needle plate – The metal section of the sewing machine that lies above the bobbin carrier. The needle passes through it to make the stitches. Needle plates often feature grid markings to aid placement of fabrics for sewing.

Needle threader – A small notion that features a loop of metal on a tag, which is used to help thread a needle.

Needles – Sharps that are used for sewing. Available in a range of various styles for different applications, for both hand and machine sewing.

Notches – Markings on a dressmakers' pattern used to help align two sections during construction.

Nylon – Man-made fibre with a soft and smooth texture.

Oilcloth – A fabric coated on the right side with a water-resistant plastic layer.

Open seam – Another name for a basic seam.

Overcasting stitch – A machine stitch worked around the raw edges of fabric to prevent it from fraying.

Overlocker – A specialist machine commonly used by dressmakers to finish and work seams. These machines can use a combination of two to four threads and feature a blade to slice the edge of a seam before sealing the cut edge with stitches.

Patch pocket – A style of pocket that sits on the right side of a garment.

Pinking shears – Large fabric shears with serrated blades that create a zigzag edging when cutting fabrics, to prevent them from fraying.

Pleat – Neat stitched-in folds, often used in skirts and dresses.

Plied – The term applied to two strands of thread twisted together to create a single thread.

Poppers – See 'snap fastenings'.

Pre-cut fabrics – A range of fabrics, usually cottons, sold in bundles cut to a set ready-to-use size. These include Charm Packs and Jelly Rolls and are commonly used in quilting projects.

Press – To smooth out or finish a section or project with an iron.

Presser foot – See 'foot'.

Quilt – A patchwork project made by piecing together a series of different sections of fabric to produce the upper surface, with a middle layer of wadding and a bottom layer of backing fabric.

Quilt block – A section of fabrics stitched together to form a certain shape. A series of such blocks are sewn together to make a quilt top.

Quilt top – The colourful section that forms the upper layer of a quilt.

Quilters' pins – Long-shafted pins used to secure the bulk of multiple layers when working with quilts.

Quilting machine – A specialist sewing machine designed for quilting projects.

Raglan – A style of sleeve that's joined to the bodice with long diagonal seams from the armhole to the neckline.

Raw edge – The cut edge of fabric. On woven materials this is prone to fraying, but can be treated with pinking shears or stitches.

Reverse appliqué – A decorative technique where a motif is stitched on to the main fabric and the inner section is cut away to reveal a contrasting fabric underneath.

Reverse stitching – Also called back tacking, this sewing machine function sets the machine to reverse back over the stitches that have just been worke,d to secure the threads.

Ribbon – A colourful haberdashery item available in a wide range of finishes and colours.

Ric rac – Also called ric-rac. A flat band of braid woven in a zigzag pattern.

Right side – The front or top surface of fabric.

Rotary cutter – A fabric-cutting tool with a disc-shaped blade, generally used in conjunction with a ruler and cutting mat. Commonly used in quilting.

Ruffle – A small section of fabric gathered up and stitched to a garment or project to add detail.

Running stitch – A long, straight hand stitch that's commonly used for joining pieces together.

Satin – A smooth luxurious fabric.

Satin stitch – A series of long hand stitches that are used to fill in sections of embroidery designs.

Seam – The section where two fabrics are joined together. There's a wide range of styles and techniques for creating seams.

Seam allowance – The section that borders each piece of fabric that needs to be joined to another. Maintaining an even seam allowance will create a neat finished item.

Seam ripper – A small tool with a point and a curved blade used to carefully remove unwanted stitches.

Seed stitch – A series of short, straight stitches often used to add detail to a needlework design.

Self-healing mat – See 'cutting mat'.

Selvedge – The woven or bound ends of fabric. In some cases these are printed with the fabric's care instructions.

Set-in – A style of sleeve that's secured to the bodice by a single seam worked in a circle around the armhole and the shoulder.

Sharps – A term used to describe general-purpose needles, which have a very sharp point.

Short and long stitch – A mixture of long and short straight stitches often used to add colour and shading to elements of an embroidery motif.

Silk – A luxurious fabric often used in dressmaking.

Skein – The name given to the wrapped bundle in which embroidery threads are sold.

Snap fastenings – Also called poppers, these metal fasteners have two parts that are sewn on to the two sections that need to be joined.

Stay stitching – A line of hand or machine stitching that's worked along the curve in a pattern piece to prevent it from becoming distorted or misshapen. Often used when working necklines, and is stitched within the seam allowance.

Stem stitch – A hand embroidery stitch where the stitches overlap partway along a sewing line to create a scrolling effect.

Stitch-in-the-ditch – A quilting term that refers to quilting stitches that sit directly in the section where two fabrics are joined.

Straight stitch – A machine stitch that creates straight, neat and even stitches. Used in the majority of sewing projects. The length can be adjusted to suit the fabric and project.

Stretch – The term used when fabrics are very flexible. Two-way stretch refers to a fabric that can be drawn out from two opposite sides when pulled. Four-way stretch is the name given to a fabric that can be pulled and drawn out from all four sides.

Stretch stitch – A machine stitch designed to be used with stretch-knit fabrics. The threads are positioned to allow the stitches movement as the fabric flexes, in order to prevent snapping.

Suffolk puff – See 'yo-yo'.

Tacking – Long, loose hand stitches used to secure two sections of fabric together during the construction process. These temporary stitches are often worked in a contrasting colour to make removing them easier.

Tailors' chalk – A chalk used to add markings on fabrics to aid the construction of garments and projects. Available in a range of colours, they can be brushed off fabrics after use.

Tailors' knot – A neat and secure knot tied to the end of thread before hand stitching.

Tape measure – A flexible ruler that usually features both imperial and metric measurements.

Tapestry needle – This has a large oval-shaped eye and a blunt tip designed to move fibres while sewing.

Tension – The balance of the two threads (spool and bobbin) that create each machine stitch. Incorrect tension can cause puckering, bagging threads and even needle breakages.

Thimble – A small notion that's worn over the tip of the finger to reduce any pain felt while pushing a needle through fabric.

Thread shank – A section of long, wrapped stitches worked to secure a button to a garment.

Threads – Available in a wide range of colours and fibres, these are used for creating the stitches in a sewing project.

Toile – A mock version of a garment, often made in calico, allowing a dressmaker to perfect any adjustments before beginning work on the final project.

Top stitching – A line of neat, straight stitches, often created with a machine. Used as a decorative addition or to provide reinforcement to a seam.

Turn through – After a seam has been worked with the right sides of the fabric facing, the item is 'turned through' so that the right sides are outermost.

Under-stitching – A line of stitching used to secure the seam allowance to the inner section of fabric. Often worked with a sewing machine, and isn't visible from the right side of the garment.

Velcro – A brand of temporary fastening with two tapes featuring hooks and loops that can be pressed together and pulled apart.

Velvet – A rich fabric with nap or pile.

Wadding – A padded layer made from either cotton or man-made materials. Used to add slight bulk and warmth to a quilt.

Warp – The threads that run vertically through fabric.

Weft – The threads running from left to right through fabric.

Without nap – A fabric that has a smooth surface, without any pile.

Woven fabric – A type of fabric that's constructed on a loom with the threads woven through a warp and a weft.

Wrong side – The back of fabric. This will be on the inside or the rear of a completed project or garment.

Yo-yo – Also known as a Suffolk puff, this is a decorative addition created by gathering up the fabric in a circle to make a slightly padded disc.

Zigzag stitch – A machine stitch made up from a series of straight stitches placed to create zigzags, with both decorative and functional properties.

Zip – A fastening that's commonly used in dressmaking. Available in a range of colours and styles. A tab is pulled up to draw two sets of teeth together to seal the fastening.

Zip foot – A specialist machine foot that's used to aid the insertion of a zip fastener into a project.

Resources

Sewing supplies

**Abakhan Fabrics,
Hobby & Home**
North Wales, Chester, Birkenhead,
Liverpool, Manchester, Preston,
Bolton & Hanley (Stoke on Trent)
www.abakhan.co.uk

Anchor Threads
01484 681 881
www.coatscrafts.co.uk

Backstitch
01480 461758
www.backstitch.co.uk

Berisfords Ribbons Limited
01260 274011
www.berisfords-ribbons.co.uk

Blooming Felt
www.bloomingfelt.co.uk

Clothkits
01243 533180
www.clothkits.co.uk

The Cotton Patch
www.cottonpatch.co.uk

Crafty Ribbons
01258 455 889
www.craftyribbons.com

Daylight
020 8964 1200
www.daylightcompany.com

DMC Creative
0116 275 4000
www.dmccreative.co.uk

Donna Flower Vintage Fabric
www.donnaflower.com

Doughty's
01432 267 542
www.doughtysonline.co.uk

Fabric Godmother
www.fabricgodmother.co.uk

Fabric Loft
www.thefabricloft.co.uk

Fabric Rehab
www.fabricrehab.co.uk

Fancy Moon
0845 519 4354
www.fancymoon.co.uk

Franklins
Colchester, Ipswich, Chelmsford,
Dovercourt, Salisbury
www.franklinsgroup.com

Gone To Earth
www.gonetoearth.co.uk

John Lewis
0845 604 9049
www.johnlewis.com

S. Nutt Sewing Machines
0121 327 2828
www.dressforms.co.uk
www.nuttsewing.co.uk

Ray Stitch
0207 704 1060
www.raystitch.co.uk

Saints & Pinners
www.saintsandpinners.co.uk

Seam Star
01829 770733
www.seamstar.co.uk

**Sew Ezi Portable
Sewing Tables**
01235 832554
www.sewezi.com/uk

Sew Over It
www.sewoverit.co.uk

Simplicity Creative Group
0161 480 8734
www.simplicitynewlook.com

Sit Kneel Chairs
www.sitkneelchairs.co.uk

Sublime Stitching
www.sublimestitching.com

Textile Garden
www.textilegarden.com

U-Handbag
www.u-handbag.com

The Village Haberdashery
www.thevillagehaberdashery.co.uk

Viva La Frida
www.vivalafrida.co.uk

Westminster Fibers
01484 681 881
www.coatscrafts.co.uk

Sewing Machines

Brother
0844 499 9444
www.brothersewing.eu

Janome
0161 666 6011
www.janome.co.uk

Juki
01206 563955
www.juki-uk.com

Singer
0207 336 7986
www.singerco.co.uk

Sewing patterns

Butterick, McCall & Vogue
www.sewdirect.com

Sew Box
www.sewbox.co.uk

Simplicity Pattern Company Inc.
www.simplicity.com

So Vintage Patterns
www.sovintagepatterns.com

Resources

www.burdastyle.com
www.thesewingdirectory.co.uk
www.urbanthreads.com

Index